AT HOME IN THE REVOLUTION

# AT HOME
# IN THE
# REVOLUTION

## WHAT WOMEN SAID
## AND DID IN 1916

## LUCY McDIARMID

At Home in the Revolution

First published 2015
Royal Irish Academy, 19 Dawson Street, Dublin 2
www.ria.ie

Text © Lucy McDiarmid

ISBN 978-1-908996-74-9

British Library Cataloguing in Publication Data. A CIP catalogue record
for this book is available from the British Library.

Printed in Ireland by SprintPrint

*for all my Irish friends*
*Do mo chairde croí in Éirinn*
*'Ar scáth a chéile a mhaireann na daoine'*

# CONTENTS

# ACKNOWLEDGEMENTS

The Marie Frazee-Baldassarre Professorship at Montclair State University has provided generous financial support for all aspects of my work on this book. As the first person to hold this professorship, I am grateful to the Department of English for honouring me with it. Three department chairs—Emily Isaacs, Johnny Lorenz and Wendy Nielsen—have encouraged my research and teaching, and I thank them all.

Over the last few years, the descendants of some of the people I've written about have been kind in expressing interest in my work, patient in answering my many questions and generous in offering family photos. I would especially like to thank Helen Litton (the Clarke and Daly families); Honor O Brolchain and Eiléan Ní Chuilleanáin (the Plunkett family); Helen Bacon (the Ryan family); Charlie Spring Rice (Mary Spring Rice); Patrick Comerford, Joe and Hilary Comerford (Máire Comerford); Deirdre McMahon (Thomas Weafer); Micheline Sheehy Skeffington (Hanna and Frank Sheehy Skeffington); Christina McLoughlin (Mary McLoughlin); Dave Foley and Fred Loane (Catherine Rooney, née Byrne); Emer Greif (Eily O'Hanrahan O'Reilly); Sarah Mahaffy, Henrietta Usherwood and Charles Baker (Elsie Mahaffy). Gertrude Parry (née Bannister), Roger Casement's cousin, had no direct descendants, but fortunately for me Jeff Dudgeon knows as much about her life as any grandson would and has given me information I could not have got otherwise. More recently, exchanges with Gerry Griffin (Eilis O'Brien and Emily Ledwith, née Elliott) and Cormac O'Malley (Ernie O'Malley) have also been useful.

I often found myself wishing that the leaders of the rebellion had waited until 1917 so I could have had another year to work on this book. Fortunately for me, many scholarly friends enabled me to complete the manuscript before 2016. The wise critiques and detailed suggestions of Nicholas Grene, Deirdre McMahon, Senia Pašeta, Linda Connolly and Patricia Coughlan improved the manuscript significantly. Fionnuala Walsh has been altogether a wonderful research assistant, and her skill in finding obscure information in tricky databases and websites has been of great use. Several close friends (and one close relative) devoted serious thought to possible titles for this book: thank you to Angela Bourke, Pat Coughlan, Nicholas Grene, Frank Miata and Lucy Schneider. I'm especially grateful to all the people who hosted talks or organised conferences where I spoke on any of the topics covered in this book, because the urgent need to produce ideas and analysis for presentation enabled me to do the thinking that went directly into my chapters, and the comments and questions I got helped me revise those ideas. My thanks to Eunan O'Halpin and Deirdre McMahon (Centre for Contemporary Irish History, Trinity College Dublin); Margaret O'Callaghan (Department of Politics and Institute of Irish Studies, Queen's University Belfast); Margaret Mills Harper, Muireann O'Cinneide and Tina O'Toole (Symposium on Women, War and Letters, 1880–1920, University of Limerick); Michael Kenneally and Rhona Richman Kenneally (International Association for the Study of Irish Literatures, Concordia University, Montreal); Eamonn Hughes (International Association for the Study of Irish Literatures, Queen's University Belfast); Brian Ó Conchubhair (Roger Casement 1864–1916: The Global Imperative, Tralee, Co. Kerry); Tony Tracy (National University of Ireland, Galway); Mary McAuliffe (Women's History Association of Ireland); Linda Connolly and Piaras Mac Éinrí (Gender, Sexuality and Culture: A Symposium in Honour of Professor Patricia Coughlan, University College Cork); Alexandra Poulain and Fiona McCann (plenary lecture at the International Association for the Study of Irish Literatures, Université de Lille); Helen Beaumont and Edith Andrees (The Howth Gun-running: 100 Years On, National Museum of Ireland, Collins Barracks); Margaret Mills Harper and Matthew Campbell (Yeats International Summer School, Sligo); Roy Foster and Senia Pašeta (Seminar in Irish History, Hertford College, Oxford University); Andrew McGowan (Yeats Society of New York, Glucksman Ireland House, New York University); Matthew Campbell (International Association for the Study of Irish Literatures, York); Linda Connolly (Merriman Summer School, Ennis, Co. Clare).

In conversations over drinks of various kinds in Buswells or on the Upper West Side or in any number of places in Ireland and New York, many friends have offered ideas, information and gossip. They brought delight to my life as I figured out what to say and how to think about the wonderful women in this book. Remembering such pleasant occasions, I would like to thank Margaret MacCurtain, Angela Bourke, Beatrice S. Bartlett, Patricia Coughlan, Nuala Ní Dhomhnaill, Margaret O'Callaghan, Deirdre McMahon, Tina O'Toole, Joe Lee, Eve Morrison, Eunan O'Halpin, Fearghal McGarry, Adrian Frazier, Nicky Grene, Theo Dorgan, Paula Meehan, Claire Bracken, Elizabeth Grubgeld, Bill Decker, Tony Tracy, James E. Kennedy, Meg Harper, Alice Kelly, Wendy Nielsen and Lauren Arrington. I am very sorry that the late Margaret Ó hÓgartaigh did not live to see this book completed; she and Eimear O'Connor led me on a somewhat furtive tour of the provost's garden in Trinity College, an escapade that enabled me to visualise many of

Elsie Mahaffy's diary entries. Table talk over many years with Declan and Beth Kiberd and the late Eithne Kiberd often paused at 1916, and I thought of them all as I wrote this book, especially when I quoted Louise Gavan Duffy. For gifts of books, for sources of quotations and for all kinds of practical help, I am grateful to James Ryan, Gerardine Meaney, Arin Gilbert, Adam Hochschild, Arlie Russell Hochschild, Gillian McIntosh, Keith Jeffery, Mike Lee, Philip O'Leary, Mary Helen Thuente, Maureen Murphy, Margaret Kelleher, Hilary Pyle, Niamh O'Mahony, Julie Dalley and Margaret Ward.

The introduction lists some of the many books on related subjects that preceded and aided my work, but five excellent recent books (and conversations with their authors) have enriched my understanding of 1916: Fearghal McGarry's *The Rising: Ireland: Easter 1916*, Senia Pašeta's *Irish nationalist women 1900–1918* and Sinéad McCoole's *Easter widows*, which I read as I was writing *At home in the revolution*; and Diarmaid Ferriter's *A nation not a rabble* and Roy Foster's *Vivid faces*, both of which I kept for dessert and read as I revised the manuscript.

Discussion and analysis of manuscript material has been important to my vision of this book from the beginning, and so I am indebted to the friendly help given me by many librarians and archivists: Rosemary King (Allen Library); Ken Bergin (Special Collections, Glucksman Library, University of Limerick); Catriona Crowe (National Archives of Ireland); James Harte (Manuscripts and Rare Books, National Library of Ireland); Harriet Wheelock (Royal College of Physicians of Ireland); Felicity O'Mahony and Aisling Lockhart (Manuscripts and Archives Research Library, Trinity College Dublin); Seamus Helferty and Orna Somerville (University College Dublin Archives); historian Samantha Brook, who consulted materials for me at the Bodleian and Rhodes House Libraries, Oxford University; and Susan Schreibman for the Letters 1916 project. I am also indebted to Joe and Hilary Comerford for a copy of the beginning of Máire Comerford's fascinating 1916 memoir.

I had long wanted to have this book published in Ireland. I am very lucky that Catriona Crowe suggested the Royal Irish Academy, because it has been a great pleasure to work with Managing Editor Ruth Hegarty. I appreciate all the good advice she has given me about this book. And without the support of my assistant, Janet Dengel, an expert in accountancy as well as in research, this book would have been a very late commemoration indeed. For wise and careful help with the proofs of this book and for years of friendship, I am grateful to Nancy Pepper.

Writing can sometimes be lonely, but work on 'what women said and did in 1916' generated (as these acknowledgements make clear) a lively social life. Frank Miata's amusing, affectionate and learned presence meant that I always had someone close by to critique and improve my ideas. Although he never quite came to love the Bureau of Military History website as much as I did, he was always willing to look up from Heidegger or *Bicycling Magazine* and contemplate a moment in 1916.

## PERMISSIONS

For permission to quote from unpublished texts, grateful acknowledgement is made to the National Library of Ireland for quotations from works by Mrs Arthur (Mary Agnes) Mitchell and Mary Spring Rice; to University College Dublin Archives for quotations from the Papers of Sighle Humphreys, P106/1; to the Glucksman Library, University of Limerick, for quotations from the Daly Papers, P2 Folder 76; to the Royal College of Physicians of Ireland for quotation from the diaries of Kathleen Lynn, KL/1; to the Bodleian Libraries, University of Oxford, for quotations from the Nathan Papers Ms. N 476, Estelle Nathan, Letters to George Nathan; to the Allen Library, Dublin, for quotation from IE/AL/1916/95/2, Elizabeth O'Farrell, 'The personal account of the surrender at the G.P.O. and other posts'; and to the Board of Trinity College Dublin for quotation from MS 2074 (1916 diary of Elsie Mahaffy).

Every effort has been made to trace copyright holders and to obtain their permission for the use of copyright material. I apologise for any errors or omissions and would be grateful to be notified of corrections that should be incorporated in future reprints or editions of this book.

# AUTHOR'S NOTE

I first met the Rising almost half a century ago through Yeats's poems; in 1968 I visited the exhibit at Kilmainham. In the intervening years, I've been teaching the literature and history of the Rising, inspired by the conflicting views of an event that was recorded and reimagined by hundreds of people. I have lived with the women (and many of the men) in this book for ages and feel as if they are my ancestors, my dead friends or literary characters in a favorite book. Their political opinions are various: some are unionists, some Home-Rulers, some moderate nationalists, some republicans; one of them says that Dublin burning looks like 'Sodom and Gomorrah'. What I admire is not their opinions so much as their energy, their idealism, and their ability to write vividly and well.

No member of my family had any connection with the Rising or with Ireland. In 1916 all my grandparents (descendants of immigrants from Germany) were living in Louisville, Kentucky, active in the city's civic life as they raised the children who would become my parents, aunts and uncles. What I would have done in the Dublin of April 1916 I have no idea; I have a rebel temperament, but bullets and explosives don't appeal to me. What interested me most in the material I studied for this book is the close view of the way women led their lives. Their accounts show how they entered public space, how they worked alongside men in a male-dominated territory, how their mothers encouraged them or tried to keep them home, how they managed household chores or romances with a war going on around them, how they expressed emotions and observed the intense feelings of others, and how during the unusual time of the Rising intimacies of all sorts—with sisters, brothers, lovers, friends and strangers—emerged and often took new forms.

The women's own words constitute the heart of my material, and except for minor silent emendations I have left their texts unchanged. Their names posed special problems: some of them married and wrote narratives of the Rising under a name different from the one they used in 1916. Others Gaelicised their names and over the years used both Irish and English versions. In most cases, the English version of the name is used. For ease of reference, the women in this book who were married at the time of the Rising are referred to by their married names (e.g. Kathleen Clarke), and those who then were single are referred to by their maiden names (e.g. Catherine Byrne). Those whose marriages occurred around the time of the Rising are called by the name they used at the date referred to in the text. To avoid confusion, all names are listed and cross-referenced in the appendix and index.

*August 2015*

*Introduction*

# JUMPING INTO THE GPO

The Irish Republic is entitled to, and hereby claims, the allegiance of every Irishman and Irishwoman. The Republic guarantees religious and civil liberty, equal rights and equal opportunities to all its citizens, and declares its resolve to pursue the happiness and prosperity of the whole nation and of all its parts, cherishing all the children of the nation equally, and oblivious of the differences carefully fostered by an alien government, which have divided a minority in the past.

'Proclamation of the Irish Republic',
24 April 1916

# I

On Monday, 24 April 1916, just after twelve noon, Catherine Byrne, 20 years old, jumped into the General Post Office in Dublin.

It was the first day of the Easter Rising, in fact the first minutes of the Rising. On her way home after a walk, Byrne had learned from a friend, Sean Flood, that 'the fight was starting that day', and when she got home her brother had already left to join his battalion of the Volunteers. At her mother's urging, Byrne (a member of Cumann na mBan) followed her brother into action, falling in behind 'a company of Volunteers led by Captain Michael Staines'. At Nelson's Pillar, 'Staines gave the order: "Right turn", so I did the "Right turn" too'.[1]

Staines (later the first commissioner of An Garda Síochána) would not let Byrne inside the Post Office with his men. Threatening her with the nearest male in her family, her older brother, he said, 'I'll tell Paddy on you', as if the brother's moral authority would weigh heavily on the sister's conscience, and as if the combined manhood of family and military would offer a sufficiently discouraging obstacle. But denied access through the main entrance to the GPO, Byrne simply waited for another opportunity. 'I hung around and...spotted Frank Murtagh...' Her entry (as she herself described it in 1952) was dramatic:

> The Volunteers had broken in the front windows of the office, but the side windows had not yet been broken. I asked Frank Murtagh to lift me up to the side window at the corner where the stamp machine is now. He did this with the aid of another Volunteer and I kicked in the glass of the window. I jumped in and landed on Joe Gahan, who

was stooping down inside performing some task. He started swearing at me, asking: 'What the bloody hell are you doing there?'[2]

Or perhaps he said 'Where the devil did you come from?' The 'swearing' was slightly different in Byrne's 1937 application for a military service pension.[3] But whatever Gahan's curse, he immediately put Byrne to work caring for the wounded Liam Clarke: 'Here is your first case,' he said.

Byrne's dramatic entry into revolutionary space is typical of the many stories told in women's accounts of the Easter Rising, in witness statements, pension applications, letters, diaries, memoirs, autobiographies, essays and journal articles. The episode is engaging, detailed, insignificant from a military point of view and therefore different in emphasis from better-known episodes about dead horses, snipers, barricades, ambushes and lucky escapes. Its difference lies in the fact that it is told by a woman and is a story about gender, though it never explicitly addresses gender as its subject. The narrative trajectory is about entrance into the GPO: 'How I came to be first Cumann na mBan member in G.P.O.' is the title Byrne gives the story in her witness statement. But every moment of which that trajectory is composed reveals Byrne negotiating small obstacles associated with gender.

What the episode shows, as so many of the women's stories do, is the ambiguous situation of women in public space. In vignettes, in instances of what sociologist Erving Goffman (in *Interaction ritual*) calls 'face-to-face behavior', women's accounts make visible the unsettled state of their political status. The 'ultimate behavioral material' of this type of episode, writes Goffman, 'are the glances, gestures, positioning, and verbal statements that people continuously feed into the situation, whether intended or not'. In the case of women's accounts of the Rising, these 'small behaviors' reveal social change in process, in miniature, not the official history of manifestoes and legislation, but the unofficial history of access to a door, threats to tell a brother, and a leap through a window.[4]

Except in the case of Staines, these surmountable obstacles do not arise from a discriminatory policy, nor does the witness statement so define them. And Staines's remark may have been provoked by Byrne's solo entry; if she had waited for her mobilisation order, delivered to her house later by Lucy Smyth, this episode might never have occurred.[5] Nevertheless, a second look shows how every stage of Byrne's progress from home to useful work inside the Post Office, tending the wounded, is characterised by a slight gender-driven delay. When Byrne returned home from a walk with her sister Alice and another girl, her mother told her that her brother Paddy had already 'left for the fight', taking his gun and equipment with him. A friend's father was there in the house in his uniform, so the news was confirmed because the men were equipped and ready: 'My mother told me to get my equipment and to follow them'. So there is a slight delay before the news reaches the women. Once out, she 'falls in behind the men'; she is 'behind', but still there. At the door of the GPO, she had to ask permission to be let in, and Staines refused. Byrne had to wait a while until she spotted a Volunteer she recognised outside the building, and she required his help and that of another Volunteer to hoist her through the window. Her arrival was greeted with an interesting expletive, whichever it was, but the surprise no doubt stemmed from the mode of her entry as much as from her gender. But moments later, she was put to work; the value of her help and the appropriateness of her presence were not questioned. These brief delays are not recorded in a tone of complaint or in the discourse of feminism. Byrne worked at a practical level: the delays were small facts that comprise part of the story, whose emphasis is on Byrne's engagement on the rebel side during the week of the Rising.

Like the story of Catherine Byrne's entry into the GPO, and often with as much drama, the narratives written by many women about their experiences in 1916, written in real time as diaries and letters or recorded later in memoirs and witness statements, focus on moments that traditional historians would consider trivial: stories of cooking with bayonets, arguing with priests, resisting sexual harassment, soothing a female prostitute, or doing sixteen-hand reels in Kilmainham Gaol. But these moments constitute part of the history of Irish women, as they negotiate entirely new situations in which gender roles are uncertain.

## II

Needless to say, in the Rising as in all wars, new strategies were required continually as circumstances evolved. Often for men as well as for women, each new situation required a gender-related decision, such as whether women would be imprisoned or how much danger they could be subjected to. But the uncertainty was not simply a result of the unpredictable nature of war; it was also a matter of the historical moment. As scholars of women's history have amply demonstrated, the results of 'first wave feminism' had long been felt in England in many feminist organisations and journals, in political activism related to social welfare especially, and in the Married Women's Property Act (1882). In 1918 property-holding women over 30, or women over 30 married to property-owning men, were given the vote; and in 1919 the Sex Disqualification (Removal) Act opened many professions and civil service jobs to women.[6] In the United States, the Women's Christian Temperance Union (established in 1874) was the 'most important organization' in moving 'mass-based women's organizations into the nation's political mainstream', and the formation of the General Federation of Women's Clubs 'channeled women's energies into concerted political action'.[7] After over 70 years of activism, American women received the vote in 1920.

In Ireland, organisations such as the Ladies Land League (established 1880) and Inghinidhe na hÉireann (established 1900), by offering a way for women to work together, raised the feminist consciousness of nationalist women. In addition, as Senia Pašeta has written, 'From an early stage, the Inghinidhe worked implicitly for women's suffrage and for increasing women's role in the political life of the country'.[8] The Irish Women's Franchise League (established 1908) worked with dedication and occasional violence to secure the vote for Irish women, disseminating information and propaganda through its organ the *Irish Citizen*, attacking government buildings in Dublin and politicians who did not support women's suffrage. By the time of the Rising, many Irish suffragists had been imprisoned for protesting and had gone on hunger strike. Debates over whether women's suffrage took priority over the national movement animated newspapers, conversations and private correspondence.[9]

The establishment of Cumann na mBan in 1914 further animated debate because of its ambiguous relation to the Volunteers. The 'Manifesto of the Irish Volunteers' said vaguely, 'There will also be work for women to do, and there are signs that the women of Ireland...are especially enthusiastic for the success of the Volunteers'.[10] The sentence was evidently intended to be welcoming and liberal, but it was unconsciously patronising. The word 'also' suggested that women were an afterthought, their 'work' somehow less central and important than the men's. The phrasing expressed at the same time men's sympathy to women's rights and the patriarchal priorities of the Volunteers.

Almost as vague in terms of gender, the stated aims of Cumann na mBan were

> 1. To advance the cause of Irish Liberty.
> 2. To organise Irishwomen in the furtherance of this object.
> 3. To assist in arming and equipping a body of Irishmen for the defence of Ireland.

4. To form a fund for these purposes to be called 'The defence of Ireland Fund'.[11]

The verb 'assist' implies a secondary role for women, and in her witness statement, Mary Josephine ('Min') Ryan, a founder member of Cumann na mBan, points out the contradiction inherent in the definition of its aims:

> We were a completely independent body from the Volunteers. People like Mrs. Wyse-Power and others used to maintain that we were not an auxiliary to the Volunteers, but an independent body; but the fact of the matter was that our activities consisted of service to the Volunteers. We had it straight in our constitution—that we were an independent organisation working for the freedom of Ireland. We had it almost the same as the Volunteers had it.[12]

Even Ryan sounds ambivalent: Cumann na mBan was both 'independent' and a 'service' organisation. Its constitution was 'almost' the same as that of the Volunteers. However 'independent' Cumann na mBan may have been, feminists like Hanna Sheehy Skeffington considered 'service' the role of a 'ladies auxiliary committee'.[13]

In both the Irish Citizen Army (established 1913), which included both sexes, and Cumann na mBan, women got training in first aid and in arms; some carried guns and some did not. In keeping with the Labour and socialist principles of the ICA, women were treated as equals to men, or so they claimed and so they felt: Constance Markievicz was second in command at the St Stephen's Green (later the College of Surgeons) garrison, and Margaret Skinnider was wounded fighting with an otherwise male squad. As Helena Molony says of the Citizen Army's policy on gender in her witness statement, '...the women in the Citizen Army were not first-aiders, but did military work, except where it suited them to be first-aiders. Even before the Russian Army had women soldiers, the Citizen Army had them'.[14]

The existence of active, vocal women's organisations in debate with one another and with male politicians meant that women's civic position was in the process of altering. Adding to the complexity of that position was the visible involvement of women in national organisations at a time when they were unable to vote. It was this unsettled situation that was expressed and embodied in the mini-dramas that appear in almost all the women's accounts of 1916, a situation evident in the series of negotiations that Catherine Byrne managed on her way to the inside of the GPO. And not long after Byrne kicked her way in, Patrick Pearse stood outside and read—for the benefit of posterity, for the ritual, if not for an immediate audience—the Proclamation with its promise of 'equal rights and equal opportunities' for all citizens. How those ideals would work in practice would be uncertain in April 1916 and, indeed, a century later.

## III

My interest lies in seeing how social change plays out in actual en-counters in the field rather than in political discussion. The nature of that change is further illuminated by first-person accounts because they express women's feelings about the encounters they describe. 'We need to find out what women did, thought, experienced', Maryann Valiulis has written, and the comprehensiveness of this book aims to make such discoveries possible.[15] It considers women's accounts of the Easter Rising, records kept by women who jumped into political action, those who wanted to jump into action but for one reason or another could not, those who performed a public function from inside the house, and those who were completely uninvolved but recorded the way they received information or misinformation about what was hap-pening. Because it is gender that interests me, I include the accounts of all classes and types of women, some with passionate political beliefs and others whose accounts never make their sympathies clear. Some of them, such as Hanna Sheehy Skeffington and Geraldine Plunkett, had gone to university. Others, teenagers from working-class families, already had jobs: according to the 1911 Census, Byrne, at age fourteen, was a grocery shop assistant, and Mary McLoughlin worked in Arnotts Department Store before the Rising.[16] One of the youngest women out in the Rising, McLoughlin had been a member of Clan na Gael, a group founded in 1911 to offer girls the same kind of military training as boys got in the Fianna Éireann.[17] Many of the women were members of Cumann na mBan or of the Irish Citizen Army. Aoife de Burca, a trained nurse who helped in the evacuation of the GPO, was not then a member of any national organisation, and Marie Perolz, a courier during the week before the Rising, was a member of both Cumann na mBan and the ICA.

The unionist women who wrote accounts of the Rising did so from varying points of view: Mary Louisa Hamilton Norway, whose husband was Secretary to the General Post Office in Ireland, expressed an ambivalent nationalism, initially condemning the rebels as 'a small body of cranks' but later entertaining the benign, patronising notion that it might be 'possible to find men who will rule with firmness and understanding this fine people—so kindly, so emotional, so clever, so easily guided, and so magnificent when wisely led'.[18] Elsie Mahaffy, daughter of the provost of Trinity College, John Pentland Mahaffy, was a strong unionist who supported the brutal style in which General Maxwell suppressed the Rising. Mary Agnes Mitchell, a Presbyterian from Tyrone then living in Herbert Park, wrote to her sister, as she watched Dublin burning, that it was 'like Sodom & Gomorrha [sic]'.[19] And Mahaffy's cousin Lilly Stokes, a young woman from a professional family in south Dublin, admired the physiques of the Volunteers from Boland's Mills as they marched past her to surrender.

I consider primarily Dublin-based accounts because women who lived in close proximity to the Rising had to position themselves in relation to it. Their diaries, letters and memoirs show them constructing selves defined by the fighting going on around them. Mahaffy never left her house, but the Rising came to her in the form of the British Army, quartered on the grounds of Trinity, and each successive diary entry reveals her evolving public persona. Mahaffy managed to stay in her own house and yet participate in public life, dining with the generals, hosting Prime Minister Asquith, and strategising with General Maxwell about public relations after the Rising.

For women less involved than Mahaffy, simply to record the Rising was to develop a relationship with a realm beyond the merely domestic. Indeed, the way the Rising permeated all parts of Dublin came to suggest that there was no such realm as the merely domestic. Even the banalities and misinformation recorded by Mary Martin, a wealthy widow in Monkstown, show the juxtaposition of the domestic with an arena of larger significance. 'It is reported', she wrote on Friday, 28 April 1916, '...that Connolly & Countess Markievicz & Sheehy Skeffington have been shot. The boys marked out the Tennis Court so I presume play will now begin for the Season'.[20] The separate realms of revolution and tennis are not connected syntactically, but their coexistence on the diarist's page indicates the way women recording events in Dublin necessarily connected their household trivia with the macro-political events playing out nearby. By 8 May, Martin's Rising narrative trails off and the tennis narrative picks up more force.

With the exception of the voyage of the *Asgard* in 1914 (see Chapter Two), an adventure that features in three women's accounts, the Rising and not earlier or later events forms the focus of this book: the shock of its occurrence, the brevity of its duration, and the drama of the fighting, surrender and executions, made it dominate the lives of the people who lived near it. While it lasted, it lasted in the foreground. Women's diaries and letters to relatives recorded in real time every detail of their daily lives under the week's unusual circumstances. And because the Rising was the first in the sequence of events that led directly to the formation of the Irish Free State, it features prominently in memoirs, autobiographies and government archives.

The women's accounts tend to focus on small interactions (like Byrne's entry into the Post Office) that reveal the way women and men improvise in new situations; the way, for instance, Mary Spring Rice and Molly Childers hung a dishcloth across the doorway of their tiny cabin on the *Asgard* so they could dress in a little privacy. To most historians, hanging a dishcloth is an event as negligible as jumping through a window, but both actions show the creative strategies women devised to share space with men. Because they record women's history with such immediacy, in episodes that foreground the practical issues involved in a gendered public sphere, the women's accounts complicate and enrich the primary military narrative of the Rising.

The chronology of the Rising is well known: the occupation of the garrisons on Easter Monday, the reading of the Proclamation in front of the GPO, engagements with the British military in various ways over the succeeding six days, the surrenders, the night on the cold, wet grass outside the Rotunda, the deportation and imprisonment of some rebels and the execution of others.[21] Over the past 30 or more years, that history has been expanded by a series of major works on women and the Easter Rising, studies emphasising women's significant presence, biographies, ideologies and the political history of Irish women's activism. The luxury of a focus exclusively on the words of women who lived through the events of Easter 1916 at close hand depends on many excellent groundbreaking books such as Margaret Ward's *Unmanageable revolutionaries: women and Irish nationalism*; Carol Coulter's *The hidden tradition: feminism, women & nationalism*; Ruth Taillon's *When history was made: the women of 1916*; Sinéad McCoole's *No ordinary women: Irish female activists in the revolutionary years 1900–1923*; Cal McCarthy's *Cumann na mBan and the Irish revolution*; Ann Matthews's *Renegades: Irish Republican women 1900–1922*; and Senia Pašeta's *Irish nationalist women 1900–1918*; as well as important essays such as Eve Morrison's 'The

Bureau of Military History and female Republican activism, 1913–1923';
Louise Ryan's '"In the line of fire": representations of women and war
(1919–1923) through the writings of Republican men'; and Beth
McKillen's 'Irish feminism and nationalist separatism, 1914–1923'.[22]

This book contributes the wealth of its material to the growing body
of work on Irish women's history not only by its focus on vignettes and
first-person sources but by its inclusion of unionist women as well as nationalists, and of women who had no immediate personal association
with the dramatic political events happening around them, such as
Dorothy Stopford, Estelle Nathan, May Fay, Mary Martin and others. It
also introduces manuscript sources that have not previously been studied
by scholars. These include major accounts written at the time of the
Rising or soon after it from notes taken as events occurred, such as Madge
Daly's 'The memoirs of Madge Daly', a typescript in the University of
Limerick Library's Special Collections, and Elsie Mahaffy's handwritten
'book' (her word for it) 'The Irish rebellion', a diary with accompanying
essays and memorabilia held in the Manuscripts and Archives Research
Library of Trinity College Library. I also consider manuscript revisions
in shorter memoirs by Mary Spring Rice and Elizabeth O'Farrell, because
the revisions, especially the deletions, offer interesting evidence of what
the women (or whoever marked the texts) considered inappropriate for
publication. Other shorter manuscripts, many of them letters, refer to
moments of contact with the Rising, contact in the form of gossip or news
or noise, that illuminate the way ordinary or conventional women attempted to comprehend what was happening around them.[23]

## I V

The accuracy of survivors' memories of 1916 has long inspired scepticism. In October 1934, when Catherine Byrne, then Mrs Rooney,
applied for a military service pension, she was required, like all appli-
cants, to submit to interviews and to provide documentary evidence
of her service.[24] Because of the unusual mode of her arrival in the GPO,
Cumann na mBan was not officially aware of her presence there; she
had arrived alone, not in response to a mobilisation order. At first, her
account of service during Easter Week was not accepted, although she
had been active in many sites preparing food, giving first aid and delivering dispatches. According to her list, she had been in the General
Post Office and the Hibernian Bank, both on O'Connell Street; in the
area of the Four Courts, King's Inns Quay, King Street, and Monk's

Bakery, Church Street.[25] Byrne felt strongly about her service in the Rising and in the War of Independence, because under the category 'Absence from duty and cause' she has written, in large upper case letters, 'NONE'.[26] By 1937, however, she was able to procure letters from many people, among them one of the two Volunteers who had hoisted her up to a side window of the Post Office, Francis Murtagh, who wrote confirming her story. The man who swore colourfully when she landed on top of him, Joe Gahan, also confirmed the incident, writing more plainly, 'I was inside when she jumped'.

In spite of letters from Murtagh and Gahan, from wounded men she had treated and from people who testified to seeing her at every Dublin location where she claimed to have served, officials at the Office of the Referee at the Department of Defence charged with determining the amount of pension to be awarded, if any, were unconvinced by Byrne's detailed narrative of her Easter Week service in particular. She was offended, writing on 26 April 1938, 'Apart from the matter of finance I feel a reflection is being cast on my National past'.[27] Judging by the long and somewhat repetitive record of documents, it appears that her account of her service during the Rising was finally accepted.[28]

A cautious approach is also taken by historians writing about some of the documents on which this book is based. Diarmaid Ferriter has urged 'scepticism' about memoirs as with 'all documentary evidence'.[29] Fearghal McGarry has written about the particular problems unique to the witness statements collected by the Bureau of Military History. Founded in 1947, the Bureau was staffed primarily by army officers. Some of the statements were presented to them already in written form, but many were taken down in interviews and 'composed into a coherent statement by the investigators'. The content of the statements is also problematic, based as they are on 'the witnesses' imperfect memory' of events. In an essay devoted particularly to the women's statements collected by the Bureau, Eve Morrison also warns that

> the lapse of over three decades between the events described and the recording of the testimonies sometimes weighed heavily on their contents. The interviewees were of advanced age, had almost always read other versions of the events recalled and frequently confused dates and details.[30]

However, the evidence provided in Byrne's pension file, as well as the detailed account she gave in 1952 to the Bureau, an account consistent in every significant detail with her pension application, seems undeniable and ought to persuade those who read all the documents that her memory was accurate. Details of later work in the national cause, such as a doctor's comments on the symptoms she suffered by carrying gelignite strapped to her arm, sound convincingly technical and not the kind of information that a young girl without medical training would be likely to know.[31]

Roy Foster notes that 'memories are not always the most reliable guide', and thus he uses 'contemporary diaries, letters and journalism' in *Vivid faces: the revolutionary generation in Ireland 1890–1923*.[32] At *home in the revolution* includes testimonies of many different kinds. No single category of life-writing covers the many genres in which the women recorded their experiences of 1916. From the explicitly polemical autobiography written for Irish–Americans to the reassuring letter sent home to a sister, from the official statement of service for a government office to the private love letters of a woman entirely unconnected to the Rising, the documents vary enormously in their sense of audience, their degrees of literary self-consciousness and their constructions of self. They also vary in proximity in time and place to the events they recount. The letters and diaries written during the Rising itself cannot be accused of forgetfulness. They were composed in real time and often tally interestingly with one another, as in the different responses of Lilly Stokes on Clyde Road in Ballsbridge and her cousin Elsie Mahaffy in Trinity to the sight of the men from Boland's Mills marching through the streets after the surrender. Mary Spring Rice's log of the *Asgard* was written daily, as were Mary Louisa Hamilton Norway's letters to her sister in England and Estelle Nathan's to her husband.

'For the historian', Helen Litton has written, 'an eye-witness account must be read as a subjective reporting of events, from one particular perspective; an eye-witness account is also an invaluable source in terms of emotions, personalities and atmosphere'.[33] Several of the longer texts I cite—those by Kathleen Clarke, Madge Daly and Elsie Mahaffy, among others—are openly ideological, written to get out the facts as they knew them but also to prove the justness of their cause, republican or loyalist or socialist–feminist. Other authors—Nora Connolly, Margaret Skinnider and Hanna Sheehy Skeffington—wrote to convey the truth about the Rising, as they experienced it, for fundraising in America. The subjective opinions of these women offer useful material as records of the way they felt. Madge Daly's account of her argument with a priest, Sheehy Skeffington's of her meeting with Asquith, or Gertrude Bannister's of her struggle to get better treatment for her cousin Roger Casement, testify to the anger these women felt and expressed, even if the texts do not give the words of the fights *verbatim*.

Although the witness statements may be more problematic than other documents, in some cases they were written at the time of the Rising or based on notes taken at that time At the end of her statement, Aoife de Burca writes, 'This account was written in June or July 1916 when these events were fresh in my mind'. The statements by Elizabeth Bloxham and Catherine Rooney contain detailed tables of contents with chapter divisions written in the first person of the woman herself (e.g. 'I go to Hibernian Bank', 'I take up work in Glasgow', or 'I protest against pulpit attack on Catholics' and 'The Rising and My Dismissal').[34] In other cases, such as the experiences of women held in Ship Street Barracks during and just after the Rising, the narratives cannot be accused of unreliability because four women's accounts tell the same stories and corroborate one another. In yet another case, the accounts of two of the Daly sisters (Madge Daly and Kathleen Clarke) describe what happened to Eily O'Hanrahan in Kilmainham Gaol in almost the same way O'Hanrahan describes it herself. In another instance, Mary McLoughlin remembers a message Thomas MacDonagh asked her to deliver to Joseph Plunkett, a recondite literary allusion she appears not to recognise and could therefore not have invented.[35]

Some of the women have definitely forgotten exactly what happened in 1916, and when they can't remember, they say so: 'I am very hazy about the early years', Louise Gavan Duffy writes about Cumann na mBan; and 'I cannot remember who the girls were' in the GPO, and 'I do not remember how we heard' about the surrender.[36] 'I don't remember how it came about that they got the chaplain', Grace Plunkett says of her famous wedding to Joseph Plunkett.[37] Some conversations in Kathleen Clarke's autobiography must be recreated from memory and are not *verbatim*, but it is unlikely she invented them altogether, because they do not show her in a patriotic light. She resisted returning to Ireland when (in 1907) she and her husband were happily living with their young sons on a small farm in Manorville, Long Island; and even more significantly, according to her narrative, on the morning of Easter Monday, she tried to dissuade her husband from joining the Rising: 'I feel I want to take you and hide you away, save you at any cost'.[38] In a few cases, Clarke in her autobiography and Madge Daly in hers claim the same conversational gambits; but whoever did the talking, the conversation's existence is at least validated.

## V

The subject matter of the chapters in this book is derived from the issues to which the women themselves devoted attention in their writing, activities of the sort that have traditionally interested women: managing a household, courtship and romance, challenging male authority, close friendships with women, and the life of the emotions. Precisely because these matters constitute women's usual concerns, they offer glimpses of what change can look like as it is being experienced or attempted. The opening chapter looks at moments when issues of gender were addressed explicitly: should women be arrested? should an unmarried woman dress a man's wound in the genital area? why weren't women allowed to pick up the rifles when the *Asgard* arrived at Howth Harbour?

The second chapter looks at the way two Protestant women, Mary Spring Rice and Elsie Mahaffy, managed two quite different kinds of domestic sites, the yacht *Asgard* (in July 1914) and the Trinity College Provost's House (in April 1916). In both cases, the sites were given over to military purposes, and they were bounded: Spring Rice could not leave the *Asgard*, nor Mahaffy the Provost's House. Adjusting to their distinct and unusual circumstances, the women took on new responsibilities in their temporary management of a semi-public space.

The next three chapters show the way intimate human relationships changed. Flirtation and courtship required new rules of engagement, because events before, during and after the Rising made trysts dangerous or impossible, disrupted plans and cast doubts over the fulfilment of romantic hopes. Confronted by hostile priests and British soldiers and bureaucrats, women under the influence of a revolution expressed their anger directly and were met with threats of violence from the men they confronted. In the midst of dangers and uncertainties, however, women offered safe and loving companionship to one another and created feminist zones of comfort.

The last two chapters study the way women engaged in what sociologist Arlie Russell Hochschild has (in a different context) called 'emotional labor': keeping the 'spirits up' of men marching off after the surrender to a fate as yet unknown to them, manifesting the appropriate and necessary control and not 'breaking down' in the cells of the men about to be executed, and generally showing a greater consciousness of emotions expressed and unexpressed.[39] Describing all these 'small behaviors', the women's records create the unofficial history of the way issues of gender were negotiated at a time of revolution.

# The petticoat heroine

Herald Staff Reporter

A DUBLIN woman who saw the Tricolour being hoisted on the G.P.O. in 1916 and carried a despatch from there to the Four Courts, recounted for me some of her experiences during the Easter Rising.

She is Mrs. Catherine Rooney (née Byrne), now a sprightly 70, who lives at 1 De Burgh Road, Parkgate Street.

Four 1916 service medals and seven War of Independence medals which Mrs. Rooney, her mother, four brothers and sister, were awarded is a striking testimony to the contribution the family made in the Irish fight for freedom. Their ages in Easter Week, 1916, ranged from Paddy Byrne, who was 24, down to Frank, who was 12. With these and Catherine there was Alice (18), Peter (16) and Jack (14).

For her services to the cause of Freedom during the Black and Tan war, their mother, Mrs. Catherine Byrne, was awarded the War of Independence medal.

## House raided

Mrs. Rooney told me that during this period, their house at 17 North Richmond Street, was used regularly by several members of Michael Collins's special squad, including Hugo McNeill, Joe Leonard, Pat McCreagh and Charlie Dalton. The house was raided on several occasions by the Tans, but luckily, nobody was ever caught there.

Mrs. Rooney, who, with sister Alice, was a member of Cumann na mBan, was in the G.P.O. on Easter Monday.

She had got into the building through a window on Princes St. And she was hardly inside when she had the first casualty to deal with—an officer in the volunteers, named Liam Clarke, who was injured when a homemade bomb accidentally exploded near him.

## Tore petticoat

"There were no bandages there at the time," said Mrs. Rooney, "and I had to tear a part of my petticoat to bandage the wounded officer."

She recalled that in the kitchenette at the G.P.O. where she was preparing some food, some cases of stout were

From left (back): Frank, Peter (dead), Paddy, Jack, now living in Limerick. Front: Alice (Mrs. Coogan), Mrs. Catherine Byrne and Catherine (Byrne) Rooney.

discovered. And she heard Thomas Clarke order that they were to be emptied down the sink.

"I was preparing some food when Joe Gahan, another

Mrs. Catherine Rooney in her Cumann na mBan uniform prior to Easter Week, 1916.

Dublin man called me and said Pearse was going to hoist the flag on the top of the building. I went up a ladder to the roof and saw him hoist the flag. He was on the

Henry Street side of the building and there was only a small group there for the ceremony.

Later, Mrs. Rooney told me, she bandaged another man in the G.P.O. with the remainder of her petticoat. The following day, she was sent from the Hibernian Bank at the corner of O'Connell St. and Middle Abbey St., where there were seven members of the Volunteers, to the G.P.O. for food.

"In the G.P.O. Pearse called me and told me he wanted me to take a despatch to Frank Fahy in the Four Courts. Joseph Plunkett wrote something on a piece of paper, which Pearse folded and gave to me. He told me to be very careful and said: "God be with you."

Mrs. Rooney said that as a precautionary measure she rolled the note in her hair bun and she saw Pearse turn to Plunkett and heard him say in Irish, "Isn't that a good idea." She delivered the note to the Four Courts but never saw Pearse after that.

## Brothers there

Mrs. Rooney told me that her brothers Paddy and Peter, who were in the G.P.O. during the Rising, were later taken to Kilmainham Jail and subsequently to Frongoch Prison. (Peter has since died).

Her sister Alice, now Mrs. Coogan, who lives in Glasgow, is coming to Dublin for the Jubilee celebrations.

---

This article from the *Evening Herald* of 13 April 1966 features Catherine Rooney (née Byrne) (who jumped through a window of the GPO in the first minutes of the Rising) recounting episodes from her experiences during Easter Week. The picture includes her brother Paddy, invoked by Michael Staines when he said 'I'll tell Paddy on you' as Byrne tried to enter the GPO through the front; her sister Alice, who headed for Liberty Hall when Catherine went to the GPO; and their mother, Mrs Byrne, who encouraged both daughters to get their equipment and follow the men into action.

44. Monepeter Hill
Dublin
20th February 1937

To Whom it may Concern.

This is to certify that I helped Mrs
Kathleen Rooney, whom I then knew as Miss
Kathleen Byrne to enter the window of the G.P.O.
in Princes St. on Easter Monday 1916.

Signed
Francis. D. Murtagh

Letter from Francis Murtagh in support of the pension application of  Catherine Rooney (née Byrne), confirming that he helped her 'enter the window of the G.P.O. in Princes [sic] St. on Easter Monday 1916' (Military Service Pensions Collection).

4o Mountjoy Sq,

Dublin 2o/2/37

This is to certify that I have known K Rooney (mee Byrne) since
1915, On Easter Monday 1916 She made her way into the G,P,O
through the window(Princes St) I was inside when she jumped and,
I assisted  She dressed Liam Clarke, and a few others,

Later we mounted the roof to see P H Pearse hoist the Flag
That night she with another Member went to the Hibernian Bank
I learned later she finished up the week in Nth King St.

I shall be only too pleased, to give any further evidence
that may be required,

Signed *Joe. Gahan .*

*( Kimmage. Garrison )*

Letter from Joe Gahan in support of the pension application of Catherine Rooney (née Byrne),
confirming that when she 'made her way into the G.P.O through the window' he 'was inside
when she jumped' (Military Service Pensions Collection).

*Chapter One*

'PROVISION FOR GIRLS'

'We haven't made any provision for girls here'.

Thomas MacDonagh, on Máire Nic Shiubhlaigh's
arrival at the garrison at Jacob's

I suppose the high ranking officer was General Lowe. The young officer stood, and we stood too. Louise [Gavan Duffy] stood up with great dignity. One of the officers said: 'We are not taking women, are we?' The other said: 'No'. ...Louise said: 'The cheek of him anyway—not taking women'.

Min Ryan, on the surrender of the
Jacob's garrison, 30 April 1916

Wherever 'girls' arrived, during Easter Week and just before and after, their arrival precipitated a discussion around gender. People were required to think about gender, to talk about it, however briefly, and often to articulate an instant policy about the presence of 'girls'. Girls would no doubt require some kind of special provision in the way of lavatories, dormitories and privacy. Girls were not the norm; men were the norm. So when Brigadier-General W. H. M. Lowe arrived at the Jacob's garrison to accept Thomas MacDonagh's surrender, his aide saw Louise Gavan Duffy and Min Ryan in the doorway and the question occurred to him: 'We are not taking women, are we?' His phrasing assumed an answer in the negative.[1]

The Rising raised consciousness: the active engagement of women was news and generated excited communication. The medical student Dorothy Stopford recorded in her diary, 'there are women SFs [Sinn Féiners] about with guns'.[2] A few weeks after it was over, Nell Humphreys, sister of The O'Rahilly, wrote to her sister-in-law in Australia, 'Did you hear at all of the part women took in the Rising?...every girl in every centre, the G.P.O., Jacobs, the College of Surgeons was cool and brave. They gave the men invaluable help and kept things normal'.[3]

According to Humphreys, her seventeen-year-old daughter Sighle challenged her mother's gendered notions of behaviour:

I used to feel ashamed of Sigle [sic] as being unwomanly, when Anna told me that at times it was difficult to keep her from taking a shot herself, that the way she gloried when the enemy fell was actually inhuman & her nerve during the whole time was wonderful. But it is only the spirit of the age...[4]

Here Nell Humphreys seems to be trying to readjust her own notions of what is 'womanly'. Her daughter's eagerness to kill 'the enemy' seems at first disturbing and 'inhuman', but when she considers it in the context of 'the spirit of the age', it seems patriotic.

That 'spirit of the age' was described in the *New York Times* by one Moira Regan, who had worked in the kitchens of the GPO during the Rising. In August 1916 she gave an interview to Joyce Kilmer in New York; the headline read 'Irish girl rebel tells of Dublin fighting':

One thing that would strike you about the conduct of the rebels was the absolute equality of the men and women. The women did first-aid work and some of them used their rifles to good advantage. They just did the work that was before them, and they were of the greatest moral aid.[5]

Kilmer (the author of the famous lines 'I think that I shall never see / A poem lovely as a tree') was impressed by Regan and wrote romantically of the Rising: '...there is a strange fire in her gray eyes when she tells of the April evening when for the first time she saw the flag of the Irish Republic floating on its staff at the head of O'Connell Street'; within two years he had died at the Second Battle of the Marne.[6]

Not all the rebel women were 'cool' and 'inhuman'. But with impressive spontaneity, in private or semi-private encounters, women often took strong feminist stands by resisting patronising or patriarchal suggestions. When, for instance, on the morning of Good Friday in 1916, Eoin MacNeill, Chief of Staff (and founder) of the Volunteers, entrusted a large package containing his private papers to Kitty O'Doherty, he 'emphasised the fact that I was to keep them under my own control—"keep them yourself"'.[7] Leaving Volunteer headquarters, O'Doherty ran into John MacDonagh, who felt obliged to help her. The exchange was short but pungent: 'He said to me: "Allow me, Madame". I said: "No, no, I carry my own parcel". He said to me: "I don't walk with a lady with a parcel". I said: "Then you don't walk with me".'[8]

As O'Doherty tells the story, her loyalty to MacNeill and her dislike of MacDonagh make it easy for her to reject his offer to carry the parcel. But because he has framed his offer in gendered language, her rejection has a feminist edge. She seems to find his apparent courtliness harassing, but it is her obligation to MacNeill and to the Volunteers that gives her the authority to rebuff MacDonagh's offer. O'Doherty evidently came from a family of strong women, because in her witness statement she mentions with pride her sister, Mother Columba, the author of 'Who fears to speak of Easter Week'.[9]

## ACCESS TO THE FIGHT

The concept of gender came up often over the basic issue of letting women 'in', in, that is, to the garrison, the room, the action.[10] On Easter Monday Máire Nic Shiubhlaigh, with five other Cumann na mBan women, deliberately went to Jacob's because she was fond of Thomas MacDonagh and his 'vivid gaiety'. 'His good humour', she writes, 'never faltered under any circumstances'.[11] When she found the entrance to the garrison and met MacDonagh there, his first response was surprise: 'My God....It's Maire Walker! How did you get in?' She writes that he 'seemed very much at ease', and then said, 'We haven't made any provision for girls here'. She made the case for her usefulness—'we could cook for the garrison and look after casualties'—and the women were allowed in. The kindly MacDonagh was not prejudiced; the possibility of helpful women in his garrison seems not to have occurred to him before.

It was not only men who were slow or reluctant to give young women access to the Rising: older women also held them back. One of the youngest women 'out' in the Rising, the fifteen-year-old Mary McLoughlin carried messages between the GPO and the Irish Citizen Army in Stephen's Green and later in the College of Surgeons. Her rebel colleagues felt a kind of parental affection for her. Julia Grenan (a member of Cumann na mBan and the Citizen Army) calls her 'a little girl', and says that when James Connolly sent both of them to get groceries for the GPO garrison, '...the little McLoughlin one bought stuff too and she had one penny left. Connolly made her keep the penny!'[12] (The annual pension granted McLoughlin by the Military Pensions committee was twenty pounds, eleven shillings—and one penny.)[13] But McLoughlin's own family was less enthusiastic about her involvement. When her brother appeared at the Post Office on Thursday he was not encouraging: 'Seán told me to go home to my mother that she was looking everywhere for me and would kill me when she saw me. Seán

McDermott [*sic*], who was standing by, said "Your mother won't kill you. She will live to be proud of you"'. Several messages later, after a trip to the garrison at Jacob's, McLoughlin went home to check in on her mother. The little drama that ensued was not what Seán MacDermott had imagined:

> ...mother opened the door and what a surprise she got when she saw me. 'Well my fine rossie, but I'm glad to see you and to have you home again and I intend to keep you safe with me', said she...She brought me upstairs, put me into a room and locked me in, saying 'You will be safer there for a few days. I will go and get you some food. You must be starving, my poor child'. With that she departed before I got the chance of saying one word. Realising I was locked in a room and that I was in possession of a gun, I turned towards the window and there I saw my opportunity of clearing out and bringing the gun back again to the G.P.O. It did not take me long to get out of the window....[14]

Mrs McLoughlin was not as enthusiastic about her daughter's involvement in the Rising as Mrs Byrne had been about hers. However, for Mary McLoughlin as for Catherine Byrne, a window was not a significant obstacle.[15]

The 24-year-old future Republican activist Máire Comerford was not as lucky as McLoughlin, though she got a good story out of her adventures anyway. Comerford had come up from the family farm in Wexford to take care of a wealthy invalid relative, Maude Mansfield, whose occupation is described on the 1911 Census form as 'independent means'.[16] On the day the Rising broke out, Comerford had to get back to Rathgar from Blackrock. Discovering there were no trams running, she followed the tramlines because 'If going home the only way I knew was going to let me see a rebellion that was a thing not to be missed!'[17]

On that first day, Comerford managed to walk past British soldiers and through barricades to talk with a Citizen Army sentry on duty at Stephen's Green. She was offered access to the garrison and to 'Madame Markievicz', but she thought of 'Poor cousin Maude in her bathchair, helpless' and went home. Cousin Maude tried to keep Comerford on a short leash: 'Back in Rathgar Maude Mansfield tried to be firm. She forbad me to leave the house again. "I'll have to go to Mass". "Well, alright, go to Mass". "Mass could be anywhere" says I to myself'.

Comerford's sorties to 'Mass' took her as far north as O'Connell Bridge but no farther. By Thursday she could no longer tour the Rising, and the Mansfield household ran out of butter. Comerford was sent away from the centre of action to Bewley's farm at Orwell Road with 'an ostrich feathered Dublin lady, a crony of my cousin's'. The woman was a unionist, and 'Under the circumstances', writes Comerford, 'with her sympathies and mine what they were, conversation was very difficult'. Nevertheless, she made a polite effort to find a subject on which they might agree:

> ...Coming up the avenue I admired Bewley's herd of beautiful Jersey cows. 'My mother would love to have a few like those' I said, by way of conversation and to change the subject. Soon we came to the place where Mr Bewley in person, a tall old man, pink faced through agitation, rage, or by nature, was slamming pounds of butter onto butter paper, wrapping them and handing them out at full speed...I would have thought angels feared to tread in the presence of his agitation, and when I heard my companion address him, and bring me into it, my heart stood still. 'This young lady wants to buy a cow', she announced as if I could buy Bewleys two or three times over.
>
> 'Just go round that way, please, I will send my herd to you', he said...We were shown around, accompanied by the lady's line of talk to a herd. My face was burning. Thank God I had secured the butter before we got into this fix. I promised to describe the cows to my mother and that she would write if she thought one of them might suit her. Then we went, as far as I was concerned, never to return no matter what butter was wanted.

Like the vignettes of McLoughlin and the 'unwomanly' Sighle Humphreys, Comerford's story shows the impatience of a young woman eager to slip away from the authorities that restrain her activity. Politely she chose to converse with the ostrich-feathered lady and find neutral common ground in Mr Bewley's cows.[18] All three women (Comerford, Humphreys, McLoughlin), restrained in various ways in 1916, would become active in the War of Independence and in the Civil War. Comerford and Humphreys were politically engaged republicans for the rest of their lives.

General Maxwell, too, had to think twice about access for women. His letter to the War Office of 10 May 1916 records the to-him-surprising fact that 'I found that about seventy women had either surrendered with the rebels or had been arrested by the police'. They were, he discovered, 'the women's brigade of the Irish Volunteers', a group 'highly seditious in its activities'.[19] Like MacDonagh, he had made 'no provision' for the women, and most were released from Kilmainham by 8 May. The eight remaining women prisoners were considered more dangerous, and 'had they been male prisoners, I would have at least recommended them for internment'. New, gender-specific policies were required. 'In view of their sex', and under a provision of the Defence of the Realm Act, Maxwell ordered that they be required 'to reside in England'. In the end, only two were deported, and five others were interned at Aylesbury Prison (Winifred Carney, Brigid Foley, Helena Molony, Marie Perolz and Nell Ryan).

## FIRSTS

Women were conscious of their 'firsts', not just Catherine Byrne, the 'first Cumann na mBan member in the GPO', and Máire Nic Shiubhlaigh, the first in the Jacob's garrison, but also Una Daly, who writes, 'I was the first woman into the Four Courts'.[20] As Ina Connolly recalled, Patrick Pearse was also conscious of such a first, even as he was about to make history himself. On Easter Monday in Liberty Hall, Pearse spoke to the 'girls from the North', Ina and Nora Connolly (daughters of James Connolly) among them:

> He carried a roll of papers in his hand. We all encircled him with anxious excitement. At last he spoke: 'You have the privilege of being the first women to read this Proclamation. Read it, study it and try to remember what is written and then you will be able to tell the men of the north that you saw and read that which will be read at the G.P.O. today at 12 o'clock, and will be posted all over the city'.[21]

Two years earlier, Ina Connolly, then only seventeen, had experienced another first. On Sunday, 26 July 1914, members of the Fianna went to Howth to pick up some of the rifles brought by the *Asgard*:

They all disappeared early on...saying they had been invited out and no girls were welcome....This was most unusual; even Madam [Constance Markievicz] had not been asked. We put in our time nicely with the Countess, listening to all her stories...Little did we realise the important happenings that were taking place, to hear that guns were being run in at Howth and us sitting looking pretty on the mountains only a few miles away nearly broke our hearts. How could we face back to Belfast and to my father and say we knew nothing and did less. It really looked as if we were not trusted. We, who had been called upon at all times and under any circumstances, turned up when we were wanted...I was overcome with joy and disappointment at the one time. My sister took me by the arm and led me away from the boys, telling me not to show my feeling so plainly—'a good soldier takes his beating with his chin up; perhaps there will be some work set aside for you to do and they wanted to leave somebody at the house to carry on in case they were all arrested'. I must say that was poor comfort, but she did her best to heal an awful wound that had been inflicted on me. Had I been a boy I would not have been overlooked.

But then Connolly learned that she had been delegated to take some of the rifles up to Belfast, and 'The dear Countess said: "You are the first woman to run guns up to the north"'. And when the guns were safely delivered, her father praised her saying, 'Bravo and well done. I could not have done it any better myself'.[22]

## ROLE MODELS

The women of 1916 had two sets of role models, men and women. To some extent, they simply followed the pattern of the men. That was quite literally true: Annie Cooney, a seamstress (according to the 1911 Census), made her own Cumann na mBan uniform: 'I had cut it on the pattern of Con Colbert's coat'.[23] As Catherine Byrne wrote, 'My mother told me to get my equipment and to follow them'.[24] Of the women in the Citizen Army who went to City Hall, Helena Molony writes, 'I, walking at the head of my nine girls, was, I believe, perhaps two or three ranks behind Sean [Connolly]. We simply followed the men'.[25]

All the women that General Maxwell had to house in prison had also 'followed' the men. Writing of the surrender at the Marrowbone Lane garrison, Annie Cooney writes, 'We Cumann na mBan fell in behind the Volunteers. They had tried to persuade us to go home, but we refused, saying that we would stick it out to the end'.[26] Rose McNamara, an officer of Cooney's section of Cumann na mBan, recorded:

> The men gave each of us their small arms to do as we liked with, thinking we were going to go home, but we were not going to leave the men we were with all the week to their fate; we decided to go along with them and be with them to the end whatever our fate might be.[27]

So also Min Ryan says of her attempt to get back to the GPO on Wednesday, even though Jennie Wyse Power insisted on the danger: '...we were determined to get back...if the men were to die, we would too; that is the way we felt'.[28] And (according to Catherine Byrne's account) this exchange took place in the Four Courts on the Saturday before the surrender: 'The men were all keyed up saying "We are not going to surrender; we'll continue to fight. Would you be game, Kate?" they said to me. I replied: "Of course, whatever you do, I'll do"'.[29]

In practical matters and in urgent situations, women followed the men. But when they were on their own, for inner strength, they looked to a gendered historical precedent. Madge Daly reminded her sisters, on their way to Kilmainham Gaol for a final meeting with their brother Ned, that they were 'the daughters and nieces of Fenians'. Eily O'Hanrahan, reporting the traumatic final meeting with her brother Micheál in his cell at Kilmainham the night before his execution, offered a different precedent: 'He told us not to fret, and we tried to reassure him that we would be all right and that the women of '98 had to endure that too'.[30] Maeve Cavanagh mentions a similar inspiration, drawn from an epithet given to her by Connolly:

> 'I wonder what we'll call you', he said. When the paper—
> 'Workers' Republic'—came out that week the placards
> were all over Dublin, 'Great Revolutionary Poem by
> Maeve Cavanagh, the Poetess of the Revolution'. I felt
> very proud that day, because I had always admired the
> women poets of '48 and longed to be like them.[31]

A few years after the Rising, Helena Concannon published *Women of 'Ninety-Eight*, but in their active participation in war and resistance, the women of 1916 had already gone beyond the conservative, secondary role models offered by the book's chapters: 'The mothers of 'Ninety-Eight', 'The wives of 'Ninety-Eight', 'Some other sisters of 'Ninety-Eight' and so forth. The women of '98 themselves were less conventional and decorative than Concannon's vocabulary made them seem: the phrases 'exquisite young girl' and 'heroic devotion' place them in conventional and non-threatening categories.[32]

## PLAYING THE WOMAN

Rebel women in 1916 were not always jumping through windows into military sites or marching jauntily to prison. Sometimes they were helpless, flirtatious and weak—strategically. Entirely conscious of men's expectations of gendered behaviour, the women played along with them. They knew how to theatricalise a position of weakness in order to construct a position of strength. In the words of Brigid Lyons, a member of Cumann na mBan, they 'had recourse' to 'feminine guile'.[33] Attempting to reach Commandant Ned Daly at the Church Street outpost of the Four Courts garrison, Phyllis Morkan and her sister-in-law met with British soldiers at every crossing. Carrying 'several rounds of ammunition' in a raincoat draped over her arm, Morkan got 'a shock' but simply 'smiled and chatted with the soldiers...and they did not question us'.[34] Mairéad Ní Cheallaigh went in the 'girl' rather than the 'young woman' direction: when she decided to go home (from the Church Street outpost on Friday of Easter Week), instead of acting the charming young woman, she disguised herself as a girl: 'I took off my nurse's apron and let down my hair in two plaits which must have made me look very young'.[35] When questioned, she presented herself as young and helpless: 'I said I had come out on Monday to look for food and there were a lot of shops down there and I got caught in the fighting and hid in the houses. I said my mother was alone at home and I was worried about her and she probably about me'.[36]

Presenting themselves in reference to a mother constructs the young women both as dependants and as caretakers: 'I always said that I was trying to get home to my sick mother': that was Catherine Byrne's story to people such as the 'kind hearted woman' of the tenements who let her spend the night, when in fact she was carrying dispatches for the Volunteers.[37] Making her way with her two sisters

to Church Street on Thursday of Easter week, Brigid Foley 'had no difficulty in getting through as we made up all sorts of pitiful stories about
sick relatives, &c.'[38]

'Plaits' served to make a woman free of suspicion. The young
Cathleen Ryan, carrying ammunition to Omagh on the Monday of
Easter Week, was advised 'if anyone questioned me I was to say I was
going north to be a priest's housekeeper. I was about 15 at the time
and generally wore my hair in two long plaits'.[39] The combination of
plaits and the words 'priest's housekeeper' sufficed to de-politicise a
woman with a suitcase of ammunition.

In a brilliant and apparently spontaneous move, Lillie Connolly
adopted a particular maternal role, that of the mother concerned for her
daughters' sexual reputation. In early 1916, two Fianna members from
Glasgow with a trunk full of gelignite spent the night at the Connollys'
Belfast house; Ina Connolly arranged for a car to drive them and their
luggage to the train station the next morning. While the Connolly
daughters were at work, detectives arrived to confront their mother:

> 'And what is it you are looking for' mother said after they
> had gone through the house and satisfied themselves there
> was nobody staying and nothing to trace of visitors
> having been.
>
> 'Well, it's like this. We expected you to have two young
> men staying here, and you say you did not see anyone
> staying here. It looks as if you're right. Now they could
> not be here without your knowing it. Would you say
> that's correct?'
>
> 'Well, as far as I know, there were no men slept here
> on Saturday night, for I saw all my family to bed and they
> were up early in the morning for early Mass and I went
> down to Crawfordsburn for the day with a friend and re-
> turned late at night and went to bed as we have to start
> early to work on Monday, so I can assure you there was
> no visitor staying any night here'.
>
> 'But, Mrs Connolly, we have information to the effect
> that two young men came off the Glasgow boat and drove
> straight here'.
>
> 'Well, that might be so,' mother innocently replied,
> 'without my knowing. You see I have a couple of girls that
> the local boys are always after, and when they get my back
> turned they bring them in and have a ceili in the parlour,

dancing and singing to their hearts' content. I never mind. I believe they're safer in the house than running wild on the streets. I thought that some of the neighbours had lodged a complaint and I would not like them to be offensive in any way. Their father would not hear tell of them losing the run of themselves like that'.

The more apologetic she became, the more the detectives tried to calm her down; the more she made a fool of them.

'If you had only told me that on your first visit I could have told you that whatever my girls did they would never keep their boy friends here all night without consulting me, and, of course, I would never put up with that'.

They finally withdrew, satisfied that there was no trace or sign of a visitor or two from Scotland in the vicinity.[40]

These cleverly constructed identities—the flirtatious young woman, the innocent girl, the priest's housekeeper, the concerned mother—were usefully available to women. In spite of the 'women of '98', a tradition not necessarily well-known to the non-nationalist, the woman overtly or covertly engaged in revolution was still, in the spring of 1916, a novelty to detectives, police and soldiers. There was always the possibility that she really was innocent, young, helpless or seriously maternal.

On the streets of Dublin during the Rising, it was unclear, at any given moment, how to 'read' an Irish woman. The soldiers might have encountered many women uninvolved in the Rising simply trying to get food for their families or to get home; women curious about the fighting, tourists at the revolution; women from the slums looting; women attempting to return home after the Easter holiday; loyalist women haranguing the rebels; or Irish Citizen Army or Cumann na mBan women in mufti.[41] The soldiers had to make quick determinations when they encountered women out on the street, based on a variety of assumptions about gender: that, for instance, women were weak and required protection; that they were young and attractive and would enjoy smiles and flirtation; that they were collaborating with the rebels and should be searched; or that they were part of the leadership of the Rising and deserved to be humiliated. In any encounter between a British soldier and an Irish woman, all of these possibilities were potentially in play. Always, of course, women were 'different', but what kind of difference obtained in any situation was a matter of conjecture.

Because women were harder to read, they were particularly useful in hiding rebellion-related items on their body. Men hid them too, of course, but women could exploit both their apparently innocent womanliness and their bodies. Their clothing, with its hems and folds and textured fabrics, could also help. There was an art to this kind of deception. On the second day of the Rising, Catherine Byrne was 'hanging around the main hall' of the GPO

> ...when Padraig Pearse asked me would I take a dispatch. I said: 'Yes, sir'. I did not know where at the time. He called me over to where Joseph Plunkett was sitting. He spoke to Joseph Plunkett. He was looking very bad, very thin and ghastly, as if he was going to pass out. He wrote the dispatch and I noticed as he was writing that he had a gold bangle on his arm. I said to myself 'I wish I had that'. I thought it very funny seeing a man wearing a bangle. He handed the dispatch to Padraig Pearse who read it. Padraig Pearse told me it was for Captain Fahy at the Four Courts and warned me to be very careful. In his presence I took off my velvet beret and pinned the dispatch inside my thick hair, pulled hair up over it and tied up the hair again with the pink ribbon and put on the beret. Both Pearse and Plunkett smiled and Pearse gave me a blessing in Irish.[42]

In this charming vignette each side admires the other: the nineteen-year-old Byrne, who had been a grocery shop assistant at age fourteen, one of eleven children of a coach trimmer, did not come from the kind of background where gold bangles were generally worn, and certainly not by men.[43] The wealthy, interestingly dressed Plunkett was exotic to her.[44] And the two rebel leaders have a moment of pleasure in the midst of their revolution, in seeing how this very young woman, in her first revolution also, spontaneously uses her natural resources to help the cause, dextrously managing her 'thick hair', her 'pink ribbon', and her 'velvet beret'. There is wonder on both sides, as people who would never otherwise have met are brought together.

Old women could be clever also, exploiting their age and apparent frailty in the national cause. Madge Daly's unpublished memoir tells how a Howth gun ceremonially given to her uncle, the Fenian John Daly, was saved during a raid on the Dalys' Limerick house:

> We had the Howth rifle which was presented to my uncle after the gun-running [inscribed by many of the men who later became signatories of the Proclamation] and two miniature rifles and some revolvers. The guns were rolled up in a large carpet, which lay against the wall. My mother sat in a large armchair in front of the roll. She was very frail and delicate looking and managed to get a weakness but when my sister went over to help her she gave a wink. My sister nearly roared laughing...The soldiers were very sympathetic and did not like to disturb her, so her wit saved the guns. The padded armchairs were packed with ammunition, but it was not discovered.[45]

Of course Mrs Daly really was a weak old woman, but a clever one who figured that gender roles might trump politics, that male respect for old mothers might trump British hostility to Irish republicans; she even managed to fool her daughter. The soldiers who raided the Dalys' house were usually not so polite, but this once they were. Mrs Daly plays the domestic role, pretending to be simply a sick old lady in her chair; but with ammunition in the upholstery and guns in the carpet, she's hiding an armoury.

## SEXUALITY

One recurrent topic in these accounts, sometimes emphasised and sometimes treated as a detour from the main narrative, is the sexualised body. With unmarried women living unchaperoned in close proximity to men for a week, and often treating wounded men, sexual issues were bound to arise. They were not discussed *per se*, but they appear in some of the witness statements. When on the first day of the Rising the British soldiers who attacked the City Hall garrison saw the women there, they thought of them in terms of their sexual vulnerability, assuming they were hostages rather than rebels. According to Helena Molony's statement, one woman in the Citizen Army exploited this assumption as 'the troops poured up the stairs and came in to where the girls were':

> The British officers thought these girls had been taken prisoner by the rebels. They asked them: 'Did they do anything to you? Were they kind to you? how many are up here?'

Jinny Shanahan—quick enough—answered: 'No, they did not do anything to us. There are hundreds upstairs—big guns and everything'. She invented such a story that they thought there was a garrison up on the roof, with the result that they did delay, and took precautions. It was not until the girls were brought out for safety and, apparently when they were bringing down some of the men, that one of the lads said: 'Hullo, Jinny, are you all right'. The officer looked at her, angry at the way he was fooled by this girl. I think that is important, because that may have delayed them, by some hours, from getting to the men on the roof. It was very natural for the British officer to take her story, and to think there were hundreds of men along the roofs of the City Hall and Dame Street, as she told them. I would not blame him for being taken in, when she said: 'There are hundreds of them with big guns'.

I thought that was something for which Napoleon would have decorated her.[46]

Like General Lowe and his aide taking the surrender at the end of the week, the British soldiers were unprepared for women soldiers. Their first response is chivalrous: 'Were they kind to you?' Whatever about Napoleon, Molony wanted to 'decorate' Shanahan for a feminist strategy. Kathleen Lynn describes the same moment without the Napoleonic allusion:

After a long time an entry was made by the British soldiers, I think through a window in the back. I was suddenly told by a voice in the dark to put up my hands which I did. I was asked by an officer who was there. I said some women and a wounded man. I found out afterwards that men were there too, but I did not know it at the time. When I told him I was a doctor, he thought I had just come in to attend to the wounded. I informed him that I belonged to the Citizen Army which surprised him very much.[47]

Lynn also omits or does not remember the soldiers' apparent concern for the women's safety, but she includes their surprise at the presence of women. The two accounts together, Molony's and Lynn's, suggest an encounter in which the element of gender is the chief feature.

Like the British soldiers, Irish priests assumed that women were in sexual danger; they became especially concerned after the surrender, when the women were left without the protection of the Volunteers. Brigid Foley mentions a night when she was the only woman in Kilmainham Gaol; all the others had been released, but a detective told her she was 'wanted', so she had to stay. She writes,

> I spent that night by myself in Kilmainham—in a different cell—so terrified that I remained on my knees behind the cell door all night. I should mention that the soldiers often were drunk and two of the Church St. priests thought it advisable one night to stay in the prison all night for the protection of the girls.[48]

In a similar situation, Brigid Lyons remained in the Four Courts garrison after the men were arrested. She was told by both Ned Daly and a British officer to stay, along with some of the other Cumann na mBan 'girls':

> We slept again in the judges' ermine, with a big guard outside the door. We had chocolate and cream crackers before we went to sleep. One of the Church St. priests, Fr. Columbus, stayed in the room with us till morning by way of protection. We were only allowed to the bathroom in twos and threes under escort. Two were allowed to the kitchen to make tea, also under escort.[49]

This curious situation shows the potential violation of several boundaries, as the male priests sleep in the room with the women, the women appropriate the judges' ermine robes and sleep in them, and all of them occupy the Four Courts.[50]

The uneasiness over even a hint of sexual transgression works both ways: the women themselves were uneasy about seeing men's nakedness. Catherine Byrne's account of treating a wound hints at such a concern:

> Before I had time to have any food myself I was told by a Volunteer that one of the guard in the storey above had been wounded and required first aid. When I went up to the guard room I found the wounded man and in the presence of Father Flanagan, who was uncovering

the soldier's wound which was near the groin (the bullet had entered there and come out through the back) I applied a large bandage, really a belly-band, and tied it at the side in an effort to stop the bleeding. There was not much blood, as the bleeding was internal. The soldier was taken immediately to hospital where I heard afterwards he died.[51]

Byrne's witness statement, which is dated 1950, appears to have been written by herself, not given orally in an interview with the Bureau of Military History as some of the others were. There is a detailed, carefully made table of contents with chapter titles such as 'I give First Aid and prepare food for the Volunteers'. Most of the other statements are not divided into chapters that way. And so the structure of the operative sentence in this passage, Byrne's own syntax, is interesting: before she uses the words 'uncovering' and 'groin', she writes the phrase 'in the presence of Father Flanagan'. She has constructed the sentence so that the priest's presence mediates between the very young woman and the wounded man's naked body; the priest desexualises the occasion. The word 'groin' forms part of a dependent clause (within another dependent clause) that describes Father Flanagan; it is he 'who was uncovering the soldier's wound which was near the groin...'. The parenthetic phrase also distances the name of the body part from the 'I' of the speaker'.

A potential contact taboo arises as well as a visual one, because Byrne had to touch the man's body in intimate places and to apply a bandage. The same concern about a woman's treating a wound near the sexual parts of a man's body occurs in Áine Heron's witness statement. Her family on both sides 'had all been Fenians', and, as she says about the Rising, '...it was what I had been looking forward to always and I wanted to be in it, though the time was not really opportune for me as I expected a baby—my third—in August'. She was 'in it'; Heron did first-aid work mostly at the Four Courts garrison, but on the Monday of Easter Week, she and another woman set up a temporary medical centre in a shop on Church Street:

It may have been Monday evening we had our first casualty. Someone came along and asked were there any Cumann na mBan here? We asked what the wound was and got the reply, 'A deep cut in the thigh'. Miss Hayes suggested that as I was a married woman I should take it on. It was Eddie

Morkan who had cut himself with his sheath knife when jumping over a barricade. I dressed the wound and Eddie told me afterwards that the dressing lasted for three weeks and was finally taken off in Knutsford Gaol.[52]

The line about 'a married woman' is only a subtext in the passage, but it forms an important part of women's narratives of the body in 1916 because it does not exist in isolation. In the previous episode, it was the priest who desexualised the man's wound and sanctioned the sight and touch of a 21-year-old woman. Here it is not the celibate asexuality of the priest but the marital, maternal sexuality of Áine Heron. 'Miss' Hayes, unmarried and therefore innocent of the naked adult male body, should not dress a wound in the thigh—or so Miss Hayes herself thought, and Heron accepted the taboo and mentions it in her statement.[53] But the focus of Heron's narrative is the work she did, so to complete the narrative, she shifts the emphasis to Eddie Morkan's gratitude for her care.[54]

In the context of these two statements, it is worth looking at what the English writer Vera Brittain says on the same subject in *Testament of youth*. In this classic First World War memoir, published in 1933, Brittain writes about her experiences during the war in which her beloved brother Edward, her fiancé and several close friends were all killed. As the war began, she was studying English literature at Somerville College, Oxford, but in 1915 she began working in a hospital in Devonshire taking care of wounded soldiers.

Throughout my two decades of life, I had never looked upon the nude body of an adult male; I had never even seen a naked boy-child since the nursery days when, at the age of four or five, I used to share my evening baths with Edward. I had therefore expected, when I first started nursing, to be overcome with nervousness and embarrassment, but, to my infinite relief, I was conscious of neither. Towards the men I came to feel an almost adoring gratitude for their simple and natural acceptance of my ministrations. Short of actually going to bed with them, there was hardly an intimate service that I did not perform for one or another in the course of four years, and I still have reason to be thankful for the knowledge of masculine functioning which the care of them gave me, and for my early release from the sex-inhibitions that even today—

thanks to the Victorian tradition which up to 1914 dictated that a young woman should know nothing of men but their faces and their clothes until marriage pitchforked her into an incompletely visualised and highly disconcerting intimacy—beset many of my female contemporaries, both married and single.[55]

At 20, Brittain is the same age as Catherine Byrne (who did her intimate nursing 'in the presence of Father Flanagan'). Brittain confronts directly and explicitly her innocence of 'the nude body of an adult male'. The subject of the paragraph is not her first-aid work but her 'early release' from Victorian 'sex-inhibitions'. Her word 'pitchforked' suggests the shock and power of the change that transforms an innocent virgin into 'a married woman', to use Áine Heron's phrase. All the force of society, custom and 'Victorian tradition' goes into that verb, implying an agency stronger than the woman's own in determining the way she encounters heterosexual intimacy.

Brittain is of course writing her own 'testament'. Her subject is her own political/spiritual/psychological development, a kind of *Bildungsroman*, not an official statement of political work for a bureau of military history accounting for her national service during the war. Given the generic convention in which she was writing, she had the luxury of constructing her subjectivity out of her own unofficial home-front experiences. The 1916 women are more concerned to construct themselves as part of a collective, as Cumann na mBan, or the Irish Citizen Army, or a descendant of Fenians. The witness statements from the Bureau of Military History show consciousness of their context, a state archive created 'to assemble and co-ordinate material to form the basis for the compilation of the history of the movement for Independence' (1913–21).[56] All of the accounts appear motivated by an interest in showing what work they did, how in a very practical way they contributed to 'the movement for Independence'. Their externality and the emphasis on material detail make even these distinctly gendered episodes emphasise their identity as part of the larger 'history of the movement for Independence'.[57]

Ina Connolly Heron (the 'first woman to run guns to the north') pictured in Irish costume with Archie Heron, whom she would later marry.

Máire Comerford (who pretended to admire Mr Bewley's cows in order to avoid discussing the Rising with a unionist) pictured here, in the centre, in 1921 with members of Cumann na mBan.

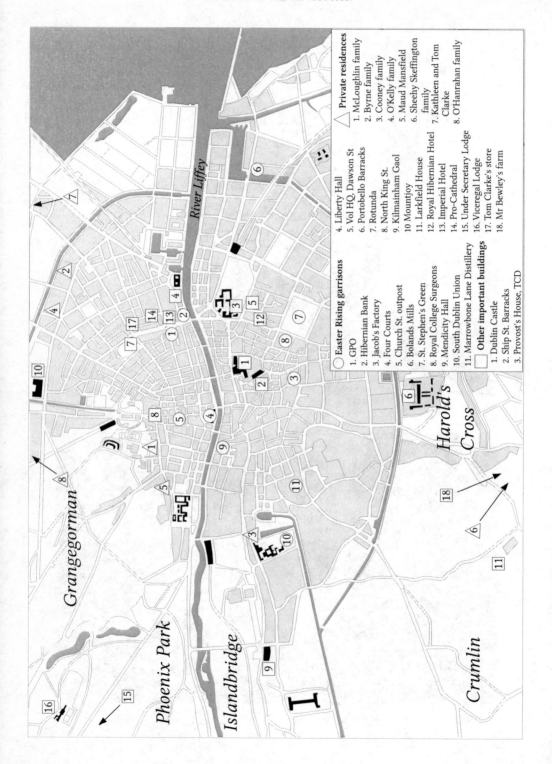

**Easter Rising garrisons**
1. GPO
2. Hibernian Bank
3. Jacob's Factory
4. Four Courts
5. Church St. outpost
6. Bolands Mills
7. St. Stephen's Green
8. Royal College Surgeons
9. Mendicity Hall
10. South Dublin Union
11. Marrowbone Lane Distillery

**Other important buildings**
1. Dublin Castle
2. Ship St. Barracks
3. Provost's House, TCD
4. Liberty Hall
5. Vol HQ, Dawson St
6. Portobello Barracks
7. Rotunda
8. North King St.
9. Kilmainham Gaol
10 Mountjoy
11. Larkfield House
12. Royal Hibernian Hotel
13. Imperial Hotel
14. Pro-Cathedral
15. Under Secretary Lodge
16. Viceregal Lodge
17. Tom Clarke's store
18. Mr Bewley's farm

**Private residences**
1. McLoughlin family
2. Byrne family
3. Cooney family
4. O'Kelly family
5. Maud Mansfield
6. Sheehy Skeffington family
7. Kathleen and Tom Clarke
8. O'Hanrahan family

*Chapter Two*

# MARY SPRING RICE, ELSIE MAHAFFY AND DOMESTIC SPACE

'Gordon' she said, 'You're ruining the guns with that coffee'.

Mary Spring Rice, 'Diary of the *Asgard*', 1914

At a little after 7:30 the 'pounding down' of Liberty Hall began—it lasted one half an hour and was indeed terrible; even the solid 'Provost's House' trembled...

Elsie Mahaffy, 'The Irish rebellion of 1916'

Guns were stashed in many intimate places in Dublin households in the years after the Howth gun-running and during the following decade: Catherine Byrne's father hid them in the fireplace.[1] In the days immediately preceding the Rising, the O'Kelly family let Patrick and Willie Pearse keep their revolvers and ammunition in the drawing room. And 'no one would enter the room without their permission', Mrs O'Kelly reassured them.[2] Annie Cooney, Lucy Smyth, Mary McLoughlin and many women hid guns on their person as they moved them from one house to another. Phyllis Morkan 'smiled and chatted' with British soldiers she met on the street while carrying a raincoat full of ammunition.[3] Weapons also had practical uses besides killing: in the Marrowbone Lane Distillery garrison, Rose McNamara picked the boiled chicken out of the pots with bayonets, 'not having any forks or utensils for cooking'.[4] And on the return gun-running voyage of the *Asgard* in 1914, during the trip back to Ireland from the Belgian coast, Mary Spring Rice and Molly Childers slept on top of rifles. As Spring Rice noted in the log, 'it is terribly easy to lose one's possessions in the cabin; they drop between the mattresses into the rifles and disappear. There will be a lot of hairpins found among them when they are unloaded'.[5]

Two detailed diaries show how women managed a household when serious weapons were in the way. Mary Spring Rice (1880–1924), only daughter of Lord Monteagle of Brandon, and Elsie Mahaffy (c.1869–1926), older daughter of Provost John Pentland Mahaffy of Trinity College, were perfectly situated as eye-witnesses to record major events in Irish history.[6] It was Spring Rice's idea to transport guns bought in Germany back to Ireland in a private yacht. Her letters to The O'Rahilly in early May 1914, the first letter written only one week after the unionist Larne gun-running, show her practical turn of mind ('It might be better to sail to Germany direct and save the difficulty of getting stuff over the frontier from Germany to France').[7] It was she who kept a daily record of the voyage of the *Asgard*. Living in the Provost's House, Mahaffy spent Easter Week surrounded by the British army and dining with the generals. Some of the rifles unloaded from the *Asgard* at Howth on 26 July 1914 no doubt shot some of the soldiers quartered in the grounds of Trinity, and some of those men from Trinity may have killed Irish rebels who, two years earlier, had marched to Dublin from Howth with their new rifles on their shoulders.

A jolly, energetic Gaelic-Leaguer, Mary Spring Rice would have been amused at a comparison between herself and Elsie Mahaffy, but Mahaffy, a unionist who considered Captain Bowen-Colthurst (notorious for shooting Frank Sheehy Skeffington without a trial) 'one of the best young men I have met', would have been appalled.[8] Yet the diary that Mahaffy so assiduously kept, recording her strong opinions for 180 hand-written pages, links her closely to Spring Rice, who kept a much briefer 'log' of the *Asgard*. Both women were engaged in the management of a household that was temporarily centred on munitions. Each account is domocentric, framed as a story about a domestic site. Spring Rice and Mahaffy oversee the transformation of these sites: the arcs of their narratives are the same, as the domestic spaces they maintain are gradually recreated as military sites and then, again gradually, become merely domestic, as the guns are unloaded at Howth or as the British army decamps.

The women who managed these unusual households were both Protestants, but different kinds of Protestants. Mary Spring Rice was an Irish-speaking, nationalist aristocrat: her father's County Limerick estate Mount Trenchard was situated on the banks of the Shannon. Members of her family had been active in public life for many centuries, though their political allegiances differed. At the same time as Mary Spring Rice was running guns for the Volunteers, her cousin Sir Cecil Spring Rice was British ambassador to the United States. It was he who wrote the hymn 'I vow to thee, my country', though the country he apostrophised was not Ireland.[9] A distant cousin was the Young Irelander William Smith O'Brien, who was found guilty of treason for his role in the failed rebellion of 1848 and transported to Van Diemen's Land. Another cousin, the famous sailor Conor O'Brien, skippered the other 1914 gun-running yacht, the *Kelpie*.

Elsie Mahaffy's family was not aristocratic; her father himself described the Mahaffys, from Donegal and Monaghan, as 'lesser landed gentry'.[10] It was he who, as provost, put the family on the cultural map. In 1859 he graduated from Trinity in Classics and philosophy and taught there for the rest of his life, becoming provost in 1914. His lit-

erary and political judgements put him on the losing side of Irish literary and political history. He was Oscar Wilde's tutor, but after
Wilde's trial in 1895, Mahaffy reportedly said, 'We no longer speak of
Mr Oscar Wilde'.[11] The revival of the Irish language was, in Mahaffy's
opinion, 'a return to the dark ages'. Of Joyce, he opined, 'James Joyce
is a living argument in defence of my contention that it was a mistake
to establish a separate university for the aborigines of this island—for
the corner boys who spit into the Liffey'.[12] And Mahaffy famously
banned 'a man called Pearse' from speaking at the Thomas Davis
Centenary meeting in 1914. A widower in 1916, he lived in the
Provost's House where his two unmarried daughters, Elsie and Rachel,
kept house for him. These and similar reactionary attitudes are ubiq-
uitous in his daughter's record of the Rising.

The genres of the two diaries are different. Although the published
version of Spring Rice's account is called 'Diary of the *Asgard*' in *The
Howth gun-running and the Kilcoole gun-running; recollections & documents*, a manuscript draft with holograph revisions typed on Mount
Trenchard stationery is titled 'Log of the gun-running cruise in the
"Asgard" July 1914'.[13] The term 'log' suggests a technical record of distances, speeds, meteorological conditions and other navigational data,
and not the cheerful, informal narrative made by Spring Rice, with
details of seasickness, accidents, uncomfortable sleeping arrangements
and the rare bath on shore.

Elsie Mahaffy's account is called a book by its author: 'When I
reread my book', she wrote in June 1917, 'many things I might have
said suggest themselves to me'.[14] The 'book', its holograph pages bound
in a single volume, is divided formally into three sections:

The Irish Rebellion of 1916

PART ONE
What I actually saw and heard from those to whom these
events happened from notes taken daily at the Provost's
House—Dublin.

PART TWO
What I have learnt from general hearsay since the
Rebellion and the results I have seen.

PART THREE
What I can learn of its Causes & Leaders.

The differentiation of the sources of information suggests a quasi-scholarly approach, an attempt at professional historical writing. Wishing her book to be of use to readers of the future, Mahaffy emphasises the authenticity of her information. On all the left-side pages are pasted documents such as maps, photographs, newspaper cuttings, Mass cards and letters, making this book one of the best sources of Rising-related primary materials. Mahaffy's book is a lengthy, detailed and serious account, but it has never been published or transcribed. It sits in the Manuscripts and Archives Research Library of Trinity College Library with no accompanying information about the circumstances under which it was donated.

One value of both accounts is their idiosyncratic and somewhat eccentric details. Spring Rice's 'log' is charming and good-humoured, with vivid stories about culinary fiascos and ablutionary strategies. Mahaffy's book is not good-humoured; every mention of a rebel or even a member of the Irish Parliamentary Party includes disparaging remarks. But it is rich with lore. Complaining about 'the deliberate and constant campaign...to set the lower classes against England and in particular the English rulers here', she asserts it was accomplished 'by the teaching of disloyal ballads in the very poor schools'.[15] And so she writes out, in long hand, many ballads that might otherwise be lost, such as one about Lady Aberdeen titled 'Herself & the microbes'.[16] In spite of herself, Mahaffy is a kind of folklorist, preserving popular nationalist culture even as she denigrates it.

## AT HOME ON THE *ASGARD*

The *Asgard* was not a battleship. A present from Dr and Mrs Hamilton Osgood of Boston to their daughter Molly and her husband Erskine Childers on their marriage in 1904, it was used for pleasure and sport. The couple 'travelled widely in the yacht, especially through Baltic and Scandinavian waters'.[17] In 1913 their friend Gordon Shephard won the Challenge Cup of the Royal Cruising Club for sailing it from Norway to Holyhead, 'covering 1,253 miles in stormy weather'.[18] The following year the *Asgard* was used to transport the weapons to Howth; 900 rifles along with 29,000 rounds of ammunition were packed and hidden in this 49-foot yacht, and six people ate, slept and worked on it during the 26 days of the voyage. The cabin, already a crowded home, became an armoury, and the guns—smelling of coffee and sprinkled with hairpins—became part of the furniture. During the night of 16 July 1914, off the coast of Devon, the *Asgard* sailed right through the middle of the British fleet: 'They seemed to be executing some night manoeuvres', noted Mary Spring Rice; 'There was one awful moment when a destroyer came very near'. Sailing with apparent nonchalance through the fleet, the yacht with a young woman 'holding up the stern light on the starboard side' did not excite any anxiety in the navy and sailed on undisturbed.[19]

As subsequent events made clear, the fleet was preparing for war with Germany. The innocent, sporty appearance of the *Asgard* served it well. In her 'Diary of the *Asgard*', Spring Rice focuses on how the limited space of the yacht was used. The diary's frame is not the story of how the guns were smuggled but of how a provisional home was constructed and reconstructed. As she tells it, the weapons form an interesting challenge to the spatial limitations of the yacht; their story becomes a secondary narrative about the maintenance of a domestic site under unusual and difficult circumstances. The political narrative is not simply subordinated to one about housekeeping; it is completely absent, either suppressed or taken for granted. At the beginning, Spring Rice, Molly and Erskine Childers, and two crew members set up house on the *Asgard* and make order out of a 'fearful scene of confusion':

> In the midst of ropes, tinned foods, marline, and clothes just unpacked, we laboured to get things straightened out before our early start. I wearily pulled my clothes out of canvas bags and holdalls and stowed them as best I could, there was a fearsome thunderstorm going on and it was breathlessly hot: however, I got to sleep at last...[20]

The diary ends on the evening of the day when the guns are landed, as Spring Rice spends the night at the Dublin house of Elsie and Augustine Henry. There she is welcomed by Alice Stopford Green, Elsie Henry's aunt and a major supporter of the gun-running; meetings planning it were held at her London house, and she contributed £700 toward the cost of the purchase. The end of the voyage is marked with superior domestic pleasures: 'I felt rather mean as I got into a glorious hot bath and thought of Molly and Erskine tired and worn out with everything upset, tossing about on the Irish Sea. But my bed was heavenly'.[21] The shape this frame gives the story of the gun-running implies that the main subject was domestic comfort (or even perhaps bathing, a repeated motif in the log). Because throughout her diary Spring Rice emphasises the instability of domestic arrangements on the *Asgard*, her arrival in a house with hot water and a comfortable bed provides closure to the story.

The difference between a housekeeping narrative and a gun-running narrative is evident in the manuscript draft of the diary in the National Library of Ireland, where Spring Rice has *crossed out* all the housekeeping minutiae and parts about clothing, and attempted to make it more 'serious' and 'political'.[22] The deleted phrases tell the story she appears to think she shouldn't tell. 'I rushed down to the cabin to shove away my last remains of clothes' becomes 'I rushed down to the cabin to stow everything'.[23] Of the space where she and Molly bed down, Spring Rice originally wrote, 'But she and I don't take much room to sleep', but that remark is crossed out as are the following:

> A roasting hot day even on the sea ~~and my pink sunbonnet was my one joy.~~
>
> ~~One has to turn down the mattress right back off the guns in our cabin to be able to turn down the basin, so one only does it when one really does feel too dirty to eat before washing.~~
>
> ~~Awfully late at breakfast, and Mr Gordon was shaving in the saloon, while I, propped up against the ammunition box in the doorway, was hoving in the breakfast things and trying to prevent them getting all mixed up with the shaving apparatus, as everything was shooting about the table.~~
>
> ~~I had a bathe before lunch, the first I have had, which was heavenly. I did envy the men their morning bathe. I never seemed to have time for it with cooking the breakfast.~~
>
> Mr Gordon never attempted to get up till everyone else was at breakfast, ~~except on the rare occasions when he shaved~~, and his food was kept hot as a matter of course.
>
> ~~How Molly manages to get about with her lameness is a constant wonder to me, I find it quite hard enough.~~

After breakfast, ~~I do a little more washing behind the dish cloth in the cabin, then~~, if fine, the mattresses and blankets are given an airing on deck, ~~and probably Molly wants the things collected — hot water etc. for dressing Erskine's hand~~.

All of the quotations deleted, in what appears to be Spring Rice's hand, together compose a narrative entirely unrelated to guns, its subjects bodily intimacy (comments about bathing, privacy, being sleepy, sleeping close to Molly Childers); housekeeping (the women's cabin, cooking, airing the bedclothes); 'girl talk' (comments about her sunbonnet or sewing a blouse); and comments about other people that might appear gossipy (e.g. comments on Molly's ability to move about the yacht in spite of her handicap or on Mr Gordon's late ar-rivals at breakfast).

The revised manuscript was not published; for whatever reason, the definitive 'Diary of the *Asgard*', as printed in the collection of docu-ments about the gun-running, contains all the sentences deleted in this manuscript. The original manuscript allows us to see that Spring Rice thought of the voyage in terms of all the practical details of personal and domestic upkeep.[24] Even Spring Rice's conversations with Erskine Childers, at least the ones she records, are on the personal subject of bathing. During a stop in Holyhead, while they have tea at a hotel, Spring Rice once again introduces the subject of a bath:

> As we sat devouring hot, buttered toast, marmalade and strawberry jam, I said to Erskine: 'That was a heavenly looking bath in the bathroom here; I was almost tempted to have a bath.' 'Why don't you?' he said. 'I've had a bath quite recently, you know—Sunday.' 'Yes,' said Erskine, 'of course you had.' 'And it's only Thursday' I said, and then we looked at each other and laughed at the thought of what our standard of washing had sunk to.[25]

The log's focus on the ordinary and the practical, on the minor dis-comforts and occasional pleasures (like strawberry jam), is refreshingly unpolemical, when one remembers the risky enterprise they've em-barked on.

## Sleeping on Rifles

Within this frame, the focus of Spring Rice's narrative is on overcoming the difficulties in maintaining a home afloat. The guns feature prominently and explicitly in the diary, but so do food, cleanliness and the daily logistics of living on a yacht: 'One of my chief duties, I found, was keeping the food hot for the late-comers, and as I sat close to the fo'-castle door and the stove was just inside, it was quite handy'.[26] Gordon Shephard, the English crew member, was never as concerned as Molly was about being tidy; at breakfast on 6 July Spring Rice 'heard a shriek from Molly—"He's pouring all the Golden Syrup on the bunk"'.[27]

Loading the guns is preceded by housekeeping work, as they make space for the new cargo. First 'we all fell to work doing the final cleaning of the saloon and cabin for the guns'.[28] Then 'We hastily hauled bags of clothes and mattresses and stowed them aft of the mizzen'.[29] In order to fit 900 guns—not the 750 they had expected—in the yacht, they had to unwrap the straw bundles of rifles packed together and hand them down, person to person, singly.[30] (And then, of course, they had to stow the ammunition 'in fearfully heavy boxes'.)[31] Everyone laboured to stow the rifles, one by one for all 900 of them, while Molly 'put pieces of chocolate literally into our mouths as we worked'.[32] Then Spring Rice

> tumbled into the fo'castle, crawling over the guns in the saloon to get to it, and got the kettle on for hot drinks while the men were fixing the tow ropes. Down they came then and we all drank cocoa and beef-tea and then shifted down the mattresses and bags of clothes, which had been stowed aft of the mizzen, and lumped them down on the guns anyhow—we were too tired to settle them properly—and lay down just as the grey light of the dawn was breaking. I remember thinking how absurd it was to go to bed in daylight and then went off into a dead sleep.[33]

The diary treats the packing of 900 rifles into small spaces on a yacht as all in a day's work. It is Spring Rice's jaunty, matter-of-fact, amused tone that makes this collective activity seem simply like a more exciting form of furniture rearrangement. So much attention is devoted to pieces of chocolate, cocoa, beef-tea, the positioning of mattresses, and the quality of sleep that it is almost possible to forget that the object of the voyage is arming the members of a paramilitary organisation.

Once the guns are loaded, the difficulties of housekeeping for six people on a small yacht become even more complicated. With so much weaponry crowding the available space on the *Asgard*, personal ablutions and other daily routines like cooking and setting the table require improvisation:

> One has to turn the mattress right back off the guns in our cabin to be able to turn down the basin, so that one only does it when one really does feel too dirty to eat before washing....

> Fried eggs are very hard on rough days; they fly about the pan and get disintegrated. Awfully late at breakfast, and Mr Gordon was shaving in the saloon, while I [,] propped up against the ammunition box in the doorway, was shoving in the breakfast things and trying to prevent them getting all mixed up with the shaving apparatus, as everything was shooting about the table.[34]

The purpose of the trip, it seems, was to challenge Spring Rice's housekeeping skills and to test the limits of everyone's need for clear spatial boundaries between eggs and shaving soap, and eggs and ammunition.

Spring Rice seems actually to enjoy the confusion of categories, but then, so did Molly Childers. They were both happy campers. Childers's letters to Alice Stopford Green emphasise, as Spring Rice's diary cannot, what a happy camper Spring Rice was: 'Mary a Spartan, helping with everything, cooking tea, wrestling with primus lamps... A heroine'. Spring Rice, says Childers, is 'cheery and a *great* companion'. Childers also indicates the way the guns became furniture: 'Below decks we sleep, crawl over, sit on, eat on guns. Guns everywhere...Our daily rub down in alcohol takes hours, one is so pitched about in the odd positions one has to take. It is all gorgeous fun and, joy of joys, Mary and I are up to it'.[35]

After her morning chores, Spring Rice writes, she would enjoy 'peace till lunch-time', and in that free time, 'I sit in the cockpit and sew or read, or learn Irish from Duggan'.[36] Charles Duggan was one of the two Gola Islanders helping out as crew on the *Asgard*, and Spring Rice's focus on labour on board the yacht reveals how sharing chores allowed class boundaries to blur. 'Pat' (she writes of Pat McGinley, the other man from Gola) 'has got to be rather good at cherishing the Primus, so I leave that to him'. When McGinley gets 'a horrible cut just over his eye' as a block falls on him that night 'Molly took a watch with Mr Gordon...as Pat was *hors de combat*'.[37]

One boundary that was retained was that of gender. The women slept in the same tiny, stuffy cabin, attempting to retain a vestige of privacy. Sleeping on guns was not the problem ('I... found my bed on top of the guns extraordinarily comfortable') but, as Spring Rice writes, it was 'sleeping in public':

> Molly and I decided it was altogether too hot to sleep with the cabin door shut and as it opened straight into the hatch and companion, it meant rather sleeping in public. The theory was that one put out the light and then no one could see in, but as it got light about 4 a.m. that rather broke down; however I don't really mind, compared to sleeping in a tug...[38]

Privacy had to be specially constructed and required improvisation:

> The cabin door had to be fixed permanently open so we had an arrangement of a dishcloth which could be hung across as a curtain when one was dressing, but it was too stuffy to keep it hung up at night and shut out the precious air that came down the companion. The worst was on a wet night when Molly insisted on shutting the companion hatch, not so much for herself as to keep the guns dry, and then the stuffiness was awful...After breakfast I do a little washing behind the dishcloth in the cabin; then, if fine, the mattresses and blankets are given an airing on deck.[39]

The sentence about 'washing behind the dishcloth in the cabin' is one of the ones Spring Rice deleted in the manuscript (though it was published in the F. X. Martin collection nevertheless). No doubt to Spring Rice and, she must have thought, to any readers, the sentence implied nakedness.

Childers's concern for the guns—that coffee and syrup not be spilled on them, that they be kept dry—is presented as a housewifely concern the way, say, protecting the finish on a mahogany table might be. The language remains the discourse of housekeeping and the labours of the two women those of spirited sisterly housewives who find the whole enterprise jolly good fun. The power of the 'Diary of the *Asgard*' comes from the utter absence of ideology and sentiment about the unmentioned purpose of the voyage.

On the final page of the manuscript, Spring Rice deletes the sentence about 'a glorious hot bath' and adds, in handwriting, 'Now our dream had come true'. This sentence, had it ever been published, would have been the one explicit indication of political sentiment. In her revisions, Spring Rice tries to make the log loftier and more conventional, in fact more gender-neutral. The presence of the deleted passages, as deletions, is a valuable indication of the way her mind worked as she thought about the 'log' from a writerly point of view: the deletions reveal both the spontaneity of Spring Rice's original observations and her second thoughts about the possible irrelevance of bodily care and household management.

The 'glorious hot bath' reappears in a postcard Alice Stopford Green wrote to her niece Elsie Henry on 27 July 1914: 'Mary Spring Rice spent last night here. <u>Very well</u> and extremely sorry not to see you. "It's an honourable thing to be a hayro" said the cook as she got the hot bath'.[40] Major historical events—perceived as 'heroic' hours after they have happened—are incorporated into the intimate spaces of the bathroom.

## ELSIE MAHAFFY'S HOSPITALITY

Elsie Mahaffy was not sleeping on top of rifles, but she was living close enough to big guns to feel them. Many of the large weapons used in the various assaults on the rebels were based just outside the Provost's House on the grounds of Trinity College. They shook the house and they terrified the birds:

> Very early on Wednesday morning we heard the noise of the heavy guns coming into Trinity with many men driving the mules. At a little after 7:30 the 'pounding down' of Liberty Hall began—it lasted one half an hour and was indeed terrible; even the solid 'Provost's House' trembled and in the garden all the birds who had sung and warbled sweetly through all the previous noises, became mute, huddling together in terrified clusters. The terrible noise was made by an '18 pounder' run out of College at the last moment into place prepared for it in Tara St. and from the guns of the 'Helga'...[41]

Like the *Asgard*, the Provost's House at Trinity College was never intended for military use. Built in 1759, Palladian in design, elegant and sturdy, it houses the chief administrative and ceremonial officer of the university and his family. In 1916, during Easter Week, the grounds of Trinity College became an armed garrison: the British army was quartered there during the Rising, and the reinforcements that arrived during the week of hostilities included 'a brigade of infantry, a battery of artillery, and a regiment of cavalry'.[42]

The diary that constitutes the middle section of Mahaffy's account of 1916 is framed by passages of domestic tranquillity. When Mahaffy heard the first news of the Rising, she was engaged in the kind of activity that Spring Rice wanted to delete from her own manuscript: 'Thus filled with happy thoughts I was completing my toilet at 12 o'clock when Rachel came into my bedroom to say that the only porter at the College gate had just come in & told her that "the Sinn Feiners had risen..."'[43] Organising the sentence as she does, Mahaffy dramatises the way her private ritual was interrupted by the news, as it travelled from outside the College gate to the porter to her sister Rachel and then upstairs to Mahaffy herself, 'completing my toilet'. Before mentioning her 'toilet', she describes in a self-consciously literary way the beauties of nature as observed from the windows of the Provost's House:

> Everyone here was in good humour and spirits as the morning was beautifully bright & sunny and in our garden the young green of grass and trees, and the flowering narcissus and tulips were beautiful. Many birds sang in the garden, and on the northern side rose the stately and beautiful Library of Trinity College.[44]

Five weeks and 94 handwritten pages later, domestic tranquillity and natural beauty are restored, when the Mahaffy family decamped to Earlscliffe, their summer house:

> On May 30th I removed to Howth where, looking over the beautiful Bay of Dublin our summers have always been spent. A sense of security and calm fell over us all which I do not think one could ever have again in Dublin—so soiled by cruelty and dishonesty.[45]

Mahaffy has carefully framed her narrative to dramatise the Rising as a disruption of routine and 'good humour and spirits'. Between these descriptive passages, the book shows the trajectory of the changing status of the Provost's House during the Rising.

The house was not the private space of the Mahaffy family, of course; they had previously lived in their own house at 38 North Great Georges Street. The house Mahaffy writes about was the professional space of the provost of Trinity College, and all members of the family living there had, by virtue of their domicile, a professional, academic role. The college itself (though not the Provost's House) had already been transformed, because the National Volunteers had been practising 'signaling in the college park' since August 1914, when the Great War began.[46] As of September 1914 members of the Officers Training Corps (OTC) of the British army reserve were encamped in 40 tents in the College Park, so that (as an undergraduate wrote) 'the hustle and bustle of military effort that has invaded our academic torpor makes us feel ill at ease in college'.[47]

By Monday afternoon of Easter Week, about 40 members of the OTC had arrived at Trinity. In the evening, the Mahaffys took in 'a little bride' who needed a place to stay. The husband, a Trinity gradu- ate, was a soldier on leave; the couple had been returning from the Fairyhouse races and found the city 'in this dangerous state'. 'While we kept his little wife in safety', Mahaffy writes, 'the husband defended Trinity'.[48] Meanwhile Professors Gwynn, Pope and Joly came regularly for meals throughout the week. And so with an increasing population, some of them hitherto strangers, the status of the house began to change. As Mahaffy writes, 'From this time on the Provost's House became practically an inn'.[49]

While some academic business was transacted, the Rising itself entered the house in various ways. Four young women who were scheduled to sit a French exam arrived, and (in the absence of their ex- aminer) the provost himself examined them, and they stayed to lunch. At 4 a.m. on Tuesday, 25 April, a dead rebel soldier was carried through the front hall; he lay 'in College' for three days before being buried in the College Park; later he was disinterred and his body sent to the city morgue.[50] On Tuesday afternoon, Colonel Bertram Portal arrived with goose-stepping soldiers who used Trinity 'as a base for operations', so Trinity was now a garrison and military headquarters.[51] Colonel Portal left mid-week but General Carleton and his 'delightful' aide de camp stayed at Trinity for twelve days 'and we saw them daily'. By Thursday there were 4,000 troops stationed in the college. On Thursday evening, 'Many people came and went in the Provost's house' and 'we had our usual undress dinner party'. At an unspecified date in late May 'our last officers General Carleton and Major Dakke left Trinity College and we settled back to our habitual academic calm'.[52]

Mahaffy marks the changing status of the house in a series of distinct phrases: the house 'became practically an Inn'; 'we settled back to our habitual academic calm'; and finally the 'removal' to Earlscliffe, the large house and gardens at Howth where the Mahaffy family spent their summers.[53] (The O'Hanrahan family, whose son Micheál had been executed, also went to Howth after the Rising; the same Dublin geopolitics obtained for both republicans and unionists.)[54]

The arrival of Colonel Portal and his men introduced military issues into the academic space of the Provost's House. Almost immediately, Portal asked the provost for a map of Dublin: he had 'never been in Dublin before and was entirely ignorant even of its streets' names'.[55] He also asked about the location of 'a high tower from which he could prospect his field of action, and he asked my father's advice as to where he ought to place the "18-pounder" to blow down Liberty Hall'.[56] From then on, the house became simultaneously the military, academic and social centre of unionist Dublin, as meals mixed military and academic guests with titled folk and politicians. On Wednesday, for instance, Elsie writes:

> At luncheon we had a big party: Colonel Portal, Col. Longridge, the Adjutant of Trinity College, Major Hill a fine tall handsome man in charge of the big guns and his 'galloper' a pretty boy of 17 Master de Robeck with pink cheeks, Mr. Eckstein, a charming young man of fashion who came into College attended by an Indian valet... besides our own old friends Dr. Gwynne [sic], Dr. Pope, and dear Dr. Joly....[57]

Meals, in fact, offered occasion for crossover moments, as the military men confided their exploits to the Mahaffy family. At the end of the week, on Friday, 28 April 1916, the officers were chatting about the rebellion over lunch: several of them discussed the 'disagreeable part of their duty: each had had to shoot someone for having arms in his house'.[58] Then 'After luncheon the time was ripe to attack the Rebel Headquarters in the General Post Office'. Mahaffy was privy to the army's strategy before it was enacted.

## HIGH POLITICS AT HOME

The Mahaffys identified the Provost's House unambiguously with counter-revolutionary politics. On the second day of the Rising, their chauffeur, Austin Whelan, left, allegedly to 'protect his mother' during the rebellion, and on the Wednesday of the following week he returned:

> He told us some cock & bull story about not being able to come back but was so entirely in sympathy with the movement, so enthusiastic over the 'patriots' that he had to be dismissed as we felt that these sentiments were out of place in the Provost's House.[59]

The rebel chauffeur's sentiments were apparently not known before the Rising, but now the Provost's House had become a political space, and the latent ideological differences between the Mahaffys and Whelan have been actualised, so 'he had to be dismissed'. Mahaffy's disgust with his enthusiasm shows in her inverted commas: 'patriots'.

Just as part of the charm of Mary Spring Rice's log is its seemingly digressive comments on baths, so one of the curiosities of Elsie Mahaffy's diary is her seemingly irrelevant concern with height. Comments on tall people and short people recur throughout the manuscript. The great tragedy of 1916 from her point of view is the loss of such a tall person as Constance Markievicz to the ranks of the Sinn Féiners. As young women, Mahaffy and Constance Gore-Booth were presented to the viceroy in the same year, and she 'was then a lovely tall creature, full of spirits and go, much admired and made love to at Dublin Castle...'[60] Unfortunately, in spite of her height, Markievicz 'lost her shame and dignity and married a Pole' and later 'took to politics and left <u>our class</u> for that of Larkin and Connolly'. On the Sunday after the Rising, Rachel and Elsie Mahaffy saw through the front railings of the Provost's House a 'band of prisoners' marching by: 'In front walked a tall fine looking lad—hatless and very pale—obviously of gentle blood. The rest were a low, motley crew...'.[61] Bowen-Colthurst, a much admired friend of Mahaffy's, is 'tall, handsome, clever'.[62]

In the days following the last of the executions, both the provost and his daughters, by virtue of the army's encampment at Trinity, became players in high politics, entertaining the prime minister and the vice-reine, reviewing the troops with General Maxwell, and attacking John Dillon in letters to the *Times* of London. Their 'saloon' and dining room became sites where political alliances were made at the highest levels. One sequence of events was generated by the visit on Friday, 12 May of Sir Henry Blake, a retired colonial administrator who lived in Youghal, Co. Cork. Blake arrived at the Provost's House and 'would not leave...until he had made my father promise to write' a letter to the *Times* 'contradicting...Dillon's lies'.[63] John Dillon, a member of the Irish Parliamentary Party, had delivered a passionate speech to the House of Commons on 11 May denouncing the government's policies in Ireland. He said among other things, 'If Ireland were governed by men out of Bedlam you could not pursue a more insane policy' and 'You are letting loose a river of blood'.[64]

The provost's letter was published on 16 May. In it, he wrote that Dillon's speech 'curried favour with the rebels', and he contradicted Dillon's statement that 'No rebellion in modern history has been put down with such blood and savagery' by citing Paris in 1848 and 1870. The language was strong ('It exceeds the bounds of ordinary patience when we see that Mr John Dillon is allowed to produce a series of foul falsehoods'), using some of the words found in his daughter's diary; he, too, referred to those who sympathised with the rebels as 'dupes'.[65]

Having read that strongly worded letter, General Maxwell wrote to the provost on the same day, accepting an invitation to dinner and adding, 'I think your letter in the Times good: but that fiend Dillon has raised the Irish question whether we like it or not. I wish you would use your influence to induce those who can write in favour of our soldiers to do so, for the tendency now is to try and attribute any death that occurred in Dublin during the revolt to the brutality of the soldiery'.[66] The letter is pasted into Elsie Mahaffy's diary, offering yet more evidence of the usefulness of the provost to the British military: on the Tuesday of Easter Week Colonel Portal had asked the provost's advice about where to station the '"18-pounder" to blow down Liberty Hall', and now after the Rising, General Maxwell has requested his help in starting a letter campaign to defend the British army in Dublin. Although Elsie does not mention how or if her father followed up this request, she was evidently pleased with the association.[67]

Meanwhile on Saturday, 13 May the Provost's House had become an even more public site, in fact an official one, when Prime Minister Asquith took tea there. The visit was announced to the hosts in a message from the vice-reine Lady Alice Wimborne: 'Her Excellency with the Prime Minister will take tea with Provost to-day at 4:30'. With this event, the Provost's House achieved its most significant public status, as the chief representative of the British government reviewed the troops at Trinity College along with General Maxwell and others; Provost Mahaffy's towering, gowned bulk is easily recognisable in photographs pasted in his daughter's album.

In her description of the house in its readiness for the 4:30 p.m. tea ordained by the vice-reine, Elsie Mahaffy emphasises the house as a public space, to be viewed by others, as it is 'decorated' for the 'distinguished guests' to admire:

> The old home was looking beautiful, decorated with tall red and white tulips...We had a large party of distinguished guests besides those from the Vice-Regal Lodge. Sir John Maxwell and his ADC Prince Alexander of Battenberg, General Carleton and General Friend and their ADCs... Lady Fitzgerald and all our OTC officers, Lady Fingall and her party, Mrs. Porter...the Bursar and Mr. Roberts.[68]

Lady Wimborne and the prime minister arrived first, and Mahaffy, in her role as hostess, 'went to receive them in the hall'. Asquith admired the silver plate and cups on display in the hall, and then Mahaffy led them to the saloon: 'At the College Green end Rachel was entertaining His Excellency so I led Mr. Asquith to the other side to divide the interest and to show him the splendid Gainsboro picture of John Duke of Bristol'.[69] Consciously organising the space of the most public room in the house, Mahaffy 'led' the prime minister to one side to 'divide the interest' between Asquith and the viceroy.

Mahaffy's conversation with Asquith, however, was not a successful one, and she used her power as hostess to introduce someone else into the conversation so she could leave it. The prime minister was not, she felt, sufficiently angered by the rebellion:

> He was just beginning to talk on the subject next my heart, anyhow with a smile—'I'm surprized to see how little harm, bad as it is, the Rebellion has done to Dublin' in a flippant tone.
>
> I felt a sort of chill because it then somehow dawned upon me that he had come here with a purpose. The harm—to him is not little. It is very great in proportion to the size of Dublin, not an enormous town. But its fine Georgian heart is largely burnt out and will never be rebuilt in the fine style and sound workmanship in which the Georgian period bequeathed it to us.

> I said 'Oh Mr Asquith! did you really expect to find us all sitting in the streets, with no roof over us?'
>
> At this moment a forward Dublin lady bounced up and told me to present her to the Prime Minister, so having obliged her I withdrew but I felt there was some evil intended to us, either to please Redmond and keep the Irish vote or to save himself the trouble of really facing the horrible facts.[70]

Mahaffy writes that she is 'sad' to feel this about 'the husband of a beloved friend'.[71] She 'felt no further interest in Mr. Asquith's visit, having gauged its import'. She records also her anger that when the prime minister visited the wounded at the Dublin Castle Red Cross station, he spoke to the wounded 'Sinn Feiners' but ignored the 'soldiers'.

The following autumn, Maxwell wrote the provost a thank-you note to which Elsie Mahaffy gives pride of place, pasting it at the beginning of her manuscript, just before the actual diary begins. General Maxwell, who had 'plenary powers' in Ireland through October, had been fortunate that the largest and best space in Dublin unoccupied by the rebels was administered by such a fiercely unionist family. From his note, dated 11 October, one would not know that he had gone to Ireland to suppress a rebellion. 'My dear Provost', he begins, and thanks him warmly for 'your hospitality to me, I will always look back on this as one of my most pleasant recollections of my short stay in Ireland'.[72] His note confirms Elsie Mahaffy's public role as hostess and makes himself sound like a personal friend and invited guest. Its tone and warmth confirm the simultaneous private and public status of the house, a family's dwelling-place and a military camp.

Neither Mary Spring Rice nor Elsie Mahaffy lived to old age. Spring Rice died of tuberculosis in 1924, aged 44, and Mahaffy died in 1926, aged 57, 'after a long illness', according to her *Irish Times* obituary.[73] Considered in terms of women's history, the 'Diary of the *Asgard*' and 'The Irish rebellion of 1916' show how the Rising offered opportunities for women as well as for men, even women not 'out' in the Rising itself. Mary Spring Rice supported the national movement in many ways, not only through the Gaelic League but also through hiding men on the run during the War of Independence. Yet she rises to prominence in the history books because of the gun-running that she initiated, the voyage in which she participated, and the log she kept. The Howth gun-running was her supreme moment. Elsie Mahaffy's knitting business looms large in her brief *Irish Times* obituary, but that work has not been mentioned in print since 1926. Almost a century after her death, it is her 'book' about the Rising that keeps her name in circulation.[74] Much as she hated the Rising of 1916, the revolution gave her the opportunity to write a work of historical significance, perhaps the kind of work she would have done professionally if she, like her more famous father, had had an academic career.

Molly Childers (on left) and Mary Spring Rice on board the *Asgard*, July 1914.

possible occasions, but we sped along so perhaps it was as well.

SAT. 11th. Much calmer, which made getting up and cooking more pleasant, but it was a bad look-out for getting to Dover. All day long we had light head-winds, and 8 p.m. found us still struggling to get round Beachy Head. A roasting hot day even on the sea. (and my pink sunbonnet was my one joy.) We had laid a lot of fruit and vegetables at Cowes, and were living much more lux-uriously than before. Mr Gordon had great ideas of being as com-fortable as possible, and he and Molly had bought lavishly But it was a depressing day, full of doubts and anxieties.

SUNDAY 12th. The day of the meeting! Should we ever get there? It certainly didn't look like it, when I came up on deck to find Erskine at the wheel in a calm sea with a light breeze ruffling the water and the fog just lifting and letting the sun through,- a heavenly summer morning- if one had no gun-running appointment at the Ruytigen Lightship, 45 knots distant? at 12 noon to make one pray for a wind. (I had slept like a top thanks to the calm night and was really hungry for breakfast.)

But we all felt rather anxious, and made calculations about the fair tide after Dover, and speculated as to how long the tug would wait if we were late, and as to what directions there might be in Figgis's letter to Dover which we had not time to call for. Then we all fell to work doing the final clearing of the saloon and cabin for the guns. This meant cutting up the two saloon bunks and Molly, Pat, and Mr Gordon were soon hard at work chop-ping and sawing. We were keeping right inshore as the tide was still against us, and when I came on deck after looking through the store of eggs, a very important part of the supplies, I saw Folkestone beach within a stone's throw, full of " the smart set" parading their best clothes in the brilliant sunshine, while on the starboard side lay 4 or 5 warships with their bells ringing for church. The Asgard slipped along between the shore and the warships , her crew making an awful noise chopping and sawing, which they devoutly hoped was not heard on either side.

Edited manuscript page from 'Log of the gun-running cruise in the "Asgard" July 1914' by Mary Spring Rice.

Above: The Saloon, Provost's House, Trinity College, where the Mahaffy family entertained Prime Minister Asquith and other dignitaries on Saturday, 13 May 1916.

Opposite: Folio 83v from Elsie Mahaffy's book 'The Irish rebellion of 1916'. At the top of the page, photo of review of the British troops in Trinity College, Saturday, 13 May 1916; as marked by Elsie Mahaffy, the people in the foreground are Provost John Pentland Mahaffy (in academic gown), Prime Minister Asquith, hidden behind Her Excellency (the vice-reine, Lady Wimborne), Her Excellency (the vice-reine), General Maxwell, and Maurice Bonham Carter (Principal Private Secretary to Asquith). At the bottom of the page is the message from the Vice-Regal Lodge to the provost.

At the Review - the Premier behind Lady Wimborne

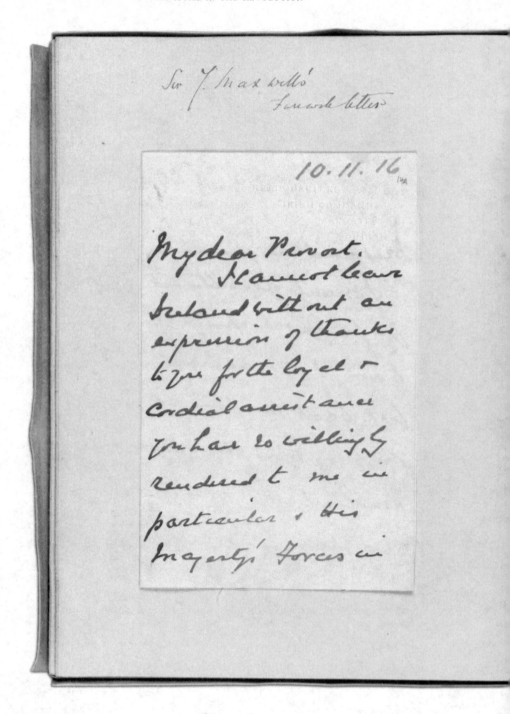

This page and opposite: Thank-you note from General Maxwell to Provost Mahaffy (10 November 1916), pasted into Elsie Mahaffy's book 'The Irish rebellion of 1916'.

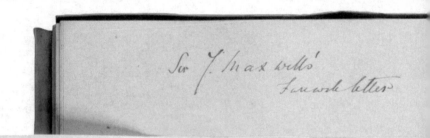

Ireland in general.

I must also thank you for your hospitality to me, I will always look back on this as one of my most pleasant recollections of my short stay in Ireland

Yours sincerely,
J. G. Maxwell

*Chapter Three*

## FLIRTATION AND COURTSHIP

Hearts with one purpose alone
Through summer and winter seem
Enchanted to a stone
To trouble the living stream.

W. B. Yeats, 'Easter 1916'

Believing that the rebels had 'hearts with one purpose alone', and that purpose was revolution, Yeats could not imagine them with any other impulse. Birds had romantic encounters—'The long-legged moor-hens dive, / And hens to moor-cocks call'—but not militant nationalists.

The play *Kathleen Ní Houlihan* by Lady Gregory and Yeats had implied that a young man seduced by Ireland would forget his wedding; after all, hadn't the old woman said, 'It is not a man going to his marriage that I look to for help'? And didn't poor Michael Gillane, who had chosen Kathleen over his fiancée Delia, have 'the look of a man who has got the touch'? Enchanted, hypnotised, without agency, almost without consciousness, Michael was taken by the fairies, or so it seemed to his mother.

In fact many of the rebels of 1916 were closer to the hens and moor-cocks than Yeats knew. Words on the subject of sexual desire written by two of the executed men show an open, playful expression of their erotic nature. In a 1908 letter to his wife Kathleen in Dublin, Tom Clarke wrote 'I'll be [back] in great shape by the time I get back to you and will be able to look after you to soothe your longing and send you off to sleep'.[1] And on the 1911 census form, under the category 'marital status', Seán MacDermott wrote, 'aonta, ach ní fada a bheith,' 'single, but will not be so for long.'[2] Although he never married the woman who was his romantic attachment, Min Ryan, he had already met her at this point, when he was 28, and he clearly felt the desire to marry. He gives the census bureaucracy more information than they requested: they only asked was he married, not what his plans were. But he says it *as Gaeilge*, and even writes it in the old Irish script: he expresses his political ideology and romantic impulse in the one phrase.

Men and women under 40 were the primary demographic of participants in the Rising, people of an age to enjoy courtship, marriage and parenthood. Of the fourteen men executed in Dublin immediately after the Rising, three left pregnant wives: Kathleen Clarke, Grace Plunkett and Agnes Mallin. The wife of The O'Rahilly, Nancy, was also pregnant, as was the wife of Volunteer Eamon Morkan, who didn't see his baby son until he returned home from Reading Gaol on Christmas Day 1916. ('My wife was particularly glad to see me so unexpectedly. However, one of her first requirements was the removal of the moustache, which most of the prisoners had begun to affect.'[3]) Sinéad de Valera was pregnant with the future archaeologist Rúaidhrí; and Una Brennan, wife of Robert (acting commandant, Wexford Brigade, Irish Volunteers), was pregnant with the future *New Yorker* writer Maeve. Volunteer John Furlong's wife Kathleen gave birth to their son in 1917.[4] At least three pregnant women were 'out' in the Rising: Áine Heron, pregnant with her third child, did first aid, cooking and dispatch work in several locations; Phyllis Morkan, a member of Cumann na mBan, did first-aid work in the Church Street outpost of the Four Courts garrison; and Una Brennan, according to her granddaughter, 'climbed up and raised the tricolor over the Athenaeum in Enniscorthy' during the Wexford Brigade's action there.[5]

The romantic lives of people 'out' in the Rising are well recorded by women and men alike. In most cases the impulse to record political events in detail led incidentally to the love stories, provided as colourful but subsidiary narratives. Courtship in the spring of 1916, as the stories show, did not assume a customary form. With no paradigm to follow for fitting romance to the demands of a revolution, the couples confronted the need to reinvent the 'rules of engagement' of courtship and romance at every stage of the relationship. The Rising disturbed the rituals and practice of romance and challenged the planning of weddings. It prevented Con Colbert and Seán MacDermott from proposing to and marrying the women they loved; it caused the hasty wedding and three-hour marriage of Joseph Plunkett and Grace Gifford; it prevented the relationship of Dorothy Stopford and Sir Matthew Nathan, undersecretary for Ireland, from becoming more than a 'friendship'; and it determined the location of Geraldine Plunkett and Tommy Dillon's wedding night, in a suite at the Imperial Hotel directly facing the General Post Office.

## THE RISING AS A COURTSHIP METAPHOR

Even couples not involved in revolution found their courtship changed. James Finn and May Fay, who had become engaged over Christmas, were taken completely by surprise when the Rising broke out; the revolution around them infiltrated the language of their love letters, in spite of their complete lack of involvement in anything revolutionary.

'Things here are very quiet and nothing at all interesting happening'. So Finn, an accountant in Dublin at the National Health Insurance Commission, wrote to his fiancée at her family farm in County Westmeath on 15 April 1916.[6] Very quiet, for Finn and Fay, meant that his sisters Moll and Nora had returned from visiting their cousin Mary Seery (Fay's neighbour) in Lockardstown with very little news.

For other people, 'things' were not at all quiet in Dublin on 15 April. At the Volunteer Headquarters, 2 Dawson Street, Patrick Pearse delivered a lecture called 'Be prepared' to the battalion officers and company captains. According to Liam O'Carroll, who wrote down the title in the minute book, the emphasis of the lecture was 'not alone being prepared militarily, but spiritually and religiously'.[7] That evening, Cumann na mBan organised a *céilí* 'to cover a meeting with men from the provinces', the Volunteer leaders to whom Seán MacDermott was explaining the plans for the imminent Rising.[8]

Unconnected with the Volunteers, Cumann na mBan or the Citizen Army, innocently focused on whether Mrs Seery would be 'vexed' with the choice of Pat Moran as best man, whether white silk would be suitable for Fay's gown, and what the weather would be for their honeymoon, Finn and Fay were shaken by the events that erupted around them and wrote anxious letters back and forth: 'I thank God that I found everything quite well at home', he wrote, and she was concerned that 'news was so very scarce and uncertain that I very soon began to look out for another letter'. But by 10 May, all was still on track for the 7 June nuptials, and 'tradesmen' were back at work putting up new wallpaper in preparation for Fay's arrival in the house in Rathmines.[9]

Nevertheless, both of them saw their existence as a couple in the light of recent events. Fay noted in the newspapers that 'all Civil Servants were to render an account of their Easter holidays, will you not be asked to render an account of all the time you spent talking to me...You need not be afraid to mention our names anyway; we are not very rebellious characters'.[10] Their unimpeachable holiday time together could hold up to official approbation; their blameless time with her family, 'on a good farm on the slopes of Uisneach', could show clearly how 'unrebellious' they were.[11] The serious, sincere James Finn even saw the Rising as somehow making him a better husband: 'I hope that the trouble through which we have all passed will eventually bring good to our poor country and that it will with God's blessing make me a better man and a more worthy one for the dear good true girl who loves me'.[12] The simultaneity of the final stages of wedding plans and the immediate consequences of the Rising created a kind of identity between the two events, marriage and revolution, so that almost every reference either separated the two ('unrebellious') or joined them ('bring good to our poor country...and...make me a better man').

In a rare moment of direct response to the turn of events, Fay wrote to Finn, 'I have great hopes Casement will turn catholic that would be grand I say a special prayer for his conversion always'.[13] Finn suggested another object of prayer. There were rumours of a second rebellion, he said, quite possibly in Kerry, where they were considering going for their honeymoon, 'so you had better start saying your prayers for both of us and don't be wasting your breath over Sir Roger Casement's conversion'.[14]

Soon both members of the couple warmed to a more explicit nationalism. Still measuring his moral worth in terms of the Rising, Finn wrote on 22 May, 'Don't worry about my being arrested. There is no fear now or indeed at any time. If I was any blooming good I'd have been arrested long ago. Men a thousand times better have a daisy quilt over them in Glasnevin now'.[15] In one of her final pre-nuptial letters to James, Fay mentioned that she was glad to get the ring-fitting card and glad to see 'Dr. O'Dwyer's letters to Maxwell'.[16] (The outspoken bishop of Limerick, Dr Edward O'Dwyer, wrote letters to General Maxwell, letters soon made public, in which he asserted among other things that the executions of the leaders had 'outraged the conscience of the country'.[17]) Fay had become somewhat less 'unrebellious'.

The Rising also affected the love-language of Diarmid Coffey and Cesca Trench in the midst of their long, unstable courtship. Both were nationalists; he sailed on the *Kelpie* and was a Volunteer, and she was an active Gaelic Leaguer and member of Cumann na mBan. In the autumn of 1914, they found themselves on different sides when the Volunteers split between John Redmond's National Volunteers and Eoin MacNeill's Irish Volunteers. Trench recorded their conversation in her diary. Anticipating a difference of opinion, Coffey said

> 'If there's a split, it seems likely that you and I will be on different sides.' I agreed. 'Well I wanted to say that it won't make any difference, before we say extremist things to each other...I'd rather anything in the world, except the disruption of Ireland, rather than a serious quarrel with you.'[18]

When they agreed not to fight, he said, '...*we* needn't make a split'. In their language, as in Finn's and Fay's, the status of their courtship and the status of Irish politics become identified. A 'quarrel with you' is made parallel to 'the disruption of Ireland', and the idea of a 'split' is transferred from the political realm to the romantic. Politics supplies the discourse for their relationship.

Trench's diary records another such usage in the middle of the Rising. On Wednesday, 26 April, she and Coffey are sitting on 'a stretch of grass' looking out at Dublin Bay and eating chocolate and an orange. '"It seems almost incredible," said D., "that there should be [a] revolution going on in Dublin, [and] that you and I should be having a picnic on Killiney Hill." I felt inclined to say that it needed a revolution to accomplish as much, but refrained'.[19] Here the 'revolution' is a simultaneous and contrastive political event ('revolution going on'), a causal factor ('a revolution to accomplish as much'), and a metaphor for the dramatic shift from quarrels to harmony in their relationship.

Both James and May Finn, and Cesca Trench and Diarmuid Coffey, had happy but tragically brief marriages, shortened by an entirely different international event, the influenza epidemic. Trench and Coffey married on 17 April 1918, and on 30 October of the same year, Trench died from the flu. 'The Rosary was recited in Irish at her graveside by members of her branch of the Gaelic League', writes Hilary Pyle. The 'inconsolable' Diarmid Coffey did not marry again for ten years, and then he married one of Trench's younger cousins.[20] Finn and Fay married on 7 June 1916 (with Patrick Moran as best man). Finn died on 6 May 1922 from endocarditis, a side effect of the flu he had caught in 1919. Four days before he died, he wrote a cheque to his wife (then pregnant with their fourth child) to cover the rent on their house, scrawling in the margin, 'May, with dearest love'.[21]

## MEN IN UNIFORM

For other courting couples, the Rising did more than supply a vocabulary, metaphors and a context in which to define their romance. Young women and men more actively involved in revolution hovered between official and unofficial identities, understanding and articulating their most private feelings always in terms of the great historical moment. In many cases, it was their common project that brought them together. The intimate proximity of young men and women working together unchaperoned for a lofty ideal meant that the possibility of attraction was ever-present, an attraction licensed and encouraged by shared revolutionary goals. It could be rejected or enjoyed, but it had to be acknowledged.

The relation between the charged political atmosphere and the inevitable heterosexual intimacy was formulated in two different ways by women who were 'out' in 1916. Marie Perolz, a member of Inghinidhe na hÉireann, Cumann na mBan and the Irish Citizen Army, was sent by Seán MacDermott on Holy Thursday with urgent dispatches. The verbal part of the message was 'Dublin is rising on Sunday evening at 6:30'. When she reached the house of Paddy O'Mahony in Dungarvan, Co. Waterford, his wife said he had been on night duty and was asleep: 'I said I did not care, I'd have to see him, and walked into his bedroom. That time we did not think about sex or anything else. We were all soldiers and I was only bothered about what I could do for Kate Houlihan'.[22] Perolz's account is supported by that of Paddy O'Mahony himself, the man awakened from rest:

> On Holy Thursday Mary Perolz brought a message from Dublin to me at Dungarvan. The message was from Liam Mellows and was to the effect that I was to carry out the mission agreed upon between us at 7 p.m. on Easter Sunday. I was in bed off duty when she came and she insisted on seeing me personally. It was between 2 and 3 p.m. on Thursday. She said to me, 'I am the bearer of an important message'. She then gave me the message from Liam Mellows and asked for a receipt for it. She had a notebook and in the notebook I wrote for her, 'Remember '65, no countermanding orders'. To Mrs. O'Mahony she said, 'Do you realize the seriousness of it. This is the most serious thing that ever happened'.[23]

Perolz clearly felt that the act of bursting into a married man's bedroom required an explanation. Her thought was that in a time of revolution, the usual social practices change: working for 'Kate Houlihan' in the cause of 'the most serious thing that ever happened' annuls both sexuality and differences in gender, especially the female gender. Respect for the boundary of the bedroom door is rendered insignificant by the enormity of the message ('Dublin is rising on Sunday...'), and so she could open it without seeming inappropriately intimate. They were all masculine—or all sexless—soldiers of 'Kate Houlihan', whose gender seems to be sexlessly female. In short, the revolution elevated intimate proximity beyond transgression and taboo.

Brigid Lyons also comments on the intimacy of men and women working together in 1916. She was a member of Cumann na mBan who had driven from Galway with her uncle Frank McGuinness to take part in the Rising. When she arrived at the Four Courts during Easter Week,

> My uncle Joe was delighted to see us and brought me to Ned Daly. I was thrilled with him and felt that although he was quiet he was very forceful. What I felt about him the first time I met him the previous summer, and also about Seamus Sullivan—they probably would not care to be told this—was that they were the nearest approach to British officers in appearance and inspired us girls with feelings of enthusiasm and caused many heart throbs. I met Frank Fahy and Peadar Clancy. He was fascinating and epitomised for me all the attractive heroes in Irish history.[24]

Lyons is charmingly honest when she suggests that the 'heart throbs' were inspired in part by the 'British' look of the Volunteer officers; it is curious that the enemy against whom they were fighting offered the macho fashion touchstone for 'us girls'. It's the uniforms that had the power, and Volunteer uniforms were modelled on the typical European male military uniform of the period, common to scouts as well as to soldiers—the boots, the Sam Browne belt, the four pockets with brass buttons. The Volunteers may have derived their sexy look from the 'British'-style uniforms, but their romantic aura was legitimised by their association with 'all the attractive heroes in Irish history'. The word 'attractive' goes for their character, of course, as well as their bodies. The sexual charm of the military man was put more directly by Kathleen Boland in a letter to her brother Harry in prison after 1916: 'There will be a great rush for all the heroes when you return. All the girls will want you'.[25]

Even unionist women were not immune to the charms of the rebel men. On Sunday, 30 April, two cousins, Elsie Mahaffy and Lilly Stokes, noticed the men marching from Boland's Mills after the surrender. As noted earlier, Mahaffy associated height with moral worth, and so when (with her sister Rachel) she peered out the windows of the Provost's House to view the men going past, it was height she noticed: 'In front walked a tall fine looking lad—hatless and very pale—obviously of gentle blood. The rest were a low, motley crew...'[26] Stokes's view was more nuanced. She, too, came from a well-known Protestant family, 'a great Irish academic and intellectual dynasty'.[27] She was a descendant of the polymath Whitley Stokes; her brother Henry was the physician who treated James Connolly while he was imprisoned in Dublin Castle. Her mother's sister had married John Pentland Mahaffy, so Elsie Mahaffy was her first cousin. On the first day of the Rising, she had tea at the Provost's House, 'where the Mahaffys gave me a welcome cup of tea'.[28] On Sunday, she saw the men at closer range and possibly about half an hour before her cousin did. She happened to be in Ballsbridge with several other people, and her brother Adrian (a future pathologist) 'would not let us hang round…so we had to quietly come home'. But she escaped from her brother's clutches when he walked ahead and so was

> just in time to see 70 prisoners from Bolands [sic] march past, fine looking fellows, swinging along in good step. Of course they looked shabby and dirty, they had been fighting for seven days. Until I saw them I thought they ought to be shot, but I don't know—it would be terrible waste of material, if it was nothing else—it made one miserable to see them. The leader in Bolands [sic] was a fine looking man called the Mexican, he is educated and speaks like a gentleman.[29]

At this time Stokes was 34 and unmarried; four years later, she married her cousin, John Boxwell. As she was watching the captured rebels march past, a feeling that was not exactly unionist expressed itself: they were 'fine looking fellows, swinging along in good step'. Apparently she had already heard that Éamon de Valera was 'educated and speaks like a gentleman'. Like the prisoners, de Valera was 'fine looking'. He was the 'tall fine looking lad' that Elsie presumed to be 'of gentle blood'. The two spinster cousins made similar judgements, but Stokes more directly appraised the men from the eugenic perspective.

## CON COLBERT'S ROMANCES

Appearances to the contrary, because one seems to deny sexuality and the other to emphasise it, the comments from Perolz and Lyons are consistent. In both cases, the physical proximity with its hint of sexuality is noted, and both women bring to their readers' attention the complications and charm of the situation. It was from such collaborative work with its collegial intimacy that an interesting romantic triangle emerged around Con Colbert, Fianna drill instructor, captain of the 4th Battalion of Volunteers in the Rising and one of the fourteen executed rebels.

his cell and told her he was going to be executed at dawn. He gave her a letter for Cooney:

> The guard said that the letter would have to be censored and Con took it back and would not let the guard have it while she was there. He must have torn it up, because the letter which I afterwards got from him and which I showed to Mrs. Murphy was much shorter—so she said— than the one he was giving her for me.[38]

Cooney and her sisters were released from Kilmainham that day. A sympathetic English sergeant asked them to come back the next morning, when he gave them the letter from Colbert, his watch and his prayer book, which was for his sister Lila. In his letter, Colbert wrote to 'My dear Annie and Lily', and told them, '...you girls give us courage, and may God grant you Freedom soon in the fullest sense'. He added, 'You wont [sic] see me again, and I felt it better not to have you see me, as you'd only be lonely, but now my soul is gone and pray God it will be pardoned all its crimes', and finished, 'Goodbye, dear friends and remember me in your prayers'.[39]

Receiving such a letter was so important to Cooney that 37 years later, she wanted to know what happened to the longer letter that was just for her (just as Lucy Smyth wanted to know what happened to the packet). In spite of the salutation to 'Annie and Lily', the address gave only her name. The giving and receiving of tokens as relics was also so important that ten years after the statement was written, when she was 'the late Anne O'Brien', her sister Lily added a supplement to the statement:

> ...in the paragraph...relating to our release from Kilmainham after Easter Week, one item does not appear on the list of articles we collected from the Sergeant at Kilmainham the morning following our release [.] I think this is an important item, as it was the Rosary Beads be-longing to Con Colbert, and he said he wanted Anne to have them. I would like to have this recorded...[40]

Although the Rosary beads are of course not 'romantic', nevertheless, as a gift just for Cooney and not shared with her sister, they acknowl-edged a special tie between them. The brown bread, the sock, the beads, the photographs, the bedroom entered without permission, the *céilithe*, the buckling of the belts, the secret last message, the lost bulky packet—all the rituals of engagement signify more intensely and also more ambiguously at a revolutionary moment. The romantic ties between Lucy Smyth and Con Colbert, and Annie Cooney and Con Colbert, different as they were, lived on in the relics the women cherished long after they were married to other men of 1916: the lock of Colbert's hair that Sheila O'Leary says her mother kept, and the Rosary beads that Lily (by then Mrs Curran) felt it important to mention when the youthful Annie Cooney who buckled Con Colbert into his Sam Browne belt Easter morning had become 'my sister the late Anne O'Brien'.

The names in these triangles are linked in the narrative of a man who knew nothing about the romances. Garry Holohan, an officer in the Fianna who fought in the Rising with the 4th Battalion, gives a clear picture in his witness statement of the way Colbert was working in collaboration with both Smyth and Cooney. As instructed by Colbert, Holohan was moving weapons around to designated locations on Good Friday. He brought

> six of the automatic pistols to a house in Palmerstown Place, near Broadstone, on the evening of Good Friday. I was told afterwards that the girl I met at Palmerstown Place was Lucy Smith [*sic*], afterwards married to Tom Byrne, later O.C. of the 1st Battalion, Dublin Brigade, and Captain of the Guard in Dáil Éireann.[41]

Later Holohan delivered bayonets 'to 2 Basin Lane, where the Cooneys lived'. His statement adds, 'You will remember that one of them was married to Dinny O'Brien, the detective who was shot some years ago'. That 'one of them' was Annie Cooney. Holohan's statement shows a pattern he was probably unaware of, the overlap in the circulation of weapons and of romantic feelings. Naming the future husbands of Smyth and Cooney, he adds the marital futures of these women to the story of their work in the Rising. Tom Byrne's own witness statement says that in looking for a safe house after the Rising, 'I decided to visit the lady who later became my wife'.[42] Suspecting that her house is soon to be raided, Smyth sent him to the Athlone Hotel. Taken together, all the witness statements show three romantic triangles. Just as Colbert was working closely with Smyth and Cooney, both sentimental attachments in different ways, so Smyth was working closely with Colbert and Byrne, both of whom were in love with her, and Cooney was in the same outpost as Colbert and her future husband. For Lucy Smyth and Annie Cooney, as for many other women, the intimate collaborations of the Rising led to the intimacy of marriage.

## Min Ryan and Seán MacDermott

Although Min Ryan and Seán MacDermott were already an acknowledged couple before the Rising, many of the same uncertainties about the relation between official and unofficial identities appear in their relationship as in the others. Writing about one of his final conversations in Kilmainham before MacDermott's death, Father Paddy Browne says, 'He spoke about Min Ryan. She was his sentimental attachment—seriously'. In MacDermott's last letter to his brothers and sisters, he wrote at the end, 'If I think of any other things to say I will tell them to Miss Ryan, she who in all probability, had I lived, would have been my wife'.

Like Cooney, Ryan found herself compelled to act in two roles simultaneously, as a member of Cumann na mBan and as the 'sentimental attachment', beloved of Seán MacDermott. The roles overlapped, and her accounts manifest her uncertainty about the appropriate way to behave at any given moment, in the role of girl-friend or in the role of a mobilised Irishwoman assisting the Volunteers. Sometimes the decision was made by others. Kathleen Clarke mentions the céilí on Palm Sunday 1916 that was actually a cover for a meeting between Seán MacDermott and the Volunteer leaders from the provinces. He had to be present but ready at any moment for a meeting when the men arrived. Waiting for the men to arrive, MacDermott had Clarke on one side of him and Sorcha MacMahon on the other:

> So we both formed a kind of bodyguard for him; many of
> his friends who would, I knew, have liked to speak to him
> passed into the hall, but with Miss MacMahon on one side
> of him and myself on the other they did not dare. I remem-
> ber three of the Misses Ryan passing, Miss Kit, Miss Min
> and Miss Phyllis; I am sure they would have [liked] to
> speak to him, but he waved them on.[43]

There must have been many such moments as this that Ryan was re-membering when she wrote after his death:

He loved his country with a passion that at times I scarcely understood. I think he is one of the few young men whom no personal passion could ever have turned away from the work he had set before himself...he worked and planned for the independence of Ireland ever since his boyhood.[44]

In those words Ryan is supporting the cultural construction of MacDermott as a martyr, but her first sentence seems just to allow the thought that she is explaining to herself why he didn't spend more time with her. In Clarke's anecdote, Ryan herself was the 'personal passion' to whom MacDermott did not 'turn' when he had work to do for Ireland. But then, the *céilí* wasn't a real *céilí* anyway; it was a meeting of the Volunteer elite, disguised as a *céilí*. (It was enough of a *céilí*, however, for the religiously observant Con Colbert to complain to Clarke about holding such an event during Lent.)[45]

Ryan's witness statement (written in 1950) emphasises her interest in getting to the GPO and staying there, where MacDermott was. She spent the Monday morning when the Rising began organising messages from Volunteers at the Four Courts and delegating various Cumann na mBan members to deliver them to the men's families. Then word came from Ned Daly that they weren't needed any more. 'I remember a certain feeling of pleasure. I said: "Now we can go around and see what is happening"'.[46]

To 'see what is happening' meant also to see MacDermott, who was of course at the centre of the action at the GPO. On Monday evening, she and another Cumann na mBan member met Seán T. O'Kelly leading a small band of men near the O'Connell monument.[47] O'Kelly asked her, 'Would you like to come into the Post Office? Would you like to see Seán MacDermott?' O'Kelly's syntax (as quoted by Ryan) acknowledged implicitly her dual and overlapping interests in entering the GPO. The tentative nature of Ryan's response—'We would love that, but we are afraid to go in'—shows her awareness that the Rising has changed the rules of engagement for herself and MacDermott. O'Kelly answered, 'Come along with me,' because his official position as Pearse's 'staff officer' gave him powers of admission, and because he had been in and out of the Post Office several times earlier in the day. Although recreated some 34 years later and perhaps not accurate to the word, this conversation nevertheless reveals the gendered social and psychological dynamic of the situation.

Once in the GPO, however, Ryan was embarrassed, because there at the centre of a revolution she was looking for her boyfriend: 'Seán T. O'Kelly told Connolly who we were and then he went off on business. I remember going to the back of the Post Office. I was looking for Seán MacDermott. I was left on my own and looked exactly like the complete camp follower'.[48] Ryan had not had practice in managing two identities simultaneously, the useful Cumann na mBan member and the 'girlfriend' following her man. Fully aware of the tricky social moment, she had no guidelines. Nor did she have an official function in the GPO at that particular moment; her only purpose was to find MacDermott. As at the Palm Sunday *céilí*, she was kept away from him by his handlers: 'I said to Gearoid O'Sullivan, who was a sort of aide-de-camp to Seán MacDermott: "I would like to see Seán MacDermott". I was told: "You can't see him. He is resting". I came out of the G.P.O. then and went back to 19, Ranelagh Road'.

MacDermott's name echoes through Ryan's witness statement, 22 times in 23 pages. She was the one 'who in all probability, had I lived, would have been my wife', but he was one of the signatories. She did not vacillate between identities; she had to figure out how to act in overlapping, simultaneous identities, official and unofficial. A new way of relating had to be invented: she subordinated the romantic relationship to their roles in the revolution. She had to be 'invited' into the GPO; she acquiesced to what the aide-de-camp said and went home. The following day, when she returned to the GPO with her sister Phyllis, she deferred to the revolutionary situation and obeyed the orders she was given.

> On Wednesday morning, I don't remember what work we did, but I remember we went down to Seán MacDermott. He said: "Come in to Pearse. There is a message to be sent". The messages we took out were really not from Pearse, but from O'Rahilly. We went with letters to the wives of three British officers.[49]

On Thursday morning, the two Ryan sisters were sent on more messages. 'We were always very sorry we got those messages', Min Ryan wrote, 'as it meant leaving the G.P.O. again'. According to the memoir of Min Ryan's son Risteárd Mulcahy, his mother described herself 'as a pusher who always wanted to be in the centre of things'.[50] In this case, the 'centre of things' was the centre of male power, the Post

Office. Ryan's statement is unashamedly honest as she acknowledges her preference for staying where the men were, especially the one she loved, rather than making herself useful away from that centre. Those Thursday messages were the last she delivered; she was unable to return to the GPO on Friday.[51]

## THE PLUNKETT WEDDINGS

The guided tour of Kilmainham begins in the room that used to be the prison chapel, and the story told to visitors is that of the midnight wedding of Grace Gifford and Joseph Plunkett, a leader of the Rising who was executed a few hours later. The idea that there would someday be tourists hearing their story probably never occurred to the bride and groom at the time, though it soon became a legend of the Rising.

The timing of the two Plunkett family weddings, those of Geraldine Plunkett and Thomas Dillon, and Joseph Plunkett and Grace Gifford, was Rising-driven: the first couple wanted to get married before the Rising started, the second before the groom was executed. When Plunkett suggested getting married during Lent, Gifford, soon to be Catholic, wanted to be liturgically correct. 'Why not at Easter?' she asked, but Plunkett responded, 'We may be running a revolution then'.[52] In fact the Rising offered the perfect opportunity for both brides to leave their difficult mothers and construct a new identity as wives. Before she was six years old, Geraldine Dillon writes 'I decided to hate my mother'. She chose to marry 'Tommy' on the morning of Sunday, 23 April because 'the Rising would put an end to my world, nothing would be the same again, and I was not going back to that hellhole of family life'.[53] Grace Gifford, in preparation for marrying Plunkett, had been received into the Catholic Church on 7 April, and her Protestant mother was not pleased. Both mothers reacted ungraciously to their daughters' marriages. On the journey to the wedding breakfast after the ceremony, Josephine Plunkett 'persuaded Mrs Dillon that I must be pregnant and succeeded in convincing her of this, but she did apologise to me a year later when my first child was born'.[54] Grace Plunkett's mother, Isabella Gifford, told an English newspaper, in words that retain their power 100 years later, that Grace 'was always a very headstrong and self-willed girl and had lived a more or less independent life for some time'.[55]

The near-simultaneity of the Rising and the weddings, one just before and the other just after the fight, created an identification of sorts between the two sets of events. Both weddings were military as well as marital sites. The two Plunkett weddings took place at the beginning and end of the Rising: Geraldine Plunkett and Thomas Dillon, and Joseph Plunkett and Grace Gifford, were supposed to have a double wedding on Easter Sunday, but Plunkett and Gifford's was postponed because he had too many pre-Rebellion meetings to go to. At Geraldine Plunkett's wedding to Dillon (her chemistry lecturer) on Easter Sunday morning, her brothers George and Jack were present in Volunteer uniform; the Plunkett brothers' close friend Rory O'Connor (not in his Volunteer uniform) was best man. And as Geraldine writes, 'Two G-men pushed their way into the sacristy but George, Jack and Rory took great pleasure in putting them out'.[56] The front line ran right through the church, right into the sacristy, a space that was invaded and defended. The Plunketts invited suspicion, and rightly so.

The site of the wedding night was determined by the battle strategy of the Rising: the Dillons' room in the Imperial Hotel was selected because its windows looked directly onto O'Connell Street opposite the GPO. Rory O'Connor went to the Imperial on Sunday afternoon to tell them 'to look out from twelve o'clock the next day'. Geraldine Dillon's final sentence for Sunday makes clear where her attention is: 'from now on we were sitting in the window, watching'. Her opening sentence for the next day emphasises a vigil rather than a honeymoon: 'From about ten o'clock on Easter Monday Tommy and I kept looking out the windows of our sitting-room in the hotel and from noon, on this beautiful day, we were sitting and watching through the open second-storey windows. It was breathless'.[57] The hotel room was not selected for its romantic atmosphere: it was a lookout point over the battlefield. The great unmentioned issue is romance.

The marriage ceremony of Grace Gifford and Joseph Plunkett had a larger and more dominant military presence: there were 'six soldiers with fixed bayonets in the little chapel', as if the groom were likely to escape, and (according to Dillon) there were soldiers in the cell later with the newly married couple when they had ten minutes together, even less of a honeymoon than the Dillons had. The passive voice in almost every sentence of Grace Plunkett's description of the wedding suggests the couple's lack of agency:

> I was brought in and was put in front of the altar; and he
> was brought down the steps; and the cuffs were taken off
> him; and the chaplain went on with the ceremony; then
> the cuffs were put on him again. I was not alone with

him—not for a minute. I had no private conversation with him at all. I just came away then.[58]

As in the case of the other Plunkett wedding, the hostilities of the Rising formed a part of the ceremony, as men with guns displayed and asserted their power in a sacred space.

## A Unionist Flirtation

Not all courting couples in 1916 were unchaperoned. The undersecretary for Ireland, Sir Matthew Nathan (a 54-year-old bachelor), had invited his close friend Dorothy Stopford (at age 26, a medical student at Trinity) to visit him over the Easter holiday and stay in the undersecretary's lodge in the Phoenix Park. Dorothy Stopford's aunt, Alice Stopford Green (she who helped fund the 1914 gun-running), had introduced Nathan and her niece. It would have been inappropriate for Dorothy to stay there without female companionship, so Sir Matthew had also invited his brother George's wife, Estelle Nathan, and her young daughters Maude and Pamela.

Her biographer has described the relationship between Nathan and Stopford as 'a friendship with possibilities that were not to be realised'.[59] It was certainly the case that no romantic possibilities were realised during the week following Easter. Sir Matthew left for the Castle on Monday morning and was not able to leave it the entire week. He telephoned daily, and the women at his lodge passed the time playing games with the children, taking short walks, and reading Sherlock Holmes ('He is our great resource', Mrs Nathan wrote to her husband in London).[60] Another activity was following sympathetically the progress of Sir Matthew's cold. Nathan told her husband that his brother had 'suffered from only having lady's small handkerchiefs'.[61]

At around 1 p.m. on Friday, 28 April, just after Volunteers in buildings on Henry Street prevented an attack by the Sherwood Foresters, and just before the South Staffordshires began to attack Volunteers in the North King Street area, the women in the undersecretary's lodge were watching a snail jump: 'Played with a snail for some hours, making it jump over a gap on the seat', Stopford wrote in her diary.[62] She felt 'mewed in', she had written on Wednesday, 26 April, and like Máire Comerford and Sighle Humphreys, she was eager to join the action but was restrained by circumstances. In the War of Independence she would serve as a medical officer to a Cork brigade of the IRA, an activity that used more of her talents and energy than playing with a snail.[63]

On Saturday, 29 April, Sir Matthew's car drove the Nathans to the boat to England and Stopford to the house of family members in Foxrock. On 3 May, Sir Matthew resigned as undersecretary. The Stopford–Nathan friendship continued fitfully in the following months—he sent her a bottle of wine, she sent him James Stephens's *Insurrection*, a book that must have given him a different perspective on the Rising—but never became more intimate.[64] In 1925 Stopford married Liam Price, 'a barrister, district justice, and local historian from Wicklow'.[65] Sir Matthew never married.

'It is not a man going to his marriage that I look to for help', Kathleen Ní Houlihan had said to the Gillane family, but Joseph Plunkett succeeded in both accomplishments, one just under the wire. Even courtship was difficult in April 1916, for those 'out' in the Rising and for those 'mewed in', as Stopford was. Yeats and Gregory formulated the relationship between political commitment and romantic love as an absolute choice of incompatible alternatives, but the realities for courting couples were more complex and more interesting. In the intimate, unchaperoned moments of collaborative nationalist work, new couplings were formed. At the same time, established romances acquired some of the characteristics of the revolution, as the Rising took over their time and their spaces. Flirtation and courtship continued with difficulty or were thwarted, registering the instability and uncertainty of a time when it was not clear what rituals of any kind were going to obtain.

Brigid Lyons Thornton, who worked in the Four Courts during the Rising and said that the Volunteers there 'inspired us girls with feelings of enthusiasm and caused many heart throbs'. The woman standing on the right is her cousin Rose McGuinness, who was wounded while working in the Four Courts in 1916. The photo was taken in 1915 or 1916.

May Fay and James Finn, whose correspondence about their June wedding continued, with interruptions, at the time of the Rising.

Self-portrait by Francesca ('Cesca') Trench (1891–1918), whose courtship and continuing political debate with Diarmid Coffey were recorded in her diary; they married in 1918.

Wedding photo of Geraldine Plunkett Dillon; the scheduling of her wedding, just before the Rising, was determined by the timing of the rebellion.

Lucy Agnes Smyth, later Mrs Tom Byrne, 'the nicest girl in Dublin', according to Con Colbert.

Above: Annie Cooney with her younger
sisters Lily and Eileen.

Right: Annie Cooney in the Cumann na
mBan uniform she patterned on Con
Colbert's Volunteer uniform.

Min Ryan, as Mary Josephine Mulcahy, with her husband, General Richard Mulcahy, in 1922. Seán MacDermott referred to her in one of his final letters as 'she who in all probability, had I lived, would have been my wife'. One of her sons was named Seán.

*Chapter Four*

# WOMEN AND MALE AUTHORITY

*Éist, a Shagairt agus seasuigh díreach,*
*Léigh an tAifreann is gheobhaidh tú díol as.*
*Níor thug sé trí ráithe in imeall do chroí agat,*
*Ná naoi mbliana déag ar fuaid an tí agat.*

Shut up, Priest, and stand up straight!
Read the Mass and you'll get paid.
He didn't spend nine months next to your heart,
Or nineteen years around your house.[1]

Traditional lament fragment

'[Y]ou think because you're a woman you can say what you like. Mind you don't get a shot through that little head of yours'. When Colonel Bertram Percy Portal addressed these words to Elizabeth O'Farrell, he might have been speaking of any number of women 'out' during the Rising who spoke their minds freely and forcefully. The women's written accounts record numerous 'sharp verbal exchanges' with men, exchanges that the women committed soon after to paper.[2]

There is ample precedent in the traditions of the Irish language for oral genres that allow for direct, belligerent verbal encounters: the *agallamh beirte* makes an art form of the short argument between two people, dramatising, for example, a debate between different genders or generations. In one such recent debate about the gendered basis of power, *Naomh Pádraig agus Naomh Bríd sna flaithis* ('St Patrick and St Bridget in heaven'), St Brigid complains about St Patrick's status as patron saint of Ireland.[3] The *caoineadh* (keen), as Angela Bourke has shown, allowed women 'to construct and transmit a rhetoric of resistance' to male domination in general. These 'subversive messages', expressed in the context of mourning, 'may be conveyed with apparent innocence'.[4]

The participants in such gendered verbal exchanges during the Rising were probably not consciously invoking these traditions or any other. They spoke nevertheless in an atmosphere in which women felt licensed to utter whatever they needed to say. Of course as political activists many of the nationalist women had experience in speaking forcefully. Hanna Sheehy Skeffington, a militant suffragist, had been imprisoned several times for protests and destruction of public property.[5] She also had much experience in public speaking and in active resistance, physical and verbal, to male authorities. Once when she and other suffragists disrupted a speech of Winston Churchill's in Belfast, two 'rough and angry' men threatened to throw her down a flight of stairs, one of them holding her over the top of the flight, but, she wrote, 'I turned and caught the lapels of his coat with each hand firmly, saying "All right, but you'll come along too!" I wasn't thrown down'.[6]

The conflict between Elizabeth O'Farrell and Colonel Portal, and the earlier one between Hanna Sheehy Skeffington and the 'rough men', are typical of women's conflicts with men during the Rising, because the men threaten physical violence but do not use it. Their belligerent words are made nastier with the threat of force, though whether they are therefore more effective is questionable. In an account of her husband's murder, Sheehy Skeffington cites the remark of English RIC officer Captain Lea Wilson regretting 'that they had not shot Mrs. Skeffington while they were about it'. Angry at the women and eager to do some violence to them, the men nonetheless restrain themselves, as if conscious of a border it would be unwise to cross.[7] In these face-to-face encounters, the aggression is always only verbal.

A rebellion in one institution creates an atmosphere in which other societal norms are questioned or defied. Joseph Plunkett dated his diary entries from the GPO '4th Day of the Republic' and a letter to Grace Gifford '6th day of the Irish Republic', so—as in the French Revolution— even the calendar was made new. The Rising unsettled and disturbed habits of deference altogether, including deference to patriarchies. It un-leashed behaviours in women as well as men: Catherine Byrne jumping through the windows of the GPO, Mary McLoughlin jumping out her bedroom window, women talking back to priests, soldiers, prison guards, government bureaucrats and the prime minister. The women did not initiate these belligerent encounters, but when they were at-tacked verbally, witnessed abuse, observed corruption or were wronged in any way, they spoke without inhibition. They were entirely conscious of their verbal freedom. Noting the murders of three men who had edited newspapers (Thomas Dickson and Patrick McIntyre as well as her husband Frank Sheehy Skeffington), Hanna Sheehy Skeffington wrote, 'Dead editors tell no tales—though sometimes their wives may'.[8]

## ATTACKING PRIESTS

A special subset of these encounters exists in episodes in which Irish women repudiate the authority of priests. Angela Bourke notes that 'In Ireland, women's traditional responsibility for funeral ritual brought them into conflict with the (male) Catholic clergy'. In several 'sharp verbal exchanges' between lamenting women and priests, 'the women came out best', as in the quatrain quoted in the epigraph: 'Shut up, Priest, and stand up straight!/Read the Mass and you'll get paid'. The recorded arguments of women with priests during the Rising are not witty or ironic debates but spontaneous rebuffs. The exchanges are not explicit attacks on the male-dominated structure of the Catholic Church, though some such notion may have been in the women's minds, but remarks to one priest alone.

The women who engaged in such confrontations were fully conscious that they were taking on a patriarchy. The account of Leslie Price, a young Cumann na mBan member, reveals her persistence in censuring a priest. From the moment Father Flanagan expressed reluctance to help the Volunteers, Price was wired to attack. On the Thursday of the Rising, Tom Clarke sent Price from the GPO to the presbytery of the Pro-Cathedral to get a priest. Having seen James Connolly brought in wounded, she thought to herself, 'Here's goodbye to you', but she looked at Tom Clarke's 'courageous old face' and said, '"Alright". I did not cry'.[9]

After a very indirect, dangerous journey, during which people shouted at Price, 'Go into a house and stay there!' and 'Go home, child!' she reached the presbytery. When she told Father Flanagan why she had come, he said, 'You are not going to the Post Office, You are staying here. No one here will go into the Post Office. Let these people be burned to death. They are murderers'.[10] She continued:

> I knew then, by some other remark Fr. O'Flanagan made, that it was the linking up with the Citizen Army he did not like. It took a certain amount of courage to fight a priest. I said, 'If no priest is going to the Post Office, I am going back alone. I feel sure that every man in the Post Office is prepared to die, to meet his God, but it is a great consolation to a dying man to have a priest near him'.
>
> Whatever effect I had on him, he said, 'Very well! I will go'. I stayed near him in the hall, and he said, 'We won't go that way. We will go out the back way'.

They made their way to Moore Street, and there they

> ...passed a man in Moore St. who had been shot and was dying on the road, but he had drink taken. The priest did

not stop for him. I was horrified. Further down Moore St. on the left we came to Henry Place I think. At that place, a white-haired man was shot but not dead. He was lying, bleeding, on the kerb. This was the second wounded man, a civilian. Someone had picked out of this old man's pocket a note, or card, or envelope; it was Eimer [*sic*] O'Duffy's father or grandfather...

   I remember the priest knelt down to give him Absolution. You see the difference! Here he knew a man who was respectable. I stood aside while he heard his Confession. Then we left him and went on. I said to Fr. O'Flanagan, 'Isn't it extraordinary you did not kneel beside the other man?'

   We got to the Post Office and I brought Fr. O'Flanagan to Tom Clarke.[11]

In the first draft of this episode, after the question to Father Flanagan, Price wrote, 'I think he thought I was an ignorant little monkey'.[12] Something about her comment must have bothered her, because she crossed it out; perhaps at a more advanced age she wanted to stand by her original question and not seem to apologise for it.

   The same fervour inspired Madge Daly, Kathleen Clarke's sister, to attack a priest in a dramatically hostile way. Daly was in Limerick during the Rising when the episode occurred:

One incident burned itself into my memory that sad week. The Prior of the Franciscan order in Limerick at that time was a brother of John Dillon's. He was a fanatical pro-Britisher, and constantly preached about the British-manufactured German 'atrocities.' While the fight was still going on, one of the Franciscan priests preached a sermon denouncing the Volunteers and ended up by asking the people 'to pray for these men who were dying in their sins.'

   Some girls, who were at the devotions, stood up and walked out as a protest...Some Cumann na mBan girls came to me with the story; they were wild with indignation. I was just raging, and I went at once to the Franciscan Friary and asked to see the Prior. He was not in, and I next asked to see one of the priests. A tall young man came to me in the convent parlour. I told him that I came to protest about the sermon preached the evening before, that it was extraordinary that an Irish Catholic priest should condemn the Volunteers in their fight for freedom when the Pope had sent a special blessing a few days before by an Irish envoy, who had explained the position in a long interview with his Holiness. I added that I knew many of the men who started the fight for freedom, that they were idealists who had sacrificed all their own interests to the dream of a free Ireland, that they had devoted their whole lives to the holy cause, and that their efforts to rid their country of the evil influence of the most ungodly empire that ever existed should win the approval of all decent Irish men and women; that my nearest relatives and dearest friends were in the fight, and if they died—they would die for a holy and just cause.

I was very excited and my words tumbled out in a torrent. The priest could not stop me, but from the first I sensed his antagonism. He made every effort to stop me, and finally became very aggressive and abusive, and ordered me to leave the convent. He raised his arm as if to strike me, and, as he did so, I looked him straight in the face and said: 'You are not worthy to be called a man. Certainly you are not worthy to wear the garb of Christ. You have no charity.' I cowed him then. I was a woman in great sorrow. From a priest I expected at least some understanding and sympathy. I got neither.[13]

Here again the man—a priest—appeared to threaten physical violence, and, like the other women, Daly fought back successfully with words: 'I cowed him then'.

In a quieter way but with typically defiant firmness, Madge Daly's sister Kathleen Clarke silenced a priest at Kilmainham in the early morning hours of 3 May, when she had just arrived to see her husband before his execution:

The first person I saw was a brown-habited priest, who was standing in the hall as I entered. He approached me and said, 'I have been waiting for you, Mrs Clarke, to use your influence with your husband to see me.' I said, 'I am afraid you waited in vain, Father. I have never interfered with my husband in anything he thinks right, and I am not going to begin now. If he will not see you, he has his reasons.' He tried to reason and argue with me, but he left me unmoved. I did not know him. I had never seen him before. He then said something about Tom going before his Judge, to which I answered that the Judge he was going before would be more merciful than the human one he had [s]een before, and as I knew what a pure soul Tom was, I was not afraid for him, or the Judgement of God for him.

...[Tom] told me that the priest had wanted him to say he was sorry for what he had done; 'unless I did he could not give me absolution. I told him to clear out of my cell quickly. I was not sorry for what I had done, I gloried in it and the men who had been with me. To say I was sorry would be a lie, and I was not going to face my God with a lie on my tongue.'

...When I heard his story, I did feel I could throttle that priest...Tom saw in the attitude of the priest the same old British official attitude he had met with in Portland, Chatham and other prisons, and quite possibly his old resentment against them flared up.[14]

Leslie Price had said openly 'It took a certain amount of courage to fight a priest', and clearly that 'courage' is inspired by and partakes of the atmosphere of the rebellion, in which old systems of deference may be defied. And having 'fought' a priest once, Price was inspired to do so a second time, with a critique (however indirect) of his pastoral negligence: 'Isn't it extraordinary you did not kneel beside the other man?' It is also a case of pastoral negligence that is a secondary disappointment to Madge Daly: 'from a priest I expected at least some understanding and sympathy'. In all three cases, it is the same paradigm: their commitment to the Rising (and in Clarke's case, to her husband) gives the women the 'courage' to attack the priests ('I have never interfered with my husband in anything he thinks right, and I am not going to begin now').

To put this matter in terms of gender: loyalty to a revolutionary group of men energises the women to attack a conservative patriarchy. There may be a feminist element in the attack, but it's not there in the language.[15] In all cases there is a spontaneous, forceful response from the women. They evince a complete understanding of the politics of their action, that the priest represents a structure of authority opposed to the revolutionary politics the women support.

# HUMILIATION

An unusual case of male verbal belligerence that stops just short of physical violence is mentioned in the witness statement of Brigid Foley, a member of Cumann na mBan who worked at two outposts of the GPO garrison, carrying dispatches and doing other work. In this episode, a physical boundary seems to have been violated, but there is no physical contact. Foley was arrested the week following the surrender during a raid on her house and was taken to a temporary women's prison at Ship Street Barracks, at the western end of Dublin Castle. Later she and other women were moved to Richmond Barracks and finally to Kilmainham.

Of the women imprisoned in Kilmainham, Foley writes:

> They were all marvellous. We sang all the national songs through the night, although the soldiers tried to shut us up. The prison was filthy as it had not been used for 16 years. There were no chairs, or forms or tables. We had to sit on the dirty floors with our backs against the dirty walls. We got skilly in bowls that night; this was a sort of watery porridge. We got the same in the morning. We had no appetite for our skilly that day as we heard the shots that killed our leaders. The military sergeant did not leave us in any doubt. He came in and told us with great satisfaction that 'four more were gone today'.
>
> When we wanted to go to the lavatory we had to knock at the door and two soldiers with fixed bayonets brought us to the lavatory which was a dry closet that had no door. The soldiers stood jeering at whatever girl was in the closet, with the result that for the eleven days I was in Kilmainham I never went to the lavatory and on my transfer to Mountjoy I had to be treated at once and for a long time after by Dr. Cook, the prison doctor. This horrible experience had a permanent effect on my constitution.[16]

Foley was not attacked by a weapon or touched by anyone, but she was injured, and the injury 'had a permanent effect on my constitution'. She was injured by the soldiers' *gaze* and by their words; that is the 'horrible experience'. She suffered bodily injury, but her body was never touched. The attack was psychological, a complete humiliation. Because Kilmainham was 'filthy' and the closet 'dry', the lavatory was no doubt already disgusting, but in addition it 'had no door'. A visual boundary is violated here: an adult woman requires privacy on the toilet, certainly privacy from men. By not only gazing but jeering, the soldiers called attention to the violation: they insisted on it. They made it impossible for Foley to ignore the fact that she was being viewed. Modestly, Foley never mentions the way she helped the other women, but Marie Perolz praises her in her witness statement: 'At Kilmainham I was very depressed when I knew the men were being executed. I could neither eat nor sleep. Only for Brighid [*sic*] Foley I would have died. She kept up my courage and tried to force me to eat'.[17]

The gaze and the jeering are also culturally complex: they express anger and contempt, the contempt of the victor for the defeated, and the male for the female. Either of these relationships would explain the jeering, but the Irish women are the locus of both despised categories. As Mary Douglas writes, 'The body is a model which can stand for any bounded system...the body is a symbol of society...the powers and dangers credited to social structure [are] reproduced in small on the human body'.[18] The national component of the humiliation is clear because the same treatment was given to men just after the surrender, when the Volunteers were lying on the grass in front of the Rotunda. As Eamonn Dore tells it, Captain Lea Wilson got Tom Clarke, Seán MacDermott, and Ned Daly to the front of the building, and 'stripped all three to the skin in the presence of us and, being broad daylight, in the presence of those nuns, etc., looking out windows'.[19] And in the words of Volunteer Joe Sweeney, Lea Wilson 'made all sorts of disparaging remarks about him'—i.e. he was jeering.[20] (In 1920, Lea Wilson was assassinated by Irish soldiers in reprisal for his actions in 1916.)

## THE SURRENDER
## AND GENERAL LOWE'S 'HONOUR'

Women who engaged in belligerent verbal encounters with officers of the military and government officials participated in the same atmosphere of licence as the women who attacked priests. These encounters were not single exchanges, brief arguments with men never to be seen again, but extended debates in which serious issues of great emotional import to the women were at stake. Especially because they endured a series of encounters, the women spoke with the consciousness that they were up against not one abusive person but an entire system. As they were sent from soldier to soldier, general to general, office to office, they perceived directly and repeatedly the pervasive corruption of the government.

Three such experiences, recorded in precise detail by the women soon after they occurred, took place in the immediate wake of the Rising. The extended argument in which the women participated, and the many obstructions they faced, constituted a continuing power struggle. Through them, the Rising was fought over again in different sites. The accounts themselves (by Elizabeth O'Farrell, Hanna Sheehy Skeffington and Gertrude Bannister) constitute a final rebuff or another counter-attack in the debate. Because the women could not be hit or bayoneted, the belligerence directed toward them had a special ferocity and was designed to humiliate as well as to threaten.

Elizabeth O'Farrell is famous as the woman who carried the white flag of the surrender and accompanied Patrick Pearse when he gave his sword to Brigadier General Lowe. Although her account is written with what sounds like great restraint, the anger is present in the details of the attacks she endured over a period of days. At her first conversation with Colonel Portal, the British officer in command of the outpost at Parnell Street, she was accused of lying:

> ...I told him the Commandant of the I.R.A. wished to treat with the C. of the B.F. in I.
> **Colonel P.** 'the Irish R. Army, the Sinn Feiners you mean?'.
> **I.** 'The I.R. Army they call themselves'.
> **Colonel Portall** [sic] 'and you think that a very good name too'.
> **Colonel P.** 'Will Pearse be able to be moved on a stretcher'.
> **I.** 'Pearse doesn't need a stretcher'.
> **Colonel P.** 'Pearse does need a stretcher Madam'.
> **I.** Pearse doesn't need a stretcher.
> **Colonel P.** 'You think because you're a woman you can say what you like; mind you don't get a shot through that little head of yours'.[21]

O'Farrell was not speaking with particular force when Portal threatened her; she was simply telling the truth—twice. The anger directed at her in gendered language derived its excessive belligerence and threatening tone from the British anger toward the Irish because of the surprise of the Rising and its bad timing (in the midst of a major war). In addition, the British military's awareness that the Irish were now in their power made it easier to treat them disrespectfully. Pearse, when he arrived to surrender, was also accused of lying:

**General Lowe to Comm. Pearse** 'The only condition I will make is I will allow the other commandants to surrender. I understand you have the Countess de Markievicz down there'.

**Comm. Pearse** 'No she is not with me'.

**B.G. Lowe** 'Oh, I know she is down there'.

**Comm. Pearse** 'Don't accuse me of speaking an untruth.'

**B.G. Lowe** 'Oh I beg your pardon Mr. Pearse, but I know she is in the area.'

**Comm. Pearse** 'Well she is not with me sir.'

Pearse was not insulted with gendered stereotypes, of course, but the title 'Mr' was no doubt intended insultingly.

O'Farrell was asked by Lowe to carry Pearse's order for the commandants to surrender to all the other garrisons. She was then in the custody of the British military, but not as a prisoner. The first night she was guarded by Lieutenant Royall, and the next night she was taken to Dublin Castle to be put up for the night 'as a guest' of General Lowe. That part of the message was not communicated, and the next day she was taken prisoner and lined up in the evening with other women prisoners. Once more she was accused of lying:

> A tall man in khaki with black trimmings took charge of us there. I went up to him and said I had B.G. Lowe's word of honour that I should not be made a prisoner and he said don't be silly. I know for a fact you shot six policemen yesterday. I knew there was no use arguing with him so I took up my place on the line.

The man in khaki was not worth the dignity of verbal argument, though he probably did not know he was insulted. In Kilmainham, when O'Farrell again insisted on her status as guest, she was ignored, but she fought back:

> On arrival there we were handed over to two officers and to those I also protested but they did not take the slightest notice of me. So I informed them if I was imprisoned I would when released publish all over the world how B.G. Lowe kept his word of honour.

O'Farrell's threat, which was ignored, was that she would speak freely and 'publish all over the world' this betrayal.

Soon, with the help of a priest, Father Columbus, O'Farrell was released, and when General Lowe came to apologise, they had—as O'Farrell recorded it—another exchange.

> B.G. Lowe also said 'I hear you have been accusing me of breaking faith'. I said 'yes I did'. B.G. Lowe 'well I'm determined my honour shall remain upheld'. Then I said it's up to you to uphold it.

In the version of O'Farrell's account published in Roger McHugh's anthology *Dublin 1916*, taken, it seems, from the *Catholic Bulletin*, someone, O'Farrell herself or an editor, has cut some of the more interesting passages in the account as it appears in the manuscript. The exchanges have been muted. O'Farrell's final retort—'it's up to you to uphold it'—is omitted, as is Portal's remark 'You think because you're a woman...'. The licensed speech of 1916 was evidently considered too 'unfettered' for the *Catholic Bulletin* in 1917.

The Rising was fought over again not only in Elizabeth O'Farrell's speech but in her body. Without actually being injured, she was treated as badly as possible. When Portal said, 'Mind you don't get a shot through that little head of yours', he obviously wanted to perpetrate some kind of violence on her body. He was restrained enough not to shoot her, but he found another way to get at her body and touch her roughly. He said to an officer, 'take that Red Cross off her and bring her over there and search her, she is a spy'. Then

> [t]he officer Lieutenant Royall, Royal Irish Regiment, then proceeded to cut the Red Cross off the front of my apron and took the Red Cross off my arm then he took me over to the hall of the National Bank on the corner of Parnell St. & Cavendish Row where he searched me & found two pairs of scissors, one of which he afterwards returned to me, some sweets, cakes, beads etc.

While the surrender order was being typed, she was taken to Tom Clarke's shop and given tea:

> During this time most of the officers came into the shop taking down the papers *Nationality, Workers Republic,*

*Honesty, Ireland* etc. off the shelves. They would flick them into my face saying 'I suppose you know this rag well'. It went so far that Lieut. Royall asked one to desist.

While O'Farrell was engaged in bringing the messages to all the commandants, she was in the custody of the British military. To reach de Valera in Boland's Mills, she had to walk through a firing line and, as she writes, 'I had to take my life in my hands several times'.

And while O'Farrell was under arrest at Kilmainham with other women, she was strip-searched:

> Our names were then called out and we were inspected, then brought upstairs and all put into the same cell. I was called out first and brought into another cell and told to take everything off. I took everything off except my knickers & stockings but even these had to come away. My clothes were then searched and no dangerous weapons being concealed on me. I put on my coat & boots, carried all my other clothes on my arms & and [*sic*] was conducted to another cell, locked in here to dress at my leisure. The prison was in charge of the military but the searching process was carried out by the wardresses of the female prisons.

This passage appears in O'Farrell's original manuscript, but it does not appear in the published version in the *Catholic Bulletin*. O'Farrell (in the manuscript) gives her readers the humiliating details that her knickers had to come off also, because the information functions as a form of protest against the authorities who refused to believe that she was General Lowe's guest. Apparently this description was considered too intimately detailed, and it was shortened to 'brought into another cell, where I was stripped of my clothing and searched by two female warders. My clothes were also searched…'. In the manuscript, O'Farrell writes that she says to Lowe, 'I protested that I had been put to the humiliation of being stripped and searched like a common criminal', but in the published version, the final phrase is 'searched while I was in the position of a "guest"'. The force of the insulting treatment in the phrase 'common criminal' is lost.

In the published version, the language used of the British military is also toned down. After her complaint about 'the humiliation of being stripped', the manuscript says simply, 'He then said he would give me a letter and that I would not have any trouble with the military', but in the published version, yet another apology is added: 'General Lowe apologized again, and vowed it was a mistake'. The account in the published version ends, 'In concluding, I would like to say that I found General Lowe, Captain Wheeler and Lieutenant Royall most courteous', but the manuscript concludes with another phrase: 'a striking contrast to their brother officers with whom I came in contact'. The phrase is muted, as is much of O'Farrell's language, but it tilts the conclusion to the negative. As published, the concluding sentence about finding the men 'most courteous' seems inappropriately polite, as if she were offering formal thanks for a visit. Nor does the manuscript say 'In concluding'; the sentence begins, 'I must say of B.G. Lowe & of Lieutenant Royall I found them most courteous...'.

O'Farrell's narrative is body-oriented: she walked through the line of fire; she had the red cross ripped from her sleeve and apron; she dodged bullets; she was guarded while she slept; she was arrested, strip-searched, fed good food or prison food; she was kept in custody for two days and then released to her own custody. Her final judgement about which officers are 'courteous' was determined by their respect for her person.

### 'A PACIFIST DIES'

Hanna Sheehy Skeffington's lecture 'A pacifist dies' tells the story of her husband's murder by a British officer while under arrest during the Rising and of physical threats made to the rest of her family. On Tuesday, 25 April Frank Sheehy Skeffington was returning home after a meeting he had called to organise a 'citizens' militia' to prevent looting and maintain civic order during the rebellion. At Portobello Bridge he was arrested by British soldiers and held as hostage for a raiding party while Captain John Bowen-Colthurst of Portobello Barracks killed a young boy and took other innocent men prisoner. On Wednesday morning, Sheehy Skeffington and two others were shot by a firing squad under Bowen-Colthurst's command. Hanna Sheehy Skeffington was not informed of her husband's arrest or death and was only able to discover what had happened on 3 May, 'pleading for information' from a priest at the barracks.[22]

Unlike O'Farrell's narrative, this one is oriented to abstract ideas: values, the law, procedures, the state, justice. The Rising was fought over and over again in attacks of different kinds on the persons of every member of the family, Frank and Hanna Sheehy Skeffington, their son

Owen, their maid, Hanna's sisters Mary Kettle and Margaret Culhane, and even on the one member of the British military who tried to help her, Sir Francis Vane. All were punished: the threatened site moved to wherever there was an attempt to redress the original crime. The larger argument of her account, however, takes place at the level of ideals.[23]

Like her husband, Hanna Sheehy Skeffington was high-minded. The story of her encounters with British military and government authority in 'A pacifist dies' is framed by eulogies of her husband. At the opening, he is described as '...an anti-militarist, a fighting pacifist, a man gentle and kindly even to his bitterest opponents, who always ranged himself on the side of the weak against the strong, whether the struggle was one of class, sex or race domination'. He had 'a great faith in humanity and a hope in the progress towards good'. In the final paragraph, she imagines her husband's reaction to his own death: 'My husband would have gone to his death with a smile on his lips, knowing that by his murder he had struck a heavier blow for his ideals than by any act of his life. His death will speak trumpet-tongued against the system that slew him'. As the word 'system' implies, the response to his death was as great a failure of justice as the death itself, with the inadequate scope of the Commission of Inquiry and the mild punishment of Captain J.C. Bowen-Colthurst, the man who ordered the firing squad to shoot Sheehy Skeffington. After only eighteen months in Broadmoor Asylum for the Criminally Insane, he was released and moved to Canada with his full pension.[24]

Sheehy Skeffington's lectures about the murder of her husband, and especially her lecture tour in America, constituted continuing examples of the 'forceful speech' in which she was already expert. 'I would pledge myself, while in the United States, "to tell the truth and nothing but the truth about Ireland, Great Britain and the War"'.[25] When, in the spring of 1917, she was denied a speaking venue in San Francisco but led a crowd to a new one, she announced, 'I have not the slightest intention to allow myself to be muzzled'.[26] Women's speech was what the 'system' didn't want: when two of Hanna's sisters went to Portobello Barracks to find out what had happened to Frank, they were arrested, court-martialled, and 'forbidden to speak till they left the premises'.[27]

In the first of Sheehy Skeffington's most important encounters with male authority in 1916, she and her household were threatened with as much force as could be used against them without killing anyone. On Friday, 28 April, 40 armed soldiers fired a volley at the front windows of her house; they shattered the windows 'with the butt-ends of their rifles', and rushed at Sheehy Skeffington, her six-year-old son Owen and their maid 'with fixed bayonets'. With typical courage and confidence, Hanna responded to her son's cry 'at the sight of the naked steel' in words: she put her arm around her son and said, 'These are the defenders of women and children'. That brief sentence, she writes, 'steadied them a little'.[28]

The raiding party took almost the entire contents of the house ('books, pictures, souvenirs, toys, linen, and household goods') and, continuing their threat of violence, left 'an armed guard on the house all night'. After another raid, Sheehy Skeffington's maid was held in custody, and one of the officers was heard to say he 'publicly regretted "that they had not shot Mrs. Skeffington while they were about it"'. Her response was typical: 'It would have saved them (and me) much trouble if they had'.[29]

In July, Sheehy Skeffington was invited to meet Prime Minister Asquith, who wanted to offer her a large amount of money for her husband's death. In this encounter, the same pattern was repeated at a higher level, as Sheehy Skeffington answered the language of power with the language of ideals. She was accompanied by the suffragist Muriel Matters as a 'witness'. There were no armed men with bayonets, but Asquith, Sheehy Skeffington writes, was a 'wily statesman' who 'carefully approached the question of "compensation"' and promises of money for 'my boy's future'. As he spoke, Asquith was 'tapping his fingers on the green baize table' and 'glancing sideways at me'. Sheehy Skeffington was not cowed in the presence of the prime minister; she wanted an official inquiry, and all his talk of 'compensation' was a waste of time for her. '…will you say yes or no?' she asked him. 'It is time that I had an answer'. (He answered later in the week, offering a commission, but a restricted one.)[30]

Sheehy Skeffington's description of Asquith's body implies the oblique dishonesty of his attitude: 'he never looked me straight in the face throughout the interview. He is mellow and hale, with rosy, chubby face and silver hair, a Father Christmas air about him'. The 'air about him' is of course false: at his 'wily' verbal level, with his 'pitiful little traps and quibbles', Asquith was the higher version of the crude physical force both Sheehy Skeffingtons had met in Dublin.

## 'THIS REQUEST SHOULD BY NO MEANS BE GRANTED'

Although Gertrude Bannister, Roger Casement's cousin, was not a suffragist, a rebel or a political activist of any kind, she was an independent working woman, a school mistress, and when the need arose, she was able, in Angela Bourke's words in another context, 'to construct and transmit a rhetoric of resistance to male domination...'.[31] Out of desperation she learned how to succeed with government officials. When she and her sister read in the newspaper that their cousin was arrested, they returned at once to London from their seaside Easter holiday. Bannister wrote a letter to the home secretary; went to the Home Office; told that Casement was in military, not civil custody, she wrote to the secretary of state for war; went to his office; was told there to go to the Home Office; was then told to 'apply to Scotland Yard', and then received only 'a formal acknowledgement'. Bannister then wrote Casement a letter, enclosing it in one to the governor of the Tower of London, where he was imprisoned, but it was never delivered.[32]

Finally, 'as a friend suggested that the Treasury were preparing the case against Roger', Bannister went to see Sir Charles Mathews, senior Treasury counsel. After a short conversation, she realised that 'it was useless begging him to give me any help, so I left him, refusing to allow him to escort me or get me a lift or anything. I hated him'.

Through the help of George Gavan Duffy, Casement's solicitor, Bannister was finally able to see her cousin. She tried to see him for lunch during the interval of the trial and was told she needed the permission of the Home Office. Once more she went there, and this time got a message that Home Secretary Herbert Samuel had no objection. When she returned to the court and met the secretary of the Lord Chief Justice, however, she saw that Samuel had deceived her, having written in red letters at the top of the message, 'This request should by no means be granted'.[33] Bannister had not yet acquired Sheehy Skeffington's power of forceful speech, but in her final such encounter, she was successful. She learned on the job.

During the trial, Bannister heard that Casement had been given inedible food for lunch and was exhausted while he was in the dock. A warder suggested she go to the Home Office, and once more she attempted to breach it. This time she saw Sir Ernley Blackwell, legal advisor to the government, a 'pale, narrow-faced, thin-lipped man with the sort of expression I knew, by much bitter experience, meant "Get through with what you have to say quickly—I will consent to nothing you want"'.[34]

> I told him I had come to ask permission to have luncheon sent in to Roger at the Law Courts. He said, 'It is impossible.' I said, 'It cannot be impossible. You mean that *you* will

forbid it.' He said, 'I have no power to allow it.' I said, 'You have. I have already inquired on that point from the officials at the Law Courts.' He said, 'I fear I cannot do it.' I said, 'You mean you will not although you could.' A long silence, then: 'Can you not imagine that this prisoner is going through a terrible strain and needs a little help—and even the knowledge that we are thinking of him and planning for him is likely to help?' Just a blank stony stare. I said, 'I beg of you to be humane enough to grant this very simple request.' He said, 'I have no power.' I said, 'But you have.' Finally he said, 'I fear I cannot continue this interview.' I said, 'I fear I cannot leave until you accede to this simple request'—and so on. I sat for a long time. He went out of the room. He returned. I was still there. He said, 'If I accede to your request it must be understood that this is the only matter in which a concession may be made.' I said, 'I agree. Will you please telephone here and now to the warder at the Law Courts saying you permit this?' He said, 'It is unnecessary. You can say I said so.' I (remembering Sir H. Samuel's trick of the day before) said, 'I should prefer you telephoned now, in my presence, or else give me a note.' He said, 'I will not give you a note.'

Then after a pause he took up the telephone and telephoned—there was no trick about it because I sent in a luncheon of roast chicken, etc., and a bottle of wine and Roger was allowed to have it.[35]

Bannister had finally figured out how to use what power she had, namely, quite literally, 'staying power'. She simply did not leave the man's office: 'I was still there'.

The women were not the only ones whose powers were temporarily released in the revolutionary moment. Clerical, military and government authorities alike appear to have felt that their obligation to control and suppress rebellious energies gave them special licence to act against women with a misogynistically tainted viciousness. They responded to women's liberated behaviours (behaviours already familiar from the suffrage movement) with such verbal violence that it might almost be said that another revolution was expressing itself through the national struggle.

Right: Elizabeth O'Farrell, who carried the news of the surrender to the garrisons but was held overnight in Kilmainham despite General Lowe's promise that she would be treated 'as a guest'.

Below: Leslie Barry (née Price), who (according to her own account) persuaded Father Flanagan to hear confessions at the GPO: 'It took a certain amount of courage to fight a priest'.

Hanna Sheehy Skeffington with her son Owen; she refused the money Prime Minister Asquith offered her–allegedly 'for my boy's future'–as compensation for her husband's death.

*Chapter Five*

# WOMEN AMONG WOMEN

*Aithnítear cara i gcruatán.*
'A friend is known in hardship'.

Irish proverb

One of the strangest sights of Easter 1916 must have been the sixteen-hand reel danced by the women prisoners in Kilmainham. It was 2 May, a cold morning, and the women had been 'awakened very early by sounds of shots'.[1] After their exercise, they 'danced and enjoyed' the reel, 'much to the alarm of the five armed soldiers on guard of us and two wardresses'. A graceful, skipping, intricate dance, with a joy built into its little leaps, chains, arches, circles and swings, the sixteen-hand reel must indeed have surprised and bewildered the guards, no doubt expecting nefarious behaviour from these rebel women and seeing instead an artful choreography.

The young women dancing in the prison, surrounded by guards but creating their own beautiful design, could serve as an emblem for the many occasions during the Rising when women created a small zone of feminist comfort within a hostile male military zone. Focusing on one another, affirming and embodying their collective identity, the women clearly enjoyed the effect they had on the Kilmainham soldiers. The sharp gender divisions of the times, made inevitable by the institutional separation of the sexes in the Volunteers and Cumann na mBan as well as in the British military's treatment of prisoners, gave the women 'out' in 1916 many opportunities to constitute themselves a community and disregard their hostile surroundings.

## 'SIN NO MORE, LEST A WORSE THING COME UNTO THEE'

Many women were 'out' in the Rising with women they were already close to. There were sets of sisters, Annie, Lily, and Eileen Cooney, Eily and Anna O'Hanrahan, Madge and Laura Daly and Kathleen Clarke, and Min and Phyllis Ryan, among many others. There were pairs and groups of friends, Kathleen Lynn and her partner Madeline ffrench-Mullen, Elizabeth O'Farrell and her partner Julia Grenan, and all 'the girls' from the North, among them two of the Connolly sisters, Nora and Ina.[2] But the connections among women that emerged during the Rising were different: they were produced by the unusual circumstances of the time. When they sang and danced, it was from a mix of excitement, youthful energy, anxiety and cultural assertiveness. On the first day of the Rising, writes Annie Cooney:

> When we arrived at the Weaver's Hall most of the section were there—24 or 25 of us in all. We had to wait there for the word to tell us where we were to go. While waiting we did a bit of Irish dancing and amused ourselves generally.[3]

And at the surrender,

> The Volunteers were marched off and we were in ranks of four behind them, keeping step...The men asked us to sing all our marching songs in which they joined. They said this kept their hearts up. This went on the whole way till we reached Richmond Barracks.[4]

Marching through Dublin, surrounded by British soldiers, the women as they sing mark their territory with sound. They claim the space for themselves and the Volunteers, their vocal power showing a force of unconquerability.

The same assertiveness drives the women's collective response to the warder at Kilmainham, described in three separate accounts:

*Brigid Lyons:*

The only really brutal individual we met during the whole time was a warder called Beatty. We were left standing in the hall for a time while he ranted and raved at us. Somebody directed him to take us to certain floors and he said 'Bring them down this way first' and he marched us down an old corridor and held up his lantern and said 'Read that' and I read out 'Sin no more lest a worse thing come unto thee'. I said 'We have not committed any sin'. He said 'Shut up, it's to the "drop" you should be taken, every one of you'.[5]

*Annie Cooney:*

The first thing that caught our eyes was an inscription inside the big gate 'Sin no more lest worse shall come to thee'. This struck us as very humorous.[6]

*Pauline Keating:*

When we arrived at Kilmainham there was an old jailer waiting for us. He brought us to a doorway and pointed to an inscription above it: 'Sin no more, lest a worse thing come to thee'. There was a violent protest from us girls. We shouted at him that we had not sinned. He retorted that if we had not come out to kill, we certainly had not come to cure. We thought it a funny incident.[7]

In all three references to this 'funny incident', the first person plural stands out: 'We have not committed any sin', 'This struck us as very humorous', 'We shouted at him that we had not sinned'. The women respond as one being, and the surrounding British penal system does not silence or frighten them. They respond with appropriate defiance and amusement to the ridiculous motto and to the Dickensian warder Beatty, a prison employee who tells the young women, 'it's to the "drop" you should be taken, every one of you'.

## BODIES IN PROXIMITY

Some connections between women emerged from accidental circumstances, especially those in which for brief periods women became intimately close to other women's bodies. In many of its minor narratives, the Rising moves into the most private places, into rooms where women are bathing, getting undressed, sleeping or using a chamber pot. And what happens in these deep interior places is a slight suspension of the 'normal' rules of intimacy. This suspension may be manifest in some subtle deviation from customary modes of behaviour, or an intimacy between strangers, or an unspoken understanding that the rules of relationship have been changed.

On the *Asgard*, for instance, as we have seen in Chapter Two, Mary Spring Rice and Molly Childers lived in close quarters. Below deck, there was a gendered division of private space: husband and wife did not sleep together. Childers and Spring Rice slept in the same cabin, and Spring Rice made many gendered comments: at one point the two women agreed that 'all men were alike about setting topsails on all possible occasions', and Spring Rice writes elsewhere, 'I did envy the men their morning bathe'.[8] This 'women's space' was so terribly crowded with themselves and most of the 900 rifles that they were necessarily intimate because their bodies were close together. The intimacy created a kind of sisterhood. As Childers wrote to Alice Stopford Green, 'Mary and I sleep on mattresses laid across our cabin over the guns....Toilet has become very difficult'.[9]

Before the guns were loaded, Spring Rice noted, 'the space certainly does look very small for all we shall have to put in but she and I don't take up much room to sleep'. One night during a huge storm, she writes that she 'crawled into the cabin where Molly and I lay, half on top of one another which seemed to make the elements less terrible'.[10] She adds, 'my bed wetter than it's ever been tonight. New leaks etc...; however Molly angelically shared hers with me, so I was only on the edge of the wet part'.[11] On another occasion, Spring Rice crawled into the cabin half on top of Childers, who was as usual 'very long suffering about it'.[12]

Their kinship was such that when Spring Rice went ashore and had a bath and Childers didn't, Spring Rice felt guilty: 'a scrumptious hot bath; but I felt rather mean at leaving Molly to do all the tidying up on board'.[13] When, after the guns were unloaded, Spring Rice was sleeping in Dublin, and Erskine and Molly were still aboard the *Asgard*, sailing it to the west of Ireland, Spring Rice writes in the diary's final entry, 'I felt rather mean as I got into a glorious hot bath and thought of Molly and Erskine tired and worn out with everything upset, tossing about on the Irish sea. But my bed was heavenly'.[14]

Kathleen Clarke's account of 1916 mentions an improvised intimate moment with a woman she barely knew. On the afternoon of 2 May 1916, as she tells it, she had had no word at all about the Rising and did not know if her husband was alive or dead. She was working in her garden just to keep occupied. A nervous elderly neighbour visited her to find out what was going on. While the 'old lady' was there, Clarke looked down the road and saw 'a detachment of British soldiers' marching up the avenue, obviously coming to her house. 'Never having experienced a military raid, I was not quite sure what they would do (though my Aunt Lollie had given me a description of a raid on her home in Fenian times...)'.[15] With about a minute to prepare, she realised quickly that the only valuable she had to worry about was the money 'held in trust' for the dependants of the men out in the Rising.

Because her domestic space was about to be invaded and disrupted, Clarke had to find a more interior space that wouldn't be disrupted.

> ...where was I to hide it? Time was short; any minute now they would be demanding admittance. Ah, sudden thought; I would give it to the old lady! She would scarcely be searched, even if I was. This was easier said

than done. She was frightened, and I had to bully her into consenting. She was so terrified at the thought that she was quite helpless, and I was shaking with pent-up excitement. She had an old-fashioned bodice, buttoned from the neck down. I opened the buttons, put the money inside and rebuttoned it. Her ample bust was not noticeably increased by the added bulk.

...The knock came at the hall door as the last button was buttoned.[16]

What's interesting here is the sudden, spontaneous creation of an intimacy that is impersonal: it involves bodily proximity but no emotional closeness. Clarke was one of eight sisters, and before her marriage to Tom Clarke, she had had a successful career in Limerick as a dressmaker, so she had some experience of working with women's bodies and clothing. But the frame of the dressmaker's store isn't operant here to give significance to the intimacy, unbuttoning the blouse of a woman she doesn't know well, a woman she doesn't even give a name to in a narrative where she usually gives names. The licence to touch another woman's body derived from the emergency of the moment. This was a moment of barely consensual but desperate intimacy: 'I had to bully her into consenting'. But even without full consent, there was nevertheless no resistance, which is a kind of tacit collaboration. The word 'ample' shows Clarke's womanly (and perhaps dressmakerly) observation of the other woman's dimensions.

When the 'old lady' was arrested along with Clarke, Clarke protested and kept protesting until she finally met a soldier with authority to let the woman go. At that point, Clarke writes, 'I breathed a sigh of relief; my money was safe'.[17] The intimacy was temporary and merely practical; it was not an intimacy like that between Childers and Spring Rice that intensified the warmth of their friendship.

Geraldine Plunkett Dillon's memoir reveals an awkward, accidental intimacy involving her newly widowed sister-in-law Grace Plunkett. In popular history, and in the official guided tour of Kilmainham, which begins in the chapel, Plunkett is the 'tragic bride of 1916'. At the time, however, Grace Plunkett's sex life was the subject of gossip. Elsie Mahaffy's diary refers to 'the "necessary" midnight marriage to make "an honest woman" of the depraved girl Grace Gifford, six months later the mother "of Plunkett's son"'.[18] Dillon's account in her diary refers to this gossip: 'It was said, of course, that Grace must have been pregnant; the curate who got permission for the marriage must have thought so.

Grace said that she told him she must get married and that he asked her, "Must you?" and she said, "Yes".[19] And the story 'put about by Dublin Castle', writes Dillon, was that 'she was going to have a baby but that Joe was not the father'. Her sex life is a matter for public speculation.

The customary modes of family relationship were already changed because of Grace's anomalous position among the Plunketts: she was an in-law and member of the Plunkett family for the rest of her life, but they didn't know her well, the marriage was sudden, and it had lasted only a few hours. Dillon took responsibility for her new sister-in-law, allowing her to stay at the Plunkett family compound at Larkfield, in south Dublin. That hospitality gave Dillon access to her sister-in-law's private space:

> Because everyone was at me to keep Grace in the public eye and in the Plunkett home, I pressed her to go to stay in Larkfield when she was thrown out of home again and I got one of our maids to stay with her. I thought Grace had many good points, and I got on better with her than the rest of the family, but while she was staying in Larkfield she took every advantage of the position; she was destructive and a messer and I thought her silly and dangerous.... She invited all her friends to stay there. I asked Marie Perolz to stay with her when she came back and Perolz said that she could not see how Grace had kept out of trouble all her life.
>
> I went out to Larkfield to see Grace and was told that she was upstairs in bed. When I went into her bedroom I saw a large white chamberpot full of blood and foetus. She said nothing and I said nothing.
>
> An ex-fiancé of Grace's named Moore sent her a postcard, congratulating her on the birth of a son, and she wrote back telling him it was not true and asking him to call on her. They made it up then but quarrelled again...[20]

This passage raises many questions, most of which no one can answer, but it should be seen in the context of the other episodes of intimacy in domestic interiors, Childers and Spring Rice sleeping in the same small bed, and Kathleen Clarke unbuttoning the other woman's 'bodice'. Here, the absence of intimacy is conspicuous. This is clearly an inadvertent violation of privacy. It seems likely that if Grace

Plunkett had had her own house, if she had not been on Geraldine Dillon's 'territory', Dillon would not have been visiting, and the secret might not have become known. By accident of timing, by a chance visit on a particular day, the secret of Grace Plunkett's sexual history and medical condition was revealed to her sister-in-law. Dillon's statement 'She said nothing and I said nothing' suggests the failure, indeed the complete absence, of personal connection between the two of them, and a deliberate reticence on both sides. Neither woman acknowledged to the other this important and traumatic fact. The air of the room must have been heavy with unarticulated feelings, one of which is expressed implicitly in the next sentence: Dillon's reference to an 'ex-fiancé' appears to be a criticism of her sister-in-law's relationships with men.

## MARGARET SKINNIDER AND CONSTANCE MARKIEVICZ

The connection between Margaret Skinnider and Constance Markievicz was more intense, at least on Skinnider's side, than any of those involved in the dancing prisoners, the singing Cumann na mBan, or the temporary physical intimacies on the *Asgard*. Skinnider worked with Markievicz to liberate Ireland, but Markievicz liberated Skinnider from the limitations of traditional 'womanly' behaviour.[21]

Skinnider was the only woman wounded in combat in the Rising, and Markievicz held the highest military position of any woman in it: she was second in command after Commandant Michael Mallin of the Irish Citizen Army division at the College of Surgeons.[22] A young maths teacher in Glasgow with Irish parents, Skinnider came down to Dublin over Christmas 1915 hiding detonators strapped to her body. She stayed with 'Madam' and took note of the Fianna:

> When I told Madam I could pass as a boy, even if it came to wrestling or whistling, she tried me out by putting me into a boy's suit, a Fianna uniform. She placed me under the care of one of her boys to whom she explained I was a girl, but that, since it might be necessary some day to disguise me as a boy, she wanted to find whether I could escape detection. I was supposed to be one of the Glasgow Fianna. We went out, joined the other Fianna, and walked about the streets whistling rebel tunes.

> Whenever we passed a British soldier we made him take
> to the gutter, telling him the streets of Dublin were no
> place 'for the likes of him'. [23]

Madam told the Fianna boy to whom she entrusted the cross-dressed Skinnider that 'it might be necessary some day' to disguise Skinnider as a boy. In other words, the transvestism was a patriotic obligation, a possible military strategy, to see if her guest could 'escape detection'. However necessary such a disguise might be for the revolution, it seemed to be fulfilling for Skinnider. She was clearly dying to be a boy and do boyish things, 'wrestling or whistling'. She was instantly successful, one of the boys: 'The boys took me for one of themselves'.

Skinnider was not only a boy; she was the best boy, the most masculine: in the shooting-gallery, 'I hit the bull's-eye oftener than any of them, much to the delight of the boy who knew I was a girl'. And in this enterprise, Skinnider had a role model: '...by her own skill Madam had accustomed them to expect good marksmanship in a woman'.[24] Markievicz had given Skinnider the space and the licence to be a boy, to act masculine, to whistle in public and make British soldiers 'take to the gutter'. Markievicz released Skinnider's talents. Skinnider had a *grá* for Markievicz and assumed the rest of the world did too: '...all the villagers on her father's estate loved Madam...When she was sent away to school or went to Paris to study painting,...they missed her'. The Fianna 'loved her and trusted her, a high compliment'.[25] Skinnider idealised the charisma, the patriotism, and the generosity of Madam, drawn especially to her unconventional hospitality: she 'kept "open house" not only for her friends, but for her friends' friends'.[26]

A large part of Skinnider's transformation was sartorial: she writes that her favourite patriotic poem was 'The jackets of green'. 'The redcoat and the green jacket!' she writes, the punctuation expressing her excitement: 'All the differences between the British and Irish lay in the contrast between those two colors'.[27] She admired the way Madam was able to disguise James Larkin as an old man and prevent the police from finding him.[28] In order to discern the lay of the land at Beggar's Bush Barracks, anticipating its possible usefulness for the imminent Rising, Skinnider planned a little drama in which she acted the part of a helpless (but curious) female:

> When I reached the spot where I thought the magazine
> ought to be, I took my handkerchief and let it blow—acci-
> dentally, of course—over this outer wall. A passing boy

gallantly offered to get it for me. Being a woman and nat-
urally curious, I found it necessary to pull myself up on
tiptoe to watch him as he climbed over the wall. The
ground between the two walls had not been paved, but
was of soft earth. I had seen enough. Thanking the boy, I
put my handkerchief carefully into my pocket so as not
to trouble anyone else by making them climb about on
Dublin walls, and went on my way.[29]

Taking into account Larkin's escape from the police, Skinnider's escape
from 'detection' when out with the Fianna, and her successful recon-
naissance of the barracks, handkerchief and all, it's clear that
cross-dressing was not her only pleasure. She enjoyed the whole street
drama of performativity, the danger, the costume elements, and the
successful deception, all grounded, as she saw it, in the larger patriotic
purpose of liberating Ireland, and all enabled by the hospitality and en-
couragement of Madam, herself liberated from Big House feminine
ways (an unfortunate liberation, as Yeats saw it another way in 'Easter
1916'). Skinnider mentions an 'Irishman' who said he never felt 'a revolution' would be 'a reality' until he saw Madam drilling the Fianna
out in the country in moonlight: 'She was in uniform, with knee-
breeches, puttees, and officer's coat, and the whole scene was martial
and intense'.[30] She was a new kind of Kathleen Ní Houlihan, persuading
men to revolt not because she was a poor old woman but because she
was a woman in breeches and puttees.

Skinnider's description of an episode from the first day of the Rising
merges the elements that excite her the most: clothing, guns and the
countess, dressed in a uniform that showily expresses both genders.
Seeing British soldiers marching up Harcourt Street, the countess

stood motionless, waiting for them to come near. She was
a lieutenant in the Irish Volunteers and, in her officer's
uniform and black hat with great plumes, looked most impressive. At length she raised her gun to her shoulder—it
was an 'automatic' over a foot long...—and took aim...I
saw the two officers leading the column drop to the street.
As the countess was taking aim again, the soldiers,
without firing a shot, turned and ran in great confusion
for their barracks. The whole company fled as fast as they
could from *two* people, one of them a woman![31]

The italicised '*two*' and the exclamation point express Skinnider's pleasure in the countess's marksmanship and in her ability to inspire fear.

The paragraph in which Skinnider describes her own uniform, donned in the College of Surgeons, emphasises its origin in Madam's generosity, its masculine style and its patriotic purpose:

> Madam had had a fine uniform of green moleskin made for me. With her usual generosity, she had made mine of better material than her own. It consisted of knee breeches, belted coat, and puttees. I slipped into this uniform, climbed up astride the rafters, and was assigned a loophole through which to shoot....More than once I saw the man I aimed at fall...Every shot we fired was a declaration to the world that Ireland, a small country but large in our hearts, was demanding her independence.[32]

Skinnider's love of shooting, indeed the pleasure she seems to take in killing, is presented as inseparable from the high-minded goal of Irish independence; the breeches, belt, puttees and gun construct the moments that she has been waiting for. All come together in a grand purpose that has been made possible by Madam.

The Rising also offered Skinnider the pleasure of changing costumes and performing both genders. 'Whenever I was called down to carry a dispatch,' she writes, '...I took off my uniform, put on my gray dress and hat, and went out the side door of the college with my message. As soon as I returned, I slipped back into my uniform and joined the firing-squad'. The thrill for her was not simply dressing as a man; it was the opportunity to dress as both sexes, to switch roles, an opportunity that allows her to dramatise to herself and to any colleagues who notice the performativity at the heart of her gender identity. She needed only to switch costumes to switch roles; she could act as either sex. Ireland might not yet be liberated at this point, but Skinnider was.

When Commandant Mallin rejected Skinnider's idea of throwing a bomb through a window of the Shelbourne Hotel, she made a feminist argument. He said he 'did not want to let a woman run this sort of risk,' and she countered, '...we had the same right to risk our lives as the men; that in the constitution of the Irish Republic, women were on an equality with men. For the first time in history, indeed, a constitution had been written that incorporated the principle of equal suffrage'.[33] This was a good argument for women's participation, but the military strategy of the suggestion was not sensible. Mallin allowed her to attempt another venture, to cut off the retreat of British soldiers by burning two buildings. This second option proved risky also, too risky: a seventeen-year-old boy was killed, and Skinnider herself was wounded.

More than the wound, Skinnider minded the destruction of her uniform and her inability to participate in other such ventures:

> They laid me on a large table and cut away the coat of my fine, new uniform. I cried over that. Then they found I had been shot in three places, my right side under the arm, my right arm, and in the back of my right side. Had I not turned as I went through that shop-door to call to the others, I would have got all three bullets in my back and lungs and surely been done for.[34]

They probed to get the bullets out, and 'all the while Madam held my hand...My disappointment at not being able to bomb the Hotel Shelbourne was what made me unhappy'. Then Markievicz went out and killed the soldiers who shot Skinnider: 'You are avenged, my dear'. Before she was taken to a hospital, she was 'in good hands' because 'Madam is a natural nurse' and took care of her. 'My beautiful uniform had entirely disappeared and I never got a button of it, but I had a whole skin so I did not worry'.[35] The wound and the destruction of her uniform ended Skinnider's temporary freedom, a freedom not so much from British rule as from definition by gender.

## SHIP STREET BARRACKS

Most women's accounts of 1916, whether in witness statements, diaries or memoirs, do not focus on interiority, as we saw in Vera Brittain's *Testament of youth*.[36] Nor are they like captivity narratives, which Elaine Showalter has called 'the first literary form dominated by women's experience'. The Irish women's captivity is brief, is collectively experienced, and—as they present it—forms part of a longer national experience of revolution and resistance. However, their representations of imprisonment do, in Showalter's words, testify to 'women's courage, resourcefulness and strength'.[37] The collective nature of those qualities, the way they are always distributed among women rather than attributed to a single hardy soul, is shown most dramatically in accounts of the temporary captivity many of them experienced together. The British military was not prepared for women rebels and had no site ready for imprisoning them. The women who surrendered with the men, such as those from the Marrowbone Lane garrison, were put in Kilmainham. Women in smaller numbers, such as the Citizen Army women from the City Hall garrison arrested on Monday, were locked in a dirty, unused room in Ship Street Barracks.

Brigid Foley, ever sensitive to the unhygienic (as we saw in her comments on the Kilmainham lavatory in Chapter Four), says Ship Street Barracks was 'a terrible place; there were no sanitary arrangements. A sergeant came with a bucket which he placed behind the door. We became infested with fleas and lice'.[38] This space recurs in many women's memoirs as a site of discomfort; but all the accounts show that the discomfort inflicted by the all-male British military inspired a temporary sisterhood among the women, even among those who were strangers to one another.

This narrative is most visible through the cameo appearances of a prostitute in the accounts of Kathleen Lynn, Brigid Foley and Kathleen Clarke. Only in Lynn's account is the woman called a prostitute, as noted in her diary for the night of Saturday/Sunday, 29/30 April, which Lynn spent in Ship Street Barracks:

> 29th April. Sat night—Sun. mg. Terribly excited drunken prostitute brought in, nearly mad, her brother shot Tues & she had gone to see body. We couldn't quiet her. Two soldiers came in, one held revolver to her head, other twisted her wrists, Emer jumped up, told him to stop & had revolver turned on her. They were brutal. D. G. they left I gave poor soul morphia [?] hypo. She lay down & slept beside me.

> 30th April…poor prostitute woman got out, with notes for E. Young & L. S. She was very grateful—I had long chat with her.[39]

Two nights later, on 2 May, Lynn was no longer there, nor was the prostitute, but she returned and appears in Foley's narrative:

> During the night a variety of people—not all of them Sinn Feiners—were brought in. There was an awful din. One woman especially was making a row. When I asked her why she was there she said she had run after one of the Volunteers with a loaf of bread and a soldier had dashed it out of her hand. She lifted a stone and threw it at the

soldiers who arrested her. I told her that one of our friends—Mrs. Clarke—was very ill and asked her to shut up and give her a chance to rest. She replied that if she made enough row and we objected, they would let her go. She told the policeman that she had left a young baby at home and wanted to feed it. She was let out.[40]

And here is Clarke's account of the same episode. Marie Perolz and Brigid Foley were brought in, and

...there was a commotion outside the door. It was banged open, and a woman with four soldiers tumbled in. She was holding them, two with each hand, and yelling, 'What did ye do with my dear, darling Doctor Lynn? Where is she?'

She was a big, powerful woman, and held the four soldiers apparently without much trouble; they were small and young. They were struggling to get free. In the struggle, her shawl fell off. To my horror her back was completely naked; the solders had torn every stitch of clothing off her in their struggles with her before they reached Ship Street. I picked up the shawl, put it around her, and whispered to her to let the soldiers go. In her surprise at my action, she let two of the soldiers go, but, looking at me suspiciously, she retained her hold on the other two. Then Miss Perolz took a hand, and persuaded her to let the other two go.

She and Miss Perolz sat down in a corner and had a heart-to-heart talk. She told Miss Perolz that her brother had been out in the Rising, got wounded during the week and managed to get home. In the street where she lived were also many of those we called 'Separation Allowance women'...some of them informed on her brother. When the British soldiers came to arrest him he made an attempt to escape and was shot dead. She became abusive to the soldiers and they arrested her. That was how she had been in Ship Street with Dr Kathleen Lynn, and other women prisoners who were there. She had been released before Dr Lynn and the others were moved elsewhere.

That day, she told Miss Perolz, a British officer was passing down her street with a squad of soldiers and she recognized him as the man who had shot her brother. She caught up a brick and flung it at him, and that was how she came to be arrested a second time. While she was telling her story to Miss Perolz, she would look across at me every now and then, and whisper to Miss Perolz, 'Are you sure she is a Sinn Feiner? Are you sure she is not one of them wans in the pay of the British?' It took some time for Miss Perolz to convince her I was all right, and could be trusted. Then she announced that she would be out of there in an hour. She asked us to keep quiet.[41]

The distressed woman banged on the door and yelled that her baby would die if she couldn't get home. She confided in the other women 'He's weaned long ago', to make it clear she was acting. The sergeant finally let her out. Clarke writes, 'The memory of her tragic story remained with us'.

This episode makes clear the non-judgemental, protective, maternal impulse of four women (Lynn, Clarke, Perolz and Foley) toward a less privileged woman. Lynn has given her morphine and let the woman sleep beside her; hence she is 'my dear, darling Doctor Lynn'. Clarke covered her nakedness, Perolz was soothing her and Foley listening to her. The same physical intimacy obtained in the sleeping arrangements for the women who remain; they slept in close proximity to keep one another warm, even though they didn't know one another well.

> The floor was the only place to lie on, and the only coverings we could find were a couple of old blankets. Both blankets and floor were filthy. We laid one blanket on the floor and used the other to cover us, and by lying very close together it barely covered us.[42]

The women got many bodily comforts from one another: morphine, warmth, and, in one episode, an education in self-defence. When Clarke was brought into the barracks, she recognised a 'young girl' (her words) who was a member of Cumann na mBan, but they didn't acknowledge one another till the soldiers had gone. Later in the evening,

> ...three or four young British soldiers came into the room...The girl was sitting on a bench, reading, with her elbows on her knees, when one of the soldiers sat down beside her, flung his arms around her and attempted to kiss her.

> She stood up without saying a word, boxed him thoroughly, resumed her seat and continued reading. I felt extremely proud of that girl; at the time I could have hugged her. From the way she tackled the young man I think she must have had boxing lessons. He was quite defeated, and made no further attempt to molest her. I only wish I could remember her name; she was a girl anyone would be proud of.[43]

Here national politics and gender politics overlap entirely in the sexual harassment of a rebel. The harassment adds an element of gender to the political alliance that already exists among the women, and of course it also increases the emotional intensity of the moment. Clarke feels what a later generation might call 'feminist solidarity'. Her word 'defeated' implies there was at least one space in which the Irish can defeat the English.

Soon Clarke, too, was harassed:

> Some time after this episode I was sitting on a bench, completely absorbed in my thoughts and fears for my husband and brother, and in a dim way hearing Miss Perolz and Miss Foley arguing with the soldiers. Then Miss Perolz asked me something about my children, and the next thing I knew I was being chucked under the chin by one of the soldiers, saying, 'Surely this kid is not old enough to have children!'
>
> I was unable to box like the girl, though speechless with indignation, but under my gaze that man slunk away; there was murder in it.[44]

Under these unpleasant circumstances, Clarke took the girl as her role model, copying her fierceness even though she put it into her face rather than her fists. There was 'murder' in her 'gaze': the belligerent response was somatic in its form of expression, and it worked in the physical realm: the man 'slunk' away. The war between the sexes in Ship Street Barracks replicates, overlaps with and repeats the struggle of the Rising, but with a better outcome. The national struggle has (temporarily) been lost, but the women's struggle has (temporarily) been won.

Above: Marie Perolz, member of Cumann na mBan and the Irish Citizen Army; while detained in Ship Street Barracks during the Rising, she had a 'heart-to-heart talk' with a prostitute agitated about her brother's death. She also took care of Grace Plunkett in the weeks after the executions.

Left: Margaret Skinnider, one of the few women actively involved in fighting during the Rising; the example of her friend Constance Markievicz liberated her from traditional 'womanly' behaviour.

Kathleen Clarke, wearing a Limerick lace shawl she herself made. While the British soldiers raided her house on 2 May, she worked on a Limerick lace handkerchief: 'the work done was very poor', she wrote, but it 'seemed to have a soothing effect' on her maid and an elderly woman who was visiting.

*Chapter Six*

# THE KILMAINHAM FAREWELL

O Fionnuala, and comely Conn, O Aodh, O Fiacra of the
beautiful arms, it is not ready I am to go away from you...

'The fate of the Children of Lir', trans. Lady Gregory

Oisín Kelly's statue of *The Children of Lir* at the Garden of Remembrance
in Dublin embodies the idea of metamorphosis by which dead rebels
become immortal heroes, or, to put it another way, by which human
beings become legendary and mythic. Fionnuala's arms and those of
her brothers hang limply over the side in the middle of the statue. At
the bottom, another brother's arms are still almost touching the earth.
Their heads also hang limply downwards, the lowest facing the ground
directly. But higher up, the huge wings and long necks and beaks of
four swans are muscular and stretched upwards, pointing to the sky. In
this way the Garden commemorates 'those who gave their lives in the
cause of Irish Freedom', as the statue makes visible the process of transformation.[1]

Of course, Irish rebels are not legendary figures who are magically
turned into birds. The culture they inhabit constructs them as martyrs,
and that construction happens after their execution. But some of it
happens before they die, and *The Children of Lir* statue shows the children in a moment where they are both human beings and swans. Yeats
wrote in 'Easter 1916' that the rebels had been 'changed, changed
utterly', but he did not mention the small steps by which the transformation took place, or the social interactions it entailed.

## 'DON'T CRY, LILLIE, YOU'LL UNMAN ME'

When the wives, sisters and other visitors conversed with the men in
their cells at Kilmainham just before the executions, the aura of the
martyr was already there. The men had begun to become swans; their
limp arms were becoming outstretched wings. The same drama was
played out in almost every cell, as the men had to indicate to the
women that the process had begun and should not be interrupted.
Preparing themselves to face the firing squad, the men did not want to
dissolve in tears during a final conversation with those they loved. The
visits took place hours and in some cases minutes before the men
would be led to the stone-breakers' yard, their hands bound behind
their backs, a blindfold over their eyes and a piece of paper pinned over
their hearts as a target. They had to be ready to endure those last penal

rituals with an appropriate dignity, because every detail would find its way to the history books.

Describing these last conversations with the men, the women's accounts reveal the different ways the men requested that emotions be controlled. Teresa Heuston, Seán Heuston's sister, writes that when she and other members of the family, including Heuston's mother, arrived to see him the night before his execution, 'On their entering the cell Seán begged them not to break down'. Father Paddy Browne says that when he arrived at the cell, 'Seán came forward to meet and welcome me. He was quite serene'.[2] Willie Pearse's sister Margaret Pearse writes that 'We talked quietly, calmly, and chiefly on personal matters...We told him how proud we were of him and of Pat, and that we were satisfied they had done right'.[3] Grace Plunkett writes of her last visit to her husband:

> When I saw him, on the day before his execution, I found him in exactly the same state of mind. He was so unselfish, he never thought of himself. He was not frightened—not at all, not the slightest. I am sure he must have been worn out after the week's experiences, but he did not show any signs of it—not in the least. He was quite calm.[4]

The last person to be with Plunkett, Father Augustine, gives the same report: 'He was absolutely calm, as cool and self-possessed as if he looked on what was passing and found it good. No fine talk. No heroics. A distinguished tranquillity...'[5]

The delicacy of the process of transformation may be noted in conversational exchanges between the men and the women. Some of these are recorded in Nora Connolly's account of the family's visit to James Connolly, lying wounded on a bed in Dublin Castle:

> When we entered the room Papa had his head turned to the door watching for our coming. When he saw Mamma he said:
> 'Well, Lillie, I suppose you know what this means?'
> 'O James! It's not that—it's not that?' my mother wailed.
> 'Yes, Lillie,' he said. 'I fell asleep for the first time to-night and they wakened me at eleven and told me that I was to die at dawn.'
> My mother broke down, laid her head on his bed and sobbed heartbreakingly.

My father patted her head and said, 'Don't cry, Lillie, you'll unman me.'

'But your beautiful life, James,' my mother sobbed. 'Your beautiful life.'

'Well, Lillie,' he said. 'Hasn't it been a full life, and isn't this a good end?' My mother still wept.

I was crying too. He turned to me at the other side of the bed and said:

'Don't cry, Nora, there is nothing to cry about.'

I said, 'I won't cry.' He patted my hand and said, 'That's my brave girl.'[6]

The details of the conversation, which are roughly the same in two other versions written by Nora Connolly, suggest another aspect of the men's demeanours: it is considered 'unmanly' to cry.[7] James Connolly was acting as he knows a future male martyr should, embracing his fate as a 'good end' and not expressing sorrow: '...there is nothing to cry about'. He was already moving toward the history books, becoming the hero whose death will be described for Irish people of the future, and such a man does not want his masculinity diminished by an account of weeping in his final hours.

This was the kind of scene Con Colbert wanted to avoid, and so, as he wrote to his sister, he did not 'call' her to visit him in Kilmainham:

My dear Lila,

I did not like to call you to this Gaol to see me before I left this world because I felt it would grieve us both too much, so I am just dropping you a line to ask you to forgive me anything I do owe you and to say 'Goodbye' to you and all my friends and to get you and them to say a prayer for my soul.

Perhaps I'd never get the chance of knowing when I was to die again and so I'll try and die well.

...May God help us—me to die well—you to bear your sorrow.[8]

The person he invited for a final visit was Kate Murphy, whose husband had been captain of 'A' Company of the 4th Battalion and in charge of the Marrowbone Lane garrison, where Colbert was second-in-command. As he wrote in a letter to his close friends Annie and Lily Cooney, he had asked for Mrs Murphy specifically because he did not know her well:

KILMAINHAM GAOL, 7.5.'16

My dear Annie and Lily,

I am giving this to Mrs. Murphy for you; she'll not mind to hear of what is happening, and she'll get you all to pray for those of us who must die. Indeed you girls give us courage, and may God grant you Freedom soon in the fullest sense. You wont see me again, and I felt it better not to have you see me, as you'd only be lonely, but now my soul is gone and pray God it will be pardoned all its crimes.[9]

The implication, of course, was that Annie and Lily would 'mind to hear of what is happening'. He preferred to remember them as they were in the garrison and at the surrender, defiantly marching with the men to prison: 'you girls give us courage'.

Murphy writes that she had never met Colbert before Easter Week, when she cooked for the garrison. A prisoner in Kilmainham when Colbert requested to see her, she writes in her account that when he greeted her in his cell, he said, 'I am one of the lucky ones' and that he

...appeared to be happy and said he was quite resigned to go before his Maker. He said he never felt happier as he never thought he would get the honour of dying for Ireland.

I said to him that he was setting an example for all soldiers of the way they should die. The soldier who was present was crying. He said: 'If only we could die such deaths.'[10]

When Murphy asked Colbert why he had not asked to see his sister, he 'said that she might find it hard to bear the strain. When leaving him I said to him that a martyr's death was a noble one. He was smiling as I was going out...'. Telling Colbert that he was 'setting an example for all soldiers', and that 'a martyr's death was a noble one', Murphy said just the right things: she sustained the transformation that Colbert himself had already set in process. 'I felt it better not to have you see me', he wrote to the Cooney sisters, and 'I felt it would grieve us both too much', he had written to his sister Lila. Murphy's words were what he wanted to hear; she did not 'break down' (as Seán Heuston was concerned his family would) or 'unman' him, as James Connolly was worried Lillie Connolly would.

## 'THE DAUGHTERS AND NIECES OF FENIANS'

For all the family members, mostly women, who were summoned to Kilmainham to say a final farewell to the men who would be executed within hours, the ride to the jail was the first traumatic part of the ritual. They describe it in almost the same language.

*Madge Daly:*

It was a terrible drive and seemed endless...Every dozen yards the car was surrounded by soldiers, who put the bayonets and lanterns close to our faces to examine us; but for them we cared not...

*Teresa Heuston:*

The night was dark and it was raining heavily.
The car, driven by a soldier, was stopped several times on the journey to Kilmainham. Each time two soldiers, with fixed bayonets, examined the car and occupants and questioned the policeman and the driver before allowing them to proceed. Their answer to inquiries each time was a cryptic 'King's messenger!'

*Min Ryan:*

A military motor car conveyed us to the prison. It would take the pen of some great Russian realist to picture that awful drive through the night, through the streets of Dublin lined with British sentries with their drawn bayonets. The houses were in darkness and there was a hushed silence in the streets. Save for the whizz of our car and the sharp cry of 'Halt!' every few yards, as we approached the sentries, there was no sound. The most awful moment was when the shout of the sentries and the noise of the car ceased and the door was silently opened for us to dismount and we found ourselves in front of a great, dark, treacherous looking building, Kilmainham Jail.

*Nora Connolly:*

> It seemed to take hours to get to the Castle. We went through the dark, deserted, burning streets encountering only the sentries. We could hardly restrain ourselves while the sentries were questioning the driver.[11]

The drive to Kilmainham was a prelude to the major trauma of the visit. It is clear from the more detailed accounts that the psychological dynamics of the visits involved more than the men's requests for emotional control. Emotional intimacies between the women emerged also in the unusual circumstances of the nocturnal visits to the jail.

In Kilmainham, the women were negotiating the narrow architectural and emotional space between two sets of men, the British military and prison authorities, and the rebels about to be executed. Their accounts of these interactions are very specific, and they correlate interestingly with one another. What they show, among other things, is that the women registered linguistic, paralinguistic and somatic signals from one another with great precision and responded accordingly. By means of these unobserved exchanges, they were operating in an informal, unofficial communications network.

This story is a hidden narrative of the revolution, one knowable only through the first-person accounts of the women who experienced it and wrote it up. The primary concern of all the women enduring the 'Kilmainham farewell' is the maintenance of an attitude they variously call 'holding up', 'bearing up' or 'not breaking down'—in other words, hiding their emotions from the men they encounter. At the same time, these emotions are expressed among themselves, noted and responded to. In short, they are hiding their emotions from men but communicating them, often covertly, to one another.

The most detailed narratives of the way women hid their emotions are in accounts by Madge Daly and her sister Kathleen Clarke, and by Eily O'Hanrahan. Daly describes the drive in the military lorry from Fairview, where the Clarkes lived, to Kilmainham, about 1 a.m. on 4 May, as three of the Daly sisters—Madge, Laura and Kathleen—are being taken to say goodbye to their brother Ned (age 25), who would be executed a few hours later. When the lorry arrived at the house, they were all in bed, and they had to get out of their nightgowns and into their street clothes quickly. Madge and Laura, who had been sharing a bedroom in the Fairview house, could barely get dressed; Madge writes, '...we shook to pieces. Our hands refused to work and it was with great difficulty and delay that we got into our clothes'. During the drive, the sisters' 'only fear' was

> that we would not be able to bear up before my brother as would become the sisters of such a hero and the daughters and nieces of Fenians. We prayed to heaven for strength but for all that, we shook to pieces and could not keep the tears back while we were in the car, when the soldiers could not see us.[12]

Madge uses the phrase 'shook to pieces' twice within the same paragraph; the imminent trauma already registers on their bodies, and they sense one another's shaking bodies and hear one another crying. She writes in the first-person plural, linking the sisters but not conveying precisely what they said.

In this emotional state, they feared 'not being able to bear up'. There were two imagined audiences for the women's demeanour, their 'brother' and 'the soldiers'. They wanted to 'bear up' before Ned 'as would become the sisters of such a hero and the daughters and nieces of Fenians'. The men's status in the nationalist pantheon conferred on the Daly sisters the obligation to act as if the dignity of the tradition depended on their deportment. (Their Uncle John Daly was imprisoned in England for years, where he met Tom Clarke; their father Edward was also a Fenian, though less active than his brother.) The family politics, with its emphasis on the male heroes, appears to replicate the gender divisions of the larger society, making the sisters' status derivative, but in a family with eight sisters and one brother, their labours and their moral support were too important to be considered secondary. Moreover, the women of the family constituted the voices of its collective memory; their Aunt Lollie's stories of the Fenians and Madge and Kathleen's autobiographies testify to that function.

In addition, the word 'Fenian' implicitly constructs a larger national unit around the family unit. It's a word to dry up tears and stop the shakes because it defines the sisters as members of a revolutionary elite. The word opens up a large historical space and time, diminishing somewhat the awful present. It is this perspective that enabled them to face their other audience, the British military, from whom emotion had to be hidden as a sign of the women's unconquerability.

> ...the minute we stepped across the gateway at Kilmainham Prison and entered into the presence of the soldiers, our pride

of race, our pride in our heroes and in their great sacrifice, strengthened our failing limbs and we walked in with heads erect, told our names with pride, and could then have faced death—anything. As we crossed the threshold, the jailer called out: 'relatives of Daly to be shot in the morning'.[13]

With words like 'hero' and 'Fenian' echoing in their heads, the sisters outfaced this rather crude welcome to Kilmainham.

The paradigm for how to behave in the condemned man's cell was set by Kathleen Clarke the night before, during her final interview with her husband. He 'faced death with a clear and happy conscience,' she writes.[14] She came close to saying things that might have upset him and then pulled back. She said, 'I don't know how I am going to live without you. I wish the British would put a bullet in me too'. Tom answered, 'It is not the British policy to shoot women since the Nurse Cavell episode. God will help you, and your own courage, also the children's need for you'. And then, writes Clarke, 'We left the subject. It was too dangerous, and might break us'.[15]

Clarke was 'conscious', she writes, of the 'very exalted state of mind he was in'. The need to avoid anything that 'might break us' remained paramount throughout the conversation. 'During the whole interview, my mind was concentrated on not breaking down. I knew that if I broke, it would break him, at least I feared it would, and perhaps leave him unfit to face the ordeal before him in the way he and I would like'.[16] The 'way he and I would like' meant for Tom Clarke, as it did for all the other men, with the dignity appropriate to an Irish martyr who will become part of collective memory. And so with that in mind, Clarke refrained from telling him an important fact: 'A baby was coming to us, but he did not know. I had not told him before the Rising, fearing to add to his anxieties, and considered if I would tell him then, but left without doing so; I was not sure how it would affect him'.[17]

This behavioural paradigm was followed the very next night when the three Daly sisters visited their brother. Although conversation with their brother was affectionate and intense, warmer than the phrase 'as would become the sisters of such a hero' implies, none of them broke down. Madge's account of the visit is moving in its detail; all the emotion that she could not express at the time comes out in the written account:

The door was then opened just as our boy jumped from the floor, where he had been lying on a half blanket or rug. He was dressed in his Volunteer suit, minus cap, belt, bandolier, sword, etc., and he looked so proud and strong and noble, with eyes alert and full of the fire of the enthusiast, that it was impossible to believe he was a doomed captive, destined to be shot in a few short hours.[18]

Kathleen Clarke's account also emphasises Ned's youth and innocence: 'He was in his uniform, and looked about eighteen years of age, his figure was so slim and boyish'.[19]

Clarke (by her account) stayed at the door to engage the soldier in conversation and give more privacy to her sisters as they talked with Ned. Madge does not mention this positioning: instead, she writes, 'We rushed to Ned and twined our arms around him, and so stood in the centre of the cell during the interview of how long I do not know, surrounded closely by the soldiers with bayonets, until the dread words, "Come—time's up," were uttered'.[20] Madge's first words, as she records them, were such as to exalt the young man who was about to die: 'Oh! Ned, why are we going to give you the highest honours? You did not sign the proclamation? You must have done great work to earn a place with Emmet and Wolfe Tone and all the others'. So saying, she was encouraging the transformation of man to martyr, helping him see beyond the terrible firing squad to the history that would place him with Wolfe Tone and Emmet. But in its passion, her interrogative seems also to be asking, 'Why are they killing you?' Ned responded modestly of course, praising the men in his garrison: 'He said such heroes—such soldiers never lived...'[21]

Like Colbert, like Clarke, like all the others, Daly embraced his fate: 'he said he was glad and proud to die for Ireland; and that he had no regrets...' Madge, by her account, spoke words that now sound hackneyed and could be seen as mere polemic, but in the immediate context, they would have given Daly strength: 'I said England might kill his body, but that his spirit and his name would live forever, as would the spirit of Ireland, which his blood would revive...'.[22]

### SISTERS AND BROTHERS

An interesting moment occurred afterwards with Laura, who was, Madge says, Ned's 'special chum':

> ...our interview was really over. The soldiers called to us: 'Time's up', so we kissed and embraced our boy—once

only, and walked from his cell without a tear or moan, with heads up....and then the cell door banged on [us] all. We walked down the endless stairs. I felt Laura's steps faltering, and feared she would faint and fall, so I whispered to her: 'Keep up, you must not break down here'. I got the answer, 'Fear not'.[23]

Those faltering steps, like the shaking or the tears in the lorry, constituted the most minimal of bodily communications, but they generated an exchange that was entirely private: of course Ned, behind the locked door, couldn't hear them, and Madge whispered, so the accompanying soldiers could not hear either. From the steps to 'Keep up' to 'Fear not' is a small corridor of communication.

As they arrived downstairs in Kilmainham, the three Daly sisters encountered the two O'Hanrahan sisters (Eily and Anna). There are three accounts of what happened next, from Madge Daly, from Kathleen Clarke and from Eily O'Hanrahan:

*Madge Daly:*

We reached the entrance hall where two pale girls waited, seemingly on a like errand. They rushed up to us and asked: 'Who are you?' and 'Who have you been to see?' We told them. They were the Misses O'Hanrahan: and when they heard of Ned's fate, one moaned: 'Oh! Micheál!' They had got a permit stating that their brother was to be deported, and so they came, quite unprepared for his death. [Eily] O'Hanrahan broke down badly, but I told her she should pull herself together for her brother's sake and before the enemy. Yet, I afterwards learned that they bore themselves bravely until they left their brother. One of the sisters afterwards became unconscious.[24]

*Kathleen Clarke:*

Before leaving the jail, I saw two sisters of Micheál O'Hanrahan. They were members of the Central Branch, Cumann na mBan. I spoke to them, and asked them why they were there. They said they had been sent for to say goodbye to Micheál. They had not the faintest idea he had been sentenced to death; they thought he had been sentenced to imprisonment, and perhaps was being sent to

England. They thought that was the reason they had been sent for. 'Eileen,' I said, 'he is being sent into the next world. This is a final goodbye.' She screamed. I had given her an awful shock, but thought it better she should get it now than in Micheál's cell. 'For God's sake, Eileen,' I said, 'control your feelings before you see Micheál. Now you know the worst, pull yourself together before you see him or you will unnerve him.' She did; both sisters did, they were wonderful. They went through the interview with Micheál bravely, but Eileen went down in a dead faint as soon as she was outside the cell. I was so sorry for those girls, as Micheál's execution was a thing they never anticipated.[25]

*Eily O'Hanrahan:*

We opened the door and the policeman gave in a letter from the O.C. of Kilmainham, to the effect that Micheál would like to see his mother and sisters before his deportation to England.

...At last we arrived at Kilmainham. We were shown into a little whitewashed room off the hall, with two candles. We were sitting there for a while. I went to the door once or twice and asked the soldiers in the hall why we were not being brought to my brother. I heard a woman's voice in the hall. 'That seems to be Mrs. Clarke', I said to Cis. I went to her and she said, 'What brings you here, Eily'. 'I don't know, except that we were told Micheál was being deported.' I said to Mrs. Clarke 'Is there anything you want to tell us?' as she seemed to hesitate. 'They are executing the men', she said. I said, 'Could it be possible that Micheál would be executed?' She then told us that she had been there the night before to see her husband before his execution, and she had been this night to see her brother, Ned Daly.[26]

This encounter happened in the hall outside the 'little whitewashed room' at a moment when there appeared not to be any British authorities around, after one visit to a brother and before another. For a brief moment, there was a 'woman's space' in which they communicated directly what is most important. All three accounts describe a trajectory of emotions over a period of minutes as one set of sisters clarifies the situation to the others. Madge's account is written with careful observation of sensory detail: 'two pale girls' and the moan whose words she hears clearly: 'Oh! Micheál!' She saw them as a mirror of the Daly sisters—'on a like errand'—and even though they seem to have just met, she notes which one 'breaks down'. But 'breaking down' was not permissible, and Daly reacts as she did to her sister Laura's 'faltering' steps, telling O'Hanrahan the Daly code of behaviour: 'I told her she should pull herself together for her brother's sake and before the enemy'. They must have listened carefully, because 'they bore themselves bravely'.

Kathleen Clarke (in her telling of the episode) identifies the O'Hanrahan sisters by their Cumann na mBan branch and presents a more precisely detailed verbal exchange: the O'Hanrahan sisters' ignorance, her own statement of fact, Eily's scream, and the need to protect their brother from all this emotion. Clarke attributes to herself—as Madge does to herself—the advice on how to manage the 'Kilmainham farewell': 'control your feelings before you see Micheál. Now you know the worst, pull yourself together before you see him or you will unnerve him'. Her prose conveys the ups and downs of the exchange more dramatically: they 'had not the faintest idea'; the information is given; Eily's scream; the advice to control themselves; praise for their deportment—'they were wonderful'—Eily's collapse ('a dead faint') and her own sympathy: 'I was so sorry for those girls'.

O'Hanrahan's own account in her witness statement omits the moan or scream but presents what she noticed about Clarke. When O'Hanrahan hazards the guess that her brother is 'being deported', she notices that Mrs Clarke 'seemed to hesitate'. Like all the women in these circumstances, she registered with extreme sensitivity every paralinguistic signal from another woman, and therefore elicited the information she needed: 'Is there anything you want to tell us?'

Micheál O'Hanrahan in his cell has the same calm that all the men have, according to the women's accounts: Grace Plunkett says that Joseph Plunkett was 'not frightened—not the slightest...He was quite calm'. Min Ryan says that Seán MacDermott showed 'no sign of mourning' and so she and her sister Phyllis 'had to hold up, of course, when he held up, and so we showed no sign of sorrow while we discussed things'. Micheál, Eily writes in her statement,

> was not in any way agitated. The only thing that worried
> him was what was to become of my mother and us.....He

told us not to fret, and we tried to reassure him that we would be all right and that the women of '98 had to endure that too.

Like Madge Daly reminding her sisters that they are 'the daughters and nieces of Fenians', Eily O'Hanrahan drew on a memorable though more remote historical precedent for comfort and resolve. A gendered tradition was useful as a response to her brother's concern, because it offered a paradigm for female autonomy, and it elevated the misery of the O'Hanrahan sisters to a noble part of Irish history, one that Constance Markievicz had drawn on recently in a lecture, 'The women of '98', delivered to the Fianna and published in December 1915.[27]

If O'Hanrahan had heard or read the story of Mary Ann McCracken, Henry Joy McCracken's sister and one of the 'women of '98', she would have seen another exemplar of 'not breaking down': McCracken noted her brother's 'serenity and composure' when he was condemned to death, and although 'falling to the ground' at the news that he was about to be executed, she pulled herself together—as a Daly would have—because

> I...knew it was incumbent on me to avoid disturbing the last moments of my brother's life, and I endeavoured to contribute to render them worthy of his whole career. We conversed as calmly as we had ever done.[28]

Just as Micheál O'Hanrahan's only concern was for the welfare of his mother and sister, so McCracken's last recorded concern was for his sister. Mary Ann writes:

> Three times he kissed me, and entreated I would go; and, looking round to recognize some friend to put me in charge of, he beckoned to a Mr. Boyd, and said, 'He will take charge of you.' Mr. B. stepped forward, and, fearing any refusal would disturb the last moments of my dearest brother, I suffered myself to be led away.[29]

O'Hanrahan's faint, like Mary Ann McCracken's fall, expresses an emotion that manifests itself physiologically before it can be articulated verbally. What is suppressed during the interview, as the women 'bear up' and do not 'break down', cannot remain suppressed. Clarke herself had a miscarriage and a near-death experience some weeks later, so the 'breaking down' which was not considered appropriate in Kilmainham took another form. O'Hanrahan says that she 'got weak' going down the stairs, 'and when I got to the ground floor I fainted'. The stairs in Kilmainham would give someone at a less difficult moment occasion to 'falter' or 'get weak'.

## 'AS IF WE WERE IN BEWLEY'S'

Min Ryan (later Mrs Richard Mulcahy) gave three accounts of her last conversation with Seán MacDermott, each with a slightly different emphasis. The latest of these (said to be based on Ryan's 1966 RTÉ interview) is consistent with the other women's narratives in its emphasis on the way the women pick up cues from the man about the emotional register he prefers. Min's sister Phyllis was with her in the cell; the two women

> ...sat down on the wooden bed, on the slightly raised board, and Sean sat between us and put one arm around each of us, and talked to us in a way that was in no way sad, I might say. We talked about everything. We kept off the evil moment of asking him anything about what was going to happen. We talked about the things that happened during the week, and about people that were in it, and people that weren't in it, and we had a good laugh about some of them. It was ridiculous in a way because there was no sign of mourning. We had to hold up, of course, when he held up, and so we showed no sign of sorrow while we discussed things.[30]

The Ryan sisters got three hours in the cell at Kilmainham, more time than any of the other women. From a comment of Grace Plunkett's in her witness statement, it is clear that the women discussed and compared the traumatic visits to the men in their cells:

> I was allowed to stay only a short time with Joe, yet I believe that Min Ryan and Father Browne were allowed to stay a long time with Seán MacDermott. Min Ryan was there with Seán MacDermott for ages and ages. In fact, she said her conversation ran out altogether. She did not know what to say to him. There would be a guard there,

and you could not talk. I can't understand how she managed to stay quite a while.[31]

Ryan gives a hint of that lengthy conversation in her account:

> We were there at twelve o'clock and we didn't leave till three. We were three hours with him and talked about everything under the sun. We talked an awful lot about the week of the Rising and about how other places had fared, as much as we knew.
>
> When the priest appeared at three o'clock—Sean was executed at a quarter to four—we stood up promptly and felt a great jerk, I am sure all three of us, to say good-bye. I was the last to say good-bye to him and he kissed me and said, just said: 'We never thought that it would end like this, that this would be the end.' Yes, that's all he said, although he knew himself long before that what the end would be for him.[32]

The three-hour conversation, as Ryan registers it, kept off 'the evil moment' of acknowledging the fact that this was a final conversation, the last they would ever have, and that MacDermott would be executed soon after it was over. Their Easter Week gossip— 'the people that were in it, and people that weren't in it'—sounds like what King Lear imagines when he says to Cordelia, 'Come, let's away to prison.'

>         ...so we'll live,
> And pray, and sing, and tell old tales, and laugh
> At gilded butterflies, and hear poor rogues
> Talk of court news; and we'll talk with them too,
> Who loses and who wins; who's in, who's out,
> And take upon's the mystery of things,
> As if we were God's spies; and we'll wear out,
> In a wall'd prison, packs and sects of great ones
> That ebb and flow by th' moon.

To which Edmund says, 'Take them away'. The arrival of the priest jolted the three people in the twentieth-century Irish prison cell back to reality, if indeed they ever left it altogether, although 'there was no sign of mourning', and like Teresa Heuston, Kate Murphy, Grace

Plunkett, the Daly sisters and the O'Hanrahan sisters, the Ryan sisters 'had to hold up, of course, when he held up...'.

In neither of her other two accounts does Min Ryan mention the final sad comment and goodbye kiss. In the narrative written only months after the event itself, Ryan describes the emotional dynamics in a slightly different way:

> As he came to the door with both hands extended, to welcome us, with a smile on his face that seemed to transcend the brutal place, one felt fortitude and confidence in oneself once more and a strong desire to show no surprise at the unusual scene. Somehow we all acted as if this was one of the places where we had been accustomed to visit each other.[33]

In this version, Ryan says that MacDermott told them everything that happened after the evacuation from the GPO, 'But it was not by way of complaint he told us these things. He merely told them as a narrative of events, and personally seemed most indifferent to all their whips and scourges'. Here Ryan uses words that characterise explicitly the emotional register MacDermott preferred:

> He did not wish to dwell on these matters. He preferred to talk of all sorts of casual matters, asking about different people we knew, referring to various happy events of the past, and enjoying little jokes and jests almost as naturally as if we were in Bewley's or in an ordinary sitting-room in one of our houses.

MacDermott does not appear to be 'exalted', like Tom Clarke, or talking about his glorious death for Ireland, though he used that patriotic discourse in his letter to his brothers and sisters ('I die that the Irish nation may live').[34] He avoids the mournful by talking in a middle register 'of all sorts of casual matters'.

It is Min Ryan herself who was emotional, although she did not show her emotions at the time:

> ...the most pathetic scene was where he tried to produce keepsakes for different girl friends of his we mentioned. He sat down at the table and tried to scratch his name and the date on the few coins he had left and on the buttons

which he cut from his clothes.... As one looked at his beautiful head assiduously bent over this work in the dim candlelight, one could scarcely keep one's feelings from surging over at the thought that in another couple of hours that beautiful head would be battered by four bullets...[35]

But these lines occur in the account she wrote in July 1916. In June 1950, in her witness statement for the Bureau of Military History, Ryan mentioned an aspect of the visit that does not appear in any of the other accounts. The military car that picked up Min and her sister Phyllis also had to pick up 'Sean Reynolds and Sean MacDermott's landlady. Sean [MacDermott] wanted Sean Reynolds to make his will for him':

> We were all there together, listening to each other's conversation. He was very anxious to have the others go. He was much more intimate with us, but there was no budge out of them. 'That is all now' Sean would say, but there was no budge at all. Then we all came out together.[36]

The 'official' witness statement for the Bureau of Military History gives no indication of the emotional register that is central to the other accounts, but it includes the fact, entirely absent from the others, that for the whole three hours, there were four visitors, not two, in MacDermott's cell. All the conversation about who was where and did what during Easter Week, all the talk about friends, took place in the hearing of two other people who were not close friends at all. At any rate, the 1916 account and the 1966 one appear to be personal, post-traumatic retellings of the event in terms of emotions, whereas the witness statement gives the facts and the personnel but never mentions the strain of maintaining the emotional register established by the prisoner himself.

## CASEMENT'S LONG MARTYRDOM

The process of metamorphosis took a lot longer for Roger Casement than for the Dublin martyrs. The final garrisons in Dublin surrendered on Sunday, 30 April, the day after Pearse surrendered, and by 12 May, all the signatories to the Proclamation and seven other leaders had been executed. Casement, however, had 103 days as a martyr-in-waiting: he was captured on 21 April 1916 and executed on 3 August.

Gertrude Bannister, Casement's cousin, was the last family member to see him, but their parting on 27 July was not at all like the Kilmainham farewells. According to her memoir, she did not control her emotions, nor did he. They were both very weepy, and she had not even then accepted that his death was inevitable:

> He was for the first time broken and sorrowful. We both tried to keep cheerful on the surface.—He then asked to be buried 'in the old churchyard in Murlough Bay'. I said, 'I will', and then I broke down, I couldn't help it, it was the only time I was in tears when I was with him. He, too, wept and said, 'I don't want to die and leave you and the rest of you dear ones, but I must.' With a superhuman effort I stopped and said, 'It won't be, we are working, all of us to prevent it—there are petitions'. But he broke in, 'No, Gee, don't delude yourself—they want my death, nothing else will do. And, after all, it's a glorious death to die for Ireland—and I could not stand long in a place like this—it would destroy my reason.'
>
> The warders broke off the interview and marched him out. I stood up and stretched out my hands to him; he turned at the door and said, 'Good-bye God bless you'—I went out and in the corridor outside I simply abandoned myself to my grief...I cried loud and uncontrollably...[37]

Accepting that he 'must' die, and speaking of his 'glorious death...for Ireland', Casement tried to speak the language of exaltation, but reluctantly.

Gradually, in the interval between his capture and his execution, Casement grew into his role, giving a speech from the dock and writing, three days before his death, in language somewhat closer to that of the Dublin rebels, '...it is a glorious death for Ireland's sake...'. At the end, to others, he looked 'exalted', to use Kathleen Clarke's word. The conscientious objector Fenner Brockway was in Pentonville Prison at the same time and left a description of Casement on his final evening:

> Casement's gaze was fixed steadfastly in the direction of the setting sun which he watched disappear below the horizon of the prison wall for the last time. His face was wonderfully calm and he seemed already to be living in

another world; there was not a trace of fear or anxiety in his features.[38]

Father McCarroll, who attended Casement while in Pentonville, said that at Mass the day before he died, Casement 'took off his shoes (as a sign of humility) and as he raised his head to receive the host, his face was transfixed and he remained a long time at prayer at the altar rail'. And Father Carey, who also attended him, said that he walked to the scaffold 'with the dignity of a prince'.[39]

Nora Connolly, who visited her father James Connolly in Dublin Castle the evening before his execution; she recorded his efforts to calm her mother and herself: 'Don't cry, Nora, there is nothing to cry about'.

Above: The O'Hanrahan sisters–Eileen, Anna, and Mary Margaret–and their mother; date unknown

Below: Mrs Daly and five of the Daly sisters in mourning after the execution of Ned Daly (the only brother in the family) and Tom Clarke, their brother-in-law.

*Chapter Seven*

EMOTIONS IN 1916

*Ní hiad bhur n-éanlaith atá mé ag éagnach,*
*An lon, an smaolach, nó an chorr ghlas,*
*Ach mo bhonnán buí, bhí lán de chroí,*
*Is gur chosúil liom féin é ina ghné is ina dhath.*

Cathal Buí Mac Giolla Ghunna, 'An bonnán buí'

It's not for the common birds that I'd mourn,
The black-bird, the corn-crake, or the crane,
But for the bittern that's shy and apart
And drinks in the marsh from the lone bog-drain.

trans. Thomas MacDonagh

Your common birds do not concern me,
The blackbird, say, or the thrush or crane,
But the yellow bittern, my heartsome namesake
With my looks and locks, he's the one I mourn.

trans. Seamus Heaney

On Easter Monday, when the seventeen-year-old Sighle Humphreys saw her uncle Michael O'Rahilly, The O'Rahilly, getting ready to join those fighting in the Rising, a 'great wish came over' her, she writes,

> to say how proud I was of being his niece and of being alive to see such a day but any display of feeling was absolutely taboo in our family. Indeed later that day when I said I just didn't feel I could eat lunch, my mother rebuked me strongly for as she put it 'giving in to myself'.

> So, knowing how any demonstration of my feelings would be frowned on, I scarcely said *Slan leat* to Michael although in my heart I knew I never would see him again.[1]

As Humphreys tells the story, her mother (Nell Humphreys, sister of The O'Rahilly) considered even so muted a display as inability to eat to be self-centred weakness, 'giving in to myself'. Yet what stands out here, in the context of other women's accounts of the Rising, is the focus on feeling at all, even unexpressed feeling. Although the emotion was not expressed at the time, it was recorded later in the prose: 'A great wish came over me to say how proud I was' and 'in my heart I knew I would never see him again'.

The week of the Rising was, after all, an emotional time: many people felt the same way Sighle Humphreys did, and they used the same words. Standing outside the GPO, watching the tricolour hoisted over the building, Connolly said to Pearse, 'Thank God, Pearse, we have lived to see this day!'[2] As Volunteers John Furlong, Sean Sinnott, and Robert Brennan were planning to leave Wexford for the Rising, Furlong's mother said, 'So yous are going out. Thanks be to God I lived to see this day'.[3] Aoife de Burca wrote of her arrival at the GPO, 'A thrill of joy and pride ran through me, and I thanked God I had lived to see such a day'.[4] Volunteer Paddy Doyle, at Mount Street Bridge, 'would say, "Boys, isn't this a great day for Ireland", and little sentences like this. He was very proud to live to see such a day'.[5]

Almost all the women who record events of 1916 in any detail write about emotion: their own emotion and other people's; expressing it, not expressing it, not being allowed to express it; feeling and not being able to feel. At the train station in Mallow, Co. Cork, near the end of Easter Week, Máirín Cregan's visible show of emotion inspired everyone around her to take sides on what was happening in Dublin. 'Rumours were rife', she writes, and

> ...one cold and miserable evening, while in the waiting room of the station, a man came in with yet another that 'the military had mown down the Volunteers in front of the G.P.O.' I, being worn out with fatigue and frustration, began to cry. To give an idea of the attitude of the general public at that time, who apparently did not realise the significance of the Rising in Dublin, one of those present turned to console me saying, 'It is only the Sinn Féiners that were killed'. This enraged me and I turned on them saying, 'But it is the Volunteers I am crying for. My friends are among them and fighting too'. It was remarkable that in a very short time, first one and then another, began to murmur, and the little crowd began to argue and take sides. This was the first public expression of any sympathy I experienced, however people may have been feeling privately.[6]

Here it was one person alone who was the conduit of emotion about the Rising: a series of responses was triggered in the random people assembled in the Mallow station by Cregan's display of feeling. The rumour of defeat led to her tears, which led to someone's sympathy, which led to her rage, which then sparked opinions and emotions in the entire 'little crowd'. It was Cregan's unrepressed, spontaneous, public expression of emotion that drove all present to express their feelings, feelings till then (it seems) not articulated in public. Her crying released the passions of everyone there.[7]

The inability to feel was also a common emotion, if emotion it can be called, in the weeks following the Rising. When Geraldine Dillon, sister of the executed Joseph Plunkett, learned that her parents were still alive, though they were imprisoned, 'this was a relief', she writes, 'though to tell the truth I could not feel very much'.[8] Around the same time, a couple of weeks after the Rising, Kathleen Clarke was so ill that at one point her heart stopped beating, but she 'was quite indifferent about what was happening to me'. When Clarke's sisters arrived from Limerick, she 'cried for the first time since the executions, cried with sheer disappointment that I was not dead'.[9] And Mary Louisa Hamilton Norway, wife of the secretary of the General Post Office in Ireland, wrote that she felt 'a total absence of thankfulness at our own escape' from bullets and snipers during the Rising, adding, 'Life as it has been lived for the past two years in the midst of death seems to have blunted one's desire for it'.[10] Wexford Brigade Acting Commandant Robert Brennan in Mountjoy after the Rising said something similar. The priest who visited him in his cell 'discoursed airily on the futility of our fight' but then sensed Brennan's anger. 'I hope I haven't hurt your feelings', he said. 'Good Lord, no', Brennan replied, 'I haven't got any'.[11]

In accounts of the Rising, emotions of any kind, joyous or sad, expressed or unexpressed, are important. They are not just ephemeral, elusive notions that float through the mind and occasionally are uttered or overheard: feelings are a category of event. Even when they seem insignificant, they are remembered; the narratives pause, and time is devoted to describing them; and they are often remarked on. The expression of a feeling is treated with as much interest as any more obviously dramatic external event, a military decision or a political pronouncement. Men's accounts mention emotions as well as women's, but because the women tend to be with the men 'behind the scenes', not in the midst of fighting or marching, they are privy to expressions of sadness or joy that occur when the men are less guarded, or so it seems from the episodes they record. These moments, as well as the women's own emotions, are worth considering because they form part of the total expressiveness of the Rising; they embody its distinctive emotional culture. The Easter Rising was not solely a military event; it was an emotional one for everyone concerned, men and women, nationalists and unionists, and the total sum of expressed feelings constitutes a narrative element within the larger narrative of the Rising.[12]

## J.J. 'Ginger' O'Connell in Tears

The phrase repeated in so many memoirs ('Thanks be to God I lived to see this day') implies an emotional participation in Irish history; 'this day', 'such a day', derives its value from all the failed risings of the past. Everyone who used that phrase was living vicariously through what the Proclamation calls 'the dead generations', imagining 'this' as the longed-for day of serious revolution. Even many of those who didn't use it felt their every action and choice during Easter Week would be understood and judged in terms of the long perspective of Irish history. Maeve Cavanagh records a conversation with Captain J.J. 'Ginger' O'Connell of the Volunteers that reveals how this historical consciousness came into play at an emotional moment.

On the Monday of Easter Week, O'Connell had had 'a bitter quarrel' with Robert Brennan of the Wexford Volunteers over whether the men and women of Wexford would join the fight in Dublin. As Brennan writes, 'I asked him not to try to stop the Waterford and Kilkenny men from joining us if we rose. He said he would have me court-martialed. As the train was steaming out, I was threatening to have him court-martialed'.[13]

On the same day, Cavanagh was sent to tell the Waterford Volunteers that 'Dublin was out'. She was unable to catch up with O'Connell until Wednesday, after he had already demobilised the men of Waterford and Kilkenny. She knew nothing of the quarrel with Brennan. O'Connell's point of view had not changed:

> 'They should have waited till there was conscription', O'Connell said. 'Look at that, it is all over already', showing me an English paper. I said, 'Sure an old woman could take Kilkenny to-day. If you are afraid to give the message, let me see the men and I'll give them the message and take the responsibility'. He replied, 'You shall certainly not see any man under my command'. To my consternation he broke down and cried, and said, 'I deserve that, I'll be called a traitor'. I was very sorry for

him as I saw he was under a terrible strain, but not of in-
decision. I said, 'Oh, Captain O'Connell, it is not as bad as
that, surely you can do something yet'. He said, 'No, it is
all over', showing me the paper again...

Afterwards at a meeting at Goold's Cross someone who
was in gaol with O'Connell told me that he—O'Connell—
wondered why they kept sending these hysterical women
after him. I was amazed because if anyone was hysterical
it certainly was not I.[14]

O'Connell had told Brennan that he 'was not going to countenance
any movement until he got a definite order from Dublin', but when it
was delivered by Cavanagh, he rejected it. To Brennan, O'Connell had
responded with hostility from the beginning, but with Cavanagh, for
whatever reason, 'he broke down and cried'.

Like Kitty O'Doherty who pointed out that John MacDonagh was
'not in No. 2 Dawson Street', meaning that he was not active in
Volunteer Headquarters, Cavanagh impugns the revolutionary commitment of O'Connell. But her discourse is gendered: O'Connell must
have felt his masculinity insulted when Cavanagh said 'sure an old
woman could take Kilkenny today', and then he cried, saying, 'I deserve
that, I'll be called a traitor'. He may have meant he deserved the humiliation of having cried, as if his public tears were a self-punishment
because he was a 'traitor' to the cause. Or perhaps he meant, if the
order of sentences is reversed, that he would go down in history as 'a
traitor' and deserves that judgement. O'Connell seemed to have seen
himself, in a flash, from the point of view of history, the history of 1916
that would someday be written, in which, even though the rebels had
lost, 'They went forth to battle...'[15] He had not gone. When the history
was written, he would be 'called a traitor'. Little did he think that the
woman he was talking to would write that history, or a part of it; that
through her witness statement his own self-condemnation would
become part of the record.

The double shame of having been told—implicitly—that he was
less manly than 'an old woman', and then of crying, led him later to
displace the feminine 'weakness' onto Cavanagh herself, one of
'these hysterical women' sent to him from Dublin. As is well known
from other sources besides this document and Yeats's poem 'Lapis
Lazuli' ('I have heard hysterical women say / They are sick of the
palate and fiddle bow'), 'hysterical' is a gendered term, not only in
etymology but in common misogynistic usage. But the only aspect

of Cavanagh's argument that was 'hysterical' was her encourage-
ment to revolution, which was simply the dominant male point of
view for which she served as a courier. She was sympathetic when
he cried and condemned himself, but wryly amused when she hears
what he said later: 'if anyone was hysterical it certainly was not I'.[16]
His comment anticipated the representation of republican women
in terms of what Margaret O'Callaghan has called 'the trope of the
nationalist harridan'.[17]

## 'My name in the song'

When former Volunteer Alf Monahan was gathering arms in the early
years of the War of Independence, he had bayonets fixed onto shot-
guns, and the man who made them would not take any money: 'The
bayonets were made by a blacksmith on the Quay in Cork City—I
forget his name. He worked overtime every night making bayonets and
the only reward he wanted was, as he said "My name in the song"'.[18]

Under the circumstances, it's too bad Monahan forgot the man's
name but his wonderful request, at least, lives after this nameless blacksmith. The kind of song he was thinking of is the kind many people
were singing in 1916. Like O'Connell's remark ('I'll be called a traitor'),
though in a different way, the songs indicated an emotional participation in Irish history. The women's accounts record many utterances
that invoke what could be called the Irish emotional imaginary, a store-
house of allusions to historical moments or to artistic expressions of
emotions, songs or poems. Many accounts of 1916, by men as well as
by women, record occasions when marching men sing 'The soldier's
song' or—when they want to be particularly annoying to the British—
'The watch on the Rhine'. They often have 'a sing-song—to keep the
fellows' hearts up' or 'to raise our spirits' or just to express solidarity.[19]
But the women are privy to solitary bursts of song, songs that are mentioned in the story because they are considered events.

Áine O'Rahilly, sister of The O'Rahilly, records some of her
brother's utterances in private life, not among Volunteers but within
his family.

> Some time before the Rising I made a remark about
> carrying out some task in a fortnight. He said in a jocose
> tone 'Ah! We'll all be either dead or in the Castle in a fort-
> night'. Another day, Palm Sunday, his wife who always

accompanied him to our house on Sundays was lying down, as she was expecting a baby in a few weeks, and he came over without her. He started singing all the national songs—he had a lovely voice. He sang 'Aghadoe' and he seemed deeply moved. Reflecting on these incidents afterwards, I concluded he knew then that the Rising was coming on.[20]

She says he sang 'all the national songs', but the one she remembers is the ballad about the young man who '...hid from the eyes of the redcoats and their spies, That year the trouble came to Aghadoe'. His lover brings him food to the 'deep and secret glen in Aghadoe', but her brother gives away the hiding place, and 'the bullets found his heart in Aghadoe'. Áine notes, 'he seemed deeply moved': possibly he was moved because The O'Rahilly was a Kerry man, born in Ballylongford, and Aghadoe is in Killarney; or possibly because of the bullets that found his heart, and the line, 'Like an Irish king he sleeps in Aghadoe':

> But they tracked me to that glen in Aghadoe, Aghadoe
> When the price was on his head in Aghadoe
> O'er the mountain through the wood as I stole to him
>     with food
> But the bullets found his heart in Aghadoe.
>
> I walked from Mallow town to Aghadoe, Aghadoe
> I took his head from the jail gate to Aghadoe
> There I covered him with fern and I piled on him
>     the cairn
> Like an Irish king he sleeps in Aghadoe.

That was Palm Sunday; by Thursday, The O'Rahilly was too sad even to sing. As Molly Reynolds records:

> My father was appointed Auditor to the Volunteers and in that connection The O'Rahilly was a frequent visitor to our office. He was of a cheerful disposition and you could always tell when he was coming because he sang on his way up the stairs. On Thursday of Holy Week, 1916, he came to the office but this time he did not sing on his way up and when I asked him why he just replied: 'Ah, I am very sad to-day.'[21]

These vignettes of The O'Rahilly show not only that the women were attuned to his expressiveness and were listening carefully to every sign of emotion, but that he made his emotions clear to those around him. Song was his discourse; not singing meant 'I am very sad to-day'.

Unlike the nameless blacksmith on the quay in Cork, The O'Rahilly got his name in the song:

> What remains to sing about
> But of the death he met
> Stretched under a doorway
> Somewhere off Henry Street;
> They that found him found upon
> The door above his head
> 'Here died The O'Rahilly.
> R.I.P.' writ in blood.[22]

Like Áine O'Rahilly and Molly Reynolds, Annie Cooney registered Con Colbert's emotion by the song he was singing, an emotion much jollier than The O'Rahilly's: 'During the time I was buckling him up Con—who had not a note in his head—was singing "For Tone is coming back again" he was so excited and charmed that at last the fight was coming off. He thought of nothing else'.[23] There is a kind of emotional contagion in the moment, as through the rollicking song Colbert expresses an excitement that Cooney picks up on in her amused parenthetic comment, 'who had not a note in his head'.

> Cheer up, brave hearts, to-morrow's dawn will see us
>     march again
> Beneath old Erin's flag of green that ne'er has known a
>     stain.
> And ere our hands the sword shall yield or furled that
>     banner be
> We swear to make our native land from the tyrant's
>     thraldom free!
>
> For Tone is coming back again with legions o'er the
>     wave,
> The scions of Lord Clare's Brigade, the dear old land to
>     save,
> For Tone is coming back again with legions o'er the
>     wave

The dear old land, the loved old land, the brave old land
   to save!

The small off-centre drama is made vivid by the song: two girls (Annie
and her sister Lily) are buckling the men (Colbert and Christy Byrne)
into their military gear, one of them singing with excitement, but
singing badly, yet through his singing identifying the 1916 moment
with the 1798 moment.

James Connolly seems to have felt the same excitement that Colbert
felt, as his daughter Nora records. On Easter Sunday morning, he was
singing:

> I went back to the Hall; and when I got back to the Hall—
> I remember very well—Daddy was in uniform. It was the
> first time I had seen him in uniform. All the time of the
> parades and exercises, he never had a uniform. I used joke
> him about going out in his navy-blue suit and slouch hat,
> and all the uniformed men behind him. But now he was
> in his uniform. He was in much better form. He felt that
> something might be done; and he was going around the
> room, singing a song which he usually sang when things
> were going well with him—'We have got another saviour
> now. That saviour is the sword'.[24]

Behind the scenes, in the days before the Rising, these men—all of
whom would die in the Rising, one way or another—express feelings
that the women consider important, and they record them. As The
O'Rahilly's remark 'Ah, I'm very sad to-day' makes clear, solo singing
for these men is a substitute for direct discourse about emotion,
emotion that the women name explicitly: Colbert is 'excited' and
'charmed', Connolly is 'in much better form'. Like Maeve Cavanagh
with O'Connell and his tears, the women remember these brief expres-
sive moments as episodes in the story of 1916.

### 'AN BONNÁN BUÍ'

On Friday, 28 April, Thomas MacDonagh in the garrison at Jacob's sent
a message to Joseph Plunkett in the GPO. The message was never delivered, because the fifteen-year-old girl to whom it was given, Mary
McLoughlin, never made it to the Post Office. She was 'taken into

custody' by a British soldier and brought to stay with the family of another soldier. The undelivered message was a verbal one: when she met MacDonagh, 'He would not give me any message except to say, if I got back to Plunkett in the G.P.O., the words "Yellow Bittern"'.[25]

McLoughlin makes no comment about the mysterious, two-word message, and it seems unlikely she recognised the reference: her witness statement does not mention that she knew Irish or MacDonagh's poems. She says 'the words', not 'the reference' or 'the title'. The allusion is so recondite that most Irish people at the time, let alone anyone in the British military, would probably not have understood it. This message is one of the most oblique expressions of emotion on record for 1916. To those who recognise it, it is richly suggestive and moving.

'The yellow bittern' is the English version of the eighteenth-century Irish poem *An bonnán buí* by Cathal Buí Mac Giolla Ghunna. MacDonagh wrote a translation of the poem that became famous, so famous that Francis Ledwidge alluded to it in his 'Lament for Thomas MacDonagh':

> He shall not hear the bittern cry
> In the wild sky, where he is lain,
> Nor voices of the sweeter birds,
> Above the wailing of the rain.

No doubt MacDonagh had discussed the poem in Irish and his own translation with Plunkett, who was also a poet. The two men had met when MacDonagh was hired to tutor Plunkett in Irish; they became close friends, worked together at the Irish Theatre Company, and married sisters, Muriel Gifford and Grace Gifford.

What exactly was the meaning of this undelivered message for which Mary McLoughlin was the conduit? Fortunately she remembered the message 38 years later and delivered it to future readers of the witness statements of the Bureau of Military History.[26] The message could refer to the bird itself or to the whole poem. If to the former, it was an oblique way of sending the sad message that MacDonagh and Plunkett were soon to be dead, like the yellow bittern of the poem:

> The yellow bittern that never broke out
> In a drinking bout, might as well have drunk;
> His bones are thrown on a naked stone
> Where he lived alone like a hermit monk.
> O yellow bittern! I pity your lot,
> Though they say that a sot like myself is curst—

I was sober a while, but I'll drink and be wise
For I fear I should die in the end of thirst.

Maybe MacDonagh was thinking of this passage:

Oh! if I had known you were near your death,
While my breath held out I'd have run to you
Till a splash from the Lake of the Son of the Bird
Your soul would have stirred and waked anew.[27]

And if the allusion was to the whole poem, it conveyed the brief narrative of someone who knew that he himself would soon be dead, like the bird he sees, and he'd like a drink ('Come, son of my soul, and drain your cup, / You'll get no sup when your life is past'), in fact a large drink: 'a dram won't stop our thirst this night'.

Either way, the message would have been a gesture of friendship, a reminder of their intimacy and love for one another, their common love of the Irish language and of poetry, and an acknowledgement of the fate they were both likely to meet soon. To invoke it at all is to catch the tone of the poem, its elegant, wry, witty, elegiac attitude to the bird's death, and to affirm comradeship with a man who was soon, though only for a brief while, to become MacDonagh's brother-in-law. According to the biography of Plunkett by his grand-niece Honor O Brolchain, Plunkett never saw MacDonagh after the surrender. Plunkett's brother Jack said that while he and Joe were 'sitting on the floor of that disgusting gymnasium in Richmond Barracks', Joe 'was worrying a lot about Tomás M[a]cDonagh'. Although MacDonagh had also been brought to Richmond Barracks, 'Joe didn't know he was there. They had not seen each other since the previous Sunday and it is almost certain that they did not see or speak to each other again'.[28] So the message remained undelivered and uninterpreted, its affection and wit preserved only by the dutiful though uncomprehending Mary McLoughlin.

## THREE KEENS

The keen (*caoineadh*), writes Angela Bourke, is

a ritual lament, led by a close woman relative of the deceased person or by a woman hired for the purpose.

Women gathered around the body, swaying back and
forth, beating their hands together, and tearing their hair,
while the chief keener or *bean chaointe* addressed the dead
person in extemporized verse interspersed with rhythmic
wailing. An essential part of funeral ritual from early
times until the nineteenth century, loud public lamentation of the dead finally disappeared in Ireland only within
living memory.[29]

There was no such ritual wailing in Dublin over the people killed
during the Rising, though the demonstrations after the memorial
Masses for the executed men were collective expressions of mourning
as well as of national solidarity. Women's lamentations took many
forms, most of them spontaneous, discrete and distinct, no two alike
in form or utterance. But considered all together, as if they were audible
and simultaneous, they would sound like a series or sequence of keens,
as J.M. Synge in *The Aran Islands* describes the way each keener in turn
takes up the cry:

> Each old woman, as she took her turn in the leading
> recitative, seemed possessed for the moment with a pro-
> found ecstasy of grief, swaying to and fro, and bending
> her forehead to the stone before her, while she called out
> to the dead with a perpetually recurring chant of sobs.
>
> All round the graveyard other wrinkled women,
> looking out from under the deep red petticoats that
> cloaked them, rocked themselves with the same rhythm,
> and intoned the inarticulate chant that is sustained by all
> as an accompaniment.[30]

The detailed accounts of mourning by women of all classes and reli-
gions constitute a narrative of feelings woven into a narrative of
external events.

The women whose statements were taken in evidence at the Military
Court of Inquiry into the North King Street murders were present at
the killings they describe, most of them hearing the shots even if they
did not see the actual killings. On Friday, 28 April, soldiers of the South
Staffordshire regiment, angry at losses they had suffered in the area,
had entered houses on North King Street and killed every male they
found, all of them, it seems, unarmed civilians with no connection to
the Rising. Much of the power of the women's accounts comes from the

direct, unadorned descriptions, the intense sympathy of the tellers, the utter innocence of all the people concerned, and the generous actions and statements of the men who were killed. Anne Fennell, an 'old woman' (age 75) who was a tenant of 174 North King Street, describes the murders of two neighbours, George Ennis (a 'coach body maker') and Michael Noonan, a messenger for Dublin Corporation:

> The soldiers rushed everywhere searching about the house and ripped up the beds with their bayonets...After a long time, it must have been a couple of hours, we heard a noise at the parlour door, and to our horror poor Mr. Ennis crawled in. I will never forget. He was dying, bleeding to death, and when the military left the house he had crept down the stairs, to see his wife for the last time. He was covered with blood and his eyes were rolling in his head. He said to his wife, 'Oh Kate they have killed me.' She said, 'O my God! for what?' He said, 'For nothing.' He asked us to go for a priest for him but we could not leave the house. I was terrified, and asked the dying man, 'would they kill us all.' He spoke very kindly to us and told us they would not touch us. We told him to lie down on the floor and we said the last prayers for the dying kneeling beside him. He said, 'They killed poor Noonan too.' I stayed with him as long as I could.—Poor Mr. Ennis did not live more than twenty minutes after he came into us. He died about two and a half hours after being shot.[31]

As Roger McHugh's book prints these statements sequentially, including that of Kate Ennis, in his collection of 1916 materials, it seems as if Mr Ennis's wife takes up the chant, like the next of the keening women to perform her 'leading recitative', her words variations on Miss Fennell's:

> At 8 o'clock my husband tumbled downstairs, struck against the parlour door which burst in, staggered over to me, and fell at my feet, a wound under his heart. He told me he was shot. I asked him who shot him, and he told me 'the soldiers.' I said 'Why did they shoot you?' and he said he did not know. I asked him where did they shoot him, and he replied 'through the heart as I asked them,' and he then asked me to go out and ask them to come in and finish him. He asked me to get a priest for him, and

just before he died he asked me to forgive the soldiers. He died at twenty minutes past eight.[32]

Then Mrs Byrne (whose brother, Michael Noonan, was also shot with Ennis) takes up her part: 'I have read the statement of Miss Fennell and it agrees in every respect with what I have heard from Mrs. Ennis. My brother was 34 years of age and was of a quiet, kindly disposition'.[33]

The surviving women of 170 North King Street also take their turns, each, in Synge's words, 'possessed...with a profound ecstasy'. First there is the statement of the 'old woman', Kate Kelly, who worked as a servant in the house. The soldiers led her and the male members of the Hickey family into the Carrolls' house through a hole in the wall.

> Mr. Hickey, as he passed, said to Mrs. Carroll, 'Isn't it too bad, Mrs. Carroll.' 'Yes indeed, Mr. Hickey,' she said, and the last thing he said to her was, 'Very often the innocent suffer for the guilty.' As I came to the hole in the wall I stumbled, was frightened, and nearly fell down. Mr. Hickey stepped forward and said, 'Wait, Kate, I'll help you,' and assisted me through.'... Both Mrs. Carroll and I heard poor Christy pleading for his father's life – 'O! don't kill father.' The shots then rung out, and I shouted, 'O, my God!' and overcome with horror, I threw myself on my knees and began to pray.[34]

Mrs Hickey (wife of Thomas Hickey, aged 38, and mother of Christopher Hickey, aged 16, both shot by the soldiers) describes the first sight of her dead son:

> When I rushed into the room, there I saw my poor angel, my darling son. He was lying on the ground, his face darkened, and his two hands raised above his head as if in silent supplication. I kissed him and put his little cap under his head and settled his hands for death.[35]

Again there is the turn-taking in the recitative: Mrs Kelly remembers Mr Hickey's polite acknowledgement of his neighbours even as he is walked through their parlour by the British soldiers ('Isn't it too bad, Mrs. Carroll') and his philosophical comment on his imminent death: 'Very often the innocent suffer for the guilty'. The artless directness of Kelly's account, which records every kind, calm sentence uttered by Hickey as he is marched to his death, gives it a documentary power. Nor does Kelly forget his thoughtful assistance to her ('Wait, Kate, I'll help you') when she stumbles going through the hole in the wall.

The son is just as thoughtful, begging the soldiers to spare his father. Mrs Hickey's first words to her son, with its series of epithets, are reminiscent of Eiblín Ní Chonaill's many apostrophes to her husband in Caoineadh Airt Uí Laoghaire ('The lament for Art O'Leary'): 'Mo ghrá thu go daingean' ('My steadfast love'), 'Mo chara is m'uan tú' ('My friend and my lamb'),'Mo chara is mo lao thu' ('My friend and my calf').[36] Anthologised as they are by Roger McHugh in his book Dublin 1916, the women's words create the ritualised effect of a collective lamentation.

## KATHLEEN CLARKE'S DREAM

Kathleen Clarke's first expression of feeling after the deaths of her husband and brother is not articulated in the direct language of grief such as the residents of North King Street used ('I shouted, "O, my God!" and overcome with horror, I threw myself on my knees and began to pray'). It is a narrative embodied in a dream vision at a time of great illness several weeks after the executions, and Clarke herself does not speak a word in it.

As is typical of women's 1916 memoirs, Clarke— usually concerned with family relationships or national politics—devotes time to talking about her feelings, tracing their history after the executions. In the weeks following the Rising, she writes in her autobiography, she was unable to feel and unable to cry. When she returned home after saying goodbye to her brother Ned Daly in his cell at Kilmainham, the day after having said goodbye to her husband, 'I remember feeling that if I could cry it would ease me. I could not'. When she went to Limerick to see her children and tell them about their father's death, 'the children were overjoyed to see me, and they were very sweet and comforting, but still I could not cry. Something hard would not break up'. After going to Limerick every weekend to see her children for several weeks, she became too sick to get out of bed. In great pain, she had a miscarriage, and, she writes, 'My baby was dead, and I hoped soon to be'.

Clarke then had what she refers to as 'a strange experience', what would later be called a 'near-death experience', which released her emotion and enabled her to mourn:

The doctor and nurse were busy with me, and while I was looking at them, suddenly everything went dark blue. 'This is the end,' I thought, and said, 'Goodbye, doctor, I'm off.' I heard him say, 'My God, nurse, she's gone.' I thought I was going to join Tom, and was very happy about it. I felt myself lifted up, through clouds which seemed to be arranged like feathers on a bird. As I passed through, they closed behind me. When I got up a certain distance I heard a great shout, like men's voices. They sounded joyous to me, and I recognised Ned's voice. Then what seemed a chorus of men were shouting joyfully, 'Here she comes.' Then there was silence.

I still kept going up, and through the clouds I saw Tom's face and then Sean MacDermott's. Sean said, 'She must go back, Tom, she must.' Tom said, 'God, Sean, we can't send her back, it is too cruel,' and Sean said, 'You know, Tom, she must go back. She has to do the work we left her to do.' On both their faces there was a look of intense sadness. I wanted to say I would not go back, but I was unable to speak. Their faces disappeared, and I felt myself being slowly but surely pushed down through the clouds of feathers. The next thing I heard was the doctor saying, in a very shocked voice, 'My God, nurse, she's coming back.' And back I was, and a more disgusted creature never arrived on this earth. But now I knew what I had to do, and gave up trying to take the easy way out. I just had to take up my burden and carry it as well as I could.

The doctor told me afterwards that for some minutes he had been sure I was dead; heart and everything had ceased for the moment.[37]

Then, she says, 'When my sisters arrived from Limerick later in the day and stooped over to kiss me, I cried for the first time since the executions, cried with sheer disappointment that I was not dead'.

This dream vision has many of the characteristics of a 'near-death' experience, the 'sense of removal from the world', the 'sense of moving up or through a passageway', and 'an intense feeling of unconditional love and acceptance'.[38] The three men she was closest to, all of them executed, greet her in a 'joyous' chorus. She hears her dead brother's voice and sees her husband's face and the face of their close friend Seán MacDermott. They debate the issue of whether she can stay with them or 'go back', and her beloved husband says, 'we can't send her back, it is too cruel'. But, says MacDermott, she must go back because 'She has to do the work we left her to do'.

Clarke's response—'I knew what I had to do...I just had to take up my burden and carry it as well as I could'—sounds like Dorothea Brooke towards the end of *Middlemarch*, feeling in spite of her misery 'the manifold wakings of men to labour and endurance'.[39] Why did this vision, with its painful sight of the joyous men she loved most in the world welcoming her to an afterlife, a heaven entered through 'clouds of feathers', precipitate her tears? It must in some way have made clear to Clarke the absolute nature of her loss, that she would never hear their voices or see their faces again, that the loss was permanent. The sudden spatial shift, as the men remain high and she moves downward away from them, dramatises their separation. Unlike the women of North King Street, she had not heard the shots, or seen her husband's or brother's dead bodies. She had not had the shock of direct confrontation with their deaths. In fact, returning to Kilmainham—the night after saying farewell to her husband—to say farewell to her brother, she had asked the guard

> if he could tell me if the man I had visited the night before was dead. 'Of course he is dead,' he said. 'Would you swear it?' I asked him. 'I would swear it,' he said, 'I was one of the firing party, and if it is any consolation to you, I can tell you I was in many a firing party, but I swear I never saw a braver man die.'[40]

In the dream vision, Clarke had no agency: she was 'lifted up' through the clouds, and then she was 'pushed down through the clouds of feathers'. She said nothing throughout the dream; only the men spoke: 'I wanted to say I would not go back, but I was unable to speak'. Her lack of agency and the narrative form of her vision may have been physiologically driven; the doctor said her heart had stopped beating, and he was sure she was dead. Her mind, not yet dead, was imagining how happy a reunion with Tom, Ned and Seán would be. When their 'faces disappeared', she has lost them all a second time.

It is at the moment when her sisters 'stooped over to kiss me' that Clarke cries 'for the first time since the executions, cried with sheer disappointment that I was not dead'. The high moral Dorothea-Brooke-ish notion that she had 'work' to do, to continue what the dead revolutionaries left unfinished, is not remembered. What she feels instead is the loss of the beautiful fantasy that she could hear the joyous, welcoming voices of the dead men she loved and join them forever. Until then, her emotions were paralysed at the time of those traumatic visits to Kilmainham; this loss was the definitive loss, a quadruple loss of husband, brother, friend and baby.

## Mary Louisa Hamilton Norway and 'the safest place in Dublin'

On Wednesday night of Easter Week, Patrick Colgan of the Maynooth Volunteers and two other men were ordered to 'smash the glass partitions' of the room they were occupying, the office of the secretary to the Post Office. They found several safes and, keeping to the ethical principles of the Volunteers, shut and secured the doors of the safes containing money. They were pleased, 'months afterward', to read 'a tribute to the Volunteers for their honesty in leaving the moneys untouched'. They continued 'to force open presses, desks and boxes in the room'. So doing, they found in one press

> the bloodstained 2/Lieutenant's British Army uniform of a son of the Secretary. He had been killed in France some short time earlier. In an envelope we found a lock of his fair hair, marked by the boy's mother. I forget the name of the boy. There were a number of letters from the boy to his mother.[41]

The 'boy' was Frederick Hamilton Norway, only nineteen when he was hit by a shell on 13 June 1915 at Epinette, near Armentières; he died three weeks later.[42] The 'lock of his fair hair' and the boy's letters were his parents' most precious possessions, and Frederick's mother, Mary Hamilton Norway, spent much of the Rising anxious about whether she would ever see them again. For her, he seemed to die all over again during the Rising. The series of letters she wrote to her sister in England giving a day-by-day account of the Rising were published in the autumn of 1916 as *The Sinn Fein rebellion as I saw it.*

In 1912, when Arthur Hamilton Norway was appointed secretary to the Post Office for Ireland, the Norways and their two sons, Frederick and Nevil, moved from Ealing, in London, to South Hill, a large house in Blackrock that 'opened up new country pleasures' for them—a pony, hay carts, greenhouses and outdoors rambling. But after

Frederick was killed in the war, the Blackrock house, in Nevil's words, 'held so many memories of Fred for my mother and myself that it [was] better to get rid of it and start again'.[43] To escape the memories, the Norways moved to the Royal Hibernian Hotel on Dawson Street. The Royal Hibernian was then (according to a 1914 London journal) 'the most fashionable first class hotel in Dublin'.[44]

From that time on, at least so long as they lived in Ireland, the Norways' domestic space was fragmented: their furniture was in storage; their clothes and a few valuable personal items remained with them in their room at the hotel; and their most treasured possessions— not only family jewellery, silver and other heirlooms, but most importantly, 'all our dear F.'s books, sword, and all his possessions, which we value more than anything else in the world'—all these were put in 'the safest place in Dublin', as Mrs Norway put it, her husband's office: the 'silver, old engravings, and other valuables were stored in the great mahogany cupboards', and Frederick's belongings and her jewel-case were locked in the safe that was built into the wall of her husband's office in the GPO on Sackville Street.[45]

During Easter Week, as Norway writes in his account of the Rising, with the exception of the Telephone Office on Dame Street, '...there was no Post Office, save the room which I had commandeered at the Hibernian Hotel, and the Telephone circuit, which I had appropriated'.[46] So the Royal Hibernian Hotel was not only their temporary home; its sitting-room was Norway's temporary office. On the Friday night of Easter Week, that temporary office, the hotel's sitting-room, also became the Norways' secondary safe-deposit box. There were so many snipers around and so many bullets flying that all the residents of the hotel were required to leave their rooms. Mrs Norway brought down the valuables she had in her room—'[Fred's] miniature and the presentation portrait of him, my despatch case with his letters, my fur coat, hat and boots'—and stored them in the sitting-room, which had now become, by default, the new 'safest place in Dublin'.[47] All the residents of the hotel were crowded into the lounge, where most of them spent the night, though the Norways 'crept' back up to their room.

Secretary Norway had put a certain amount of time and energy into reconstructing the GPO, and both he and his wife felt a vested interest in its new elegance:

> When we came here H. was scandalised at the condition
> of the G.P.O. The whole frontage was given up to sorting
> offices, and the public office was in a side street, a miser-

able, dirty little place, that would have been a disgrace to a small country town.—H. found that plans had been drawn up and passed for the complete reconstruction of the interior...So H. hustled, and the work was completed and opened to the public six weeks ago.—It was really beautiful. The roof was a large glass dome, with elaborate plaster work, beautiful white pillars, mosaic floor, counters all of red teak wood, and bright brass fittings everywhere—a public building of which any great city might be proud; and in six weeks all that is left is a smoking heap of ashes![48]

The rebels had commandeered this building not because of its interior decoration, of course, but because they considered it strategically central. They could not have known (or cared) that a tiny part of the building was one of the scattered fragments of the Norways' domestic site.

Joyce wrote of Mrs Kearney in 'A Mother' that she thought her husband 'as secure and fixed as the General Post Office'. The reverse could be said of Mrs Norway, that she thought the General Post Office 'as secure and fixed' as her husband. He was in charge of it; he had redecorated it; and after the Great War began, by his order, it had a guard of soldiers ordered 'to shoot to stop' any 'unidentified person' heading toward the Instrument Room. The safe that Mrs Norway considered so 'safe', a space within a space within a space, was nested within that large stone building, protected by British armed soldiers (whose guns, it turned out, had no ammunition). She maintained a kind of faith even when, on Friday of Easter Week, she thought the fire had destroyed everything; she was pleased that 'When the rebels took possession they demanded the keys from the man who had them in charge. He quietly handed over the keys, having first abstracted the keys of H's room!'[49]

The family's belongings were dispersed in so many cases, boxes and buildings, that Mrs Norway couldn't keep track of them, and her access to them seems always to be at several removes and mediated by someone else. On the Sunday after the surrender, she discovered to her immense relief that some of the valuables she feared were in the GPO were in fact in the hotel in another case:

When we came back from Italy in March, H. brought back from the office my large despatch-case in which I keep all [Fred's] letters. I did not remember what else was in it, so I investigated and found my necklet with jewelled cross

and the pink topaz set, also the large old paste buckle...
But, best of all, there were the three little handkerchiefs
F. sent me from Armentières with my initial worked on
them; for these I was grieving more than for anything, and
when I found them the relief was so great I sat with them
in my hand and cried.[50]

Such is one of many of Mary Norway's keens: 'I sat with them in my
hand and cried'. The pathos here and in so many places in her letters
comes from her apparent lack of agency: the possessions that mean
the most to her seemed to disappear and reappear as if almost of their
own volition.

That 'safest place in Dublin' was ground zero of a surprise revolution, and when Mrs Norway believed there was nothing left of the
things she had stored in the safe, she writes, 'I think I am past caring
about any possessions now. F. and all his precious things are gone.
Nothing else seems worth considering'.[51] But on 20 May, as she watched
the excavations of her husband's office, some of those things emerged.
A Mr Noblett, her husband's trusted employee, showed her 'a great
lump of molten glass' which she realised must have been 'the cut-
glass bottles in the large rosewood and brass-bound dressing-case in
which I had packed all my jewellery'. Then

When I went down again in the afternoon Noblett produced three little brooches that F. had given me on various
birthdays when a wee boy. He always went out with his
own sixpence, and nearly always returned with a brooch,
which I used to wear with great pride. One, a Swastika
brooch, he gave me when he was at Margate after that terrible illness, and he used to go on the pier in his bath-chair.
The blue enamel on it was intact in several places; the
other two were intact in form, but charred and black, with
the pins burnt off. But how glad I was to see them again![52]

This vignette of the mourning mother rejoicing over the return of her
dead son's childhood birthday presents to her, rejoicing in the ruins of
a building where a rebellion has just taken place, forms an image that
is startling because of its juxtapositions. Its peculiar power comes from
juxtapositions of scale: the small brooches and the vast vacant shell of
the GPO, the tiny moment of personal memory and the large forces of
national history. And also, of course, from each side's obliviousness:

Mary Norway was as unaware of the rebels' griefs and joys as they were of hers. And what of the building itself? For this brief time, it was no longer a rebel bastion; it was not yet restored as a working post office; nor was it yet restored as a monument to Irish nationalist struggles. Enclosing as it did the relics of Frederick Norway, as well as the ashes of whatever the rebels left there, the entire building had become, in effect, a giant reliquary.

Because the headquarters of the revolution and the location of the Norways' 'most treasured possessions' were one and the same, Mary Norway mourned her son Frederick throughout the Rising. He was never absent from her thoughts. Her maternal feelings for young manhood modified her attitude to the Rising generally. Although at the beginning she felt the 'Sinn Fein movement' was populated by 'a small body of cranks...thirsting for notoriety', by Friday, 28 April, she was writing, 'One of the most awful things in this terrible time is that there must be scores of dead and dying Sinn Feiners, many of them mere lads, that no one can get at in the houses, and where they will remain till after the rebellion...'.[53] Those 'mere lads' inspired her sympathy. In this passage and throughout her letters to her sister, Norway, along with the widows and mothers of North King Street and Kathleen Clarke, took her turn 'in the leading recitative'.

## EMOTIONAL CONTAGION

A professional nurse tending the wounded in the Hibernian Bank outpost of the GPO and in the GPO, Aoife de Burca wrote her account of the Rising in 'June or July 1916', when it was fresh in her mind. She had treated the dying Volunteer Captain Thomas Weafer on Wednesday, and on Friday she treated James Connolly's wound. Her account of the evacuation from the Post Office on Friday treats the emotional aspects as much as the military ones. At seven in the evening, she left in a small group of nine wounded men (three of them on stretchers), two doctors, a few nurses and eight Volunteers. They walked through the Wax Works 'and on through passages which had been blasted for the purpose of retreat' until they got to the Coliseum Theatre, 'As long as I live I shall never forget that night', de Burca writes:

> The most awful period came now, and I certainly thought
> very few of us (if any) would live to tell the tale. As we
> were arranging the wounded comfortably for a short rest

bullets began falling like rain around the building—the noise was deafening—it seemed as if bombs were being thrown by the dozen about us and we expected every moment would be our last. Our Captain Captain Doyle and Fr. [ ] with some of the men, were in another part of the theatre trying to force open a door. We thought we would never see them again. Suddenly Captain D–[Doyle] rushed in, ordering lights to be extinguished, (we had two candles) and everyone to lie flat on the floor; we did so, every man and woman of us, heads and heels all huddled together in the most bewildering confusion, for the space was small for such a number. It was pitch dark. One man began to light a cigarette and the Captain ordered him to put it out at once. Another young chap was standing beside me, not thinking there was another inch of ground to be found, and I gave him a chuck, saying to him to lie down somehow or another as I felt every minute a bullet would send him toppling over. The girl that was nearest to me was trying to prepare for death, and I thought I would do likewise. I tried to make an Act of fervent Contrition, but the situation was bordering on the comical as well as tragedy, so I burst out laughing instead. Another girl did likewise, and very soon we were all at it. I remember one wounded Volunteer saying 'That's right, let's keep our spirits up though we are facing death'. Anyway, that laugh did us good and I recollect wishing not to die so that I could relate it all some day.[54]

For de Burca, this instance of emotional contagion (not mentioned by anyone else who evacuated the GPO through the Coliseum) was so important that it made her wish 'not to die' so she could 'relate it all some day'.[55] The inappropriate but unavoidable touching of male and female bodies, 'heads and heels all huddled together in the most bewildering confusion', with two Acts of Contrition being recited, not exactly in unison, triggers a series of emotions: first a laugh in the midst of the unusual intimacy, expressing embarrassment and anxiety at the same time; then an epidemic of laughing, as the mixed emotions of the first laugh spread to everyone lying on the floor; then a feeling of gratitude, as the wounded man praises the group for keeping 'our spirits up'; and then de Burca's own wish to survive. The entire episode is reminiscent of Máirín Cregan's story of the Mallow train station, in which one person's audibly expressed emotion (in that instance tears) generates emotional expressiveness in an entire room of people who barely know one another. The feelings were there waiting to be released, and one woman's spontaneous release of her own feelings liberated those of everyone else.

In her First World War memoir *The forbidden zone*, Mary Borden says that as a nurse, she felt 'it was my business to create a counter-wave of life', and that's clearly what Aoife de Burca's laugh did here, not from duty but from impulse, quite spontaneously.[56] The burst of laughter inspired solidarity ('soon we were all at it'). By leading the men and women in laughter and thereby helping to 'keep our spirits up', de Burca was performing what Arlie Russell Hochschild has called 'emotional labour', though hers was not 'managed' or commercialised.[57]

The following day de Burca managed to get safely from Jervis Street home to Drumcondra. As her nephew Éanna de Búrca said in an interview, she was very relaxed about walking through the city: 'Sure what would they want to shoot me for? was her attitude and she walked across O'Connell Street'.[58]

The O'Rahilly and his sister Nell Humphreys: she chastised her daughter Sighle for 'giving in to' herself by refusing to eat lunch on the day The O'Rahilly left to fight in the Rising. However, she later wrote to her sister-in-law about women's participation, '...every girl in every centre, the G.P.O., Jacobs, the College of Surgeons was cool and brave'.

Left: Mary McLoughlin (on right, wearing her 1916 medal), Kathleen Lynn (center) and Hanna Sheehy Skeffington; date unknown (possibly 1941 at the 25th anniversary of the Rising). McLoughlin carried the last message from Thomas MacDonagh in the Jacob's garrison to Joseph Plunkett in the GPO; the message was the title of a poem, an allusion McLoughlin did not recognise. She was not able to reach the GPO, so the message was never delivered, but she remembered it for the rest of her life.

Below: Máirín Cregan (with her husband, Dr James Ryan), whose tears in the Mallow train station during Easter Week triggered an outpouring of emotional discussion about the Rising.

*Conclusion*

# WORKING THE REVOLUTION

'There will also be work for women to do...'
*Manifesto of the Irish Volunteers*, 1913


In 1950, when some members of Cumann na mBan said they would rather 'burn anything they had' than give it to the Bureau of Military History, Pauline Keating tried to persuade them otherwise, suggesting 'that the information might be of interest to future generations'.[1] The information—the stories, anecdotes, quotations, the details about daily life—is indeed of interest, as is all the content of women's diaries, letters and memoirs studied in the previous chapters. They look especially valuable a century later, when Irish women and women in every nation of the world are more conscious of their histories.

The nature of women's status in the years that followed their active participation in the Rising, the War of Independence and the Civil War has been described in various ways, all of them emphasising the legal limits placed on women's citizenship. In strong language, Margaret Mac Curtain invokes 'the illiberal legislation and stifling provincialism of the post-Civil War decades in the Irish Free State' and 'the total exclusion of women from public life, and from responsibility for public morality'.[2] In the words of Maryann Gialanella Valiulis, 'the Free State enacted gender legislation which tried to remove women from participating in the economic and political life of the state'.[3] Eve Morrison cites Bridget O'Mullane's 1937 complaint to de Valera about a draft of the proposed new constitution:

> ...this clause about the inadequate strength of women is... particularly hurtful to us who in the various phases of the struggle for National Independence, were so frequently called on...to undertake tasks entailing heavy muscular toil...One of our proudest achievements is that we conveyed safely from place to place machine guns, heavy explosives and rifles...without any loss or capture of same in transit.[4]

O'Mullane's precise and vivid memories must have had some effect, because the offending language was 'removed from the final version of the 1937 Constitution'.[5] Nevertheless, those 'proudest achievements' were not recognised in any legislation that granted women what the Proclamation had called 'equal rights and equal opportunities'.

In the last few decades of the past century, Irish women, like women in many parts of the world, became active contributors to the second and third 'waves' of feminism, agitating for power in the fields of the workplace, sexuality and the family.[6] In that third 'wave', two women have been elected as presidents of Ireland and three women have been tánaiste. Yet 99 years after the Rising, Micheline Sheehy Skeffington, the granddaughter of Ireland's most famous feminist, Hanna Sheehy Skeffington, won a case against the National University of Ireland, Galway, when the Equality Tribunal found that she had been denied promotion on the basis of gender. As Sheehy Skeffington said, 'I'm a feminist. I come from a family of feminists. I had to take this case to honour them all'.[7]

Looking back at 1916 from the perspective of the present moment, almost a century later when problems relating to Irish women's citizenship are not yet entirely resolved, we can observe how the Rising functioned to some extent like any bounded territory or site that men dominate and that women wish to enter. This is of course to see the Rising purely in terms of gender politics, but such a view makes visible patterns present in many of the women's accounts. The spatial metaphor of words like 'site' or 'territory' is not a metaphor in the case of Dublin in April 1916: although the fighting was potentially anywhere, women who wanted to be 'out' had to associate themselves with a particular garrison or outpost. The 'small behaviors' detailed in the women's memoirs reveal the kinds of difficulties that Irish women would continue to confront, and the choices they would make, as they entered a primarily male public sphere.

For those women who arrived singly, and not with a branch of Cumann na mBan or a division of the Citizen Army, the Rising often appeared to be someone else's space, an area that posed special problems of entry. The example of Catherine Byrne, the young woman who jumped through a window of the GPO, dramatises the unconventional and precipitous route a woman took to enter the public and predominantly male space of a war. The example of Min Ryan (granted entry to the GPO by Seán T. O'Kelly, then wandering around inside the building, 'looking for Seán MacDermott' and 'feeling like the complete camp follower') shows the unease a woman felt, uncertain how to manage private and public selves in a military headquarters. Her embarrassment at searching for the man she loves in such a place expresses itself in the suggestive sexual term she applies to herself, 'camp follower'.[8]

The account of a less aggressive young woman, Mairéad Ní Cheallaigh, represents the Rising as a space to be entered not with a jump but with a series of tentative attempts. Her narrative makes especially clear the gendered nature of both domestic and military sites in 1916. Ní Cheallaigh was the sister of future President Seán T. O'Kelly, and according to a brief notice of her death in 1971, she 'led a very quiet life and was rarely seen publicly'.[9] During Easter Week she was constantly trying to find a good point of entry and a place to do useful work, as she entered the Rising in different sites. Her witness statement is indeed one of those 'of interest to future generations', as her activities show the many subtle lines of demarcation between women's and men's spaces.

For the four days before the Rising, the O'Kelly family was host to Patrick and Willie Pearse, whose school the O'Kelly brothers attended. The drawing-room was given over to the Pearses, and their weapons and ammunition were hidden there: 'I did not see the revolvers which must have been in the haversacks which were buckled up and were never opened in my presence. Pádraig asked my mother would their stuff be safe there. My mother reassured them, saying no one would enter the room without their permission'.[10] Mrs O'Kelly created a hidden male space for weapons within her house; she also purchased 'nice linen' towels 'for these important and distinguished guests'.

In a memorable passage, Ní Cheallaigh described serving the Pearse brothers what must have been their last home-cooked meal.[11]

> My mother...called me to give me instructions about the breakfast for the Pearses. She said she had prepared a tureen of bacon and eggs which she had left on a trivet in front of the dining-room fire. She had also a tureen of mutton chops. She said they must be very hungry and God knows when they will get a meal again. She must have known more than I did. She went out and I went into the dining-room where the table was set. Shortly afterwards I heard the Pearses come down stairs. They stood shyly outside the door until I called them in. I informed them that my mother had been worried about their taking so little food and had prepared their breakfast herself. I said I hoped they would enjoy it. I placed the two tureens on the table and they ate every bit of the food on the table including a whole loaf of bread.[12]

The men about to begin an armed revolution were too shy or too polite to enter the dining-room uninvited. It was a women's space, managed by mother and daughter, and the men felt they must be invited into it. Once at breakfast, the men ate 'every bit of food on the table including a whole loaf of bread'. Ní Cheallaigh was 'dumbfounded', she adds, 'to see all they had eaten'.[13] Her account gives a charming vignette of the brothers leaving for the revolution, their last moments in domestic space of any kind: 'They took their bicycles which were in the hall, wheeled them down the four steps. They mounted the bicycles and turned to wave to me'.[14] She adds, 'I have kept the table and tablecloth that were used by the Pearses at the last meal they ate in our house'.[15] The cloth and the furniture were touched by history, as the whole house was.

When Ní Cheallaigh went out herself to join the Rising, she found it difficult to discover how to get into it. No one was at the meeting place she had been ordered to go to, so she and some other members of Cumann na mBan she met went to a store north of Parnell Square and 'decided to turn the drawing-room over the shop into an emergency hospital'. Soon they realised that 'the fighting was not likely to come our way', so they disbanded. At a loss for what to do next, Ní Cheallaigh went home to see how her mother was doing and went out again the next morning 'where I guessed my brothers were, down in the North King Street area'; the males in her family would perhaps show her a route in. There she ran into 'five or six strange girls...cooperating with the Volunteers, always dying to be told to do something'. Dying to do something herself, Ní Cheallaigh decided to stay in that area, and the women 'cooked meals, potatoes, meat and vegetables in one of the houses near Halston Street' for the Volunteers in 'F' Company, 1st Battalion. Over the following days, as ordered by the Volunteers, they distributed food and tea to the civilian residents of the houses near them.[16]

In so far as the men were giving the orders, this site—like other outposts in the Rising—replicated in its gender hierarchies the more conservative contemporary practices of the Irish home (and most other homes in Europe and the United States at that time). Ní Cheallaigh's witness statement records small spatial distinctions that limn further divisions of gender:

> I think it was on Wednesday the Volunteers started to burrow through the houses and after that they did not let us go on the street at all. The Volunteers made an attack on the Broadstone on that day as far as I recollect and we followed them with dressings but we were not let go too near them.[17]

As these memories indicate, the public space she and the other women occupied was marked by degrees of proximity to the front line. The men did not allow the women to leave the house where they were cooking and go 'on the street', and when the men attacked the enemy, the women 'were not let go too near them'. The women in that group were 'out', but they were not as far 'out' as the men.

By Friday, Ní Cheallaigh 'was getting restless' because 'I did not appear to be doing work of any great value'. She was worrying about her mother, and her younger brother Michael (19 to her 23 years) 'kept telling me that I ought to be at home with her as she was quite alone'. Going home to mother seems to have been Ní Cheallaigh's default option; she left because her work was not 'of any great value'. In order to get home safely Ní Cheallaigh (still in her nurse's uniform) took on another identity, letting down her hair in 'plaits which must have made me look very young'. On her way home, she had to use the all-purpose lie many of the women used, which in her case was true—'I said my mother was alone at home and I was worried about her and she probably about me'—and after a two-hour arrest by British soldiers and a night spent alone in an empty building, she reached home again.[18]

Mairéad Ní Cheallaigh's memories of dates may be vague; she thinks 'it was on Wednesday', and she acknowledges it was 'on that day as far as I recollect'. But her locational memories are precise, and those details map a woman's participation in the Rising. The realm in which she and so many other women in 1916 acted exists in what historian Seth Koven has called a borderland or overlap between 'the private, female world of household and family' and 'the public, male-dominated world of politics'.[19] The women Ní Cheallaigh writes about in her witness statement were positioned in an area between the 'house' and the front line. Whether she is cooking for the Volunteers, distributing food to civilians or following behind the battle lines with medical dressing, she is operating in a borderland, a territory in which women are using domestic skills to serve the military purposes of men. Ní Cheallaigh is neither as 'out' as the men nor as 'in' as an uninvolved woman such as Mary Martin, watching for the good tennis weather to come.[20]

This borderland was not unique to rebel women. Mary Louisa Hamilton Norway, wife of the secretary to the Post Office in Ireland, also operated in a borderland during Easter Week. As we saw in Chapter Six, she and her husband were living in the Royal Hibernian Hotel on Dawson Street, and together they recreated the work of the Post Office within the hotel. Mary Norway herself modestly does not praise her own labours, but her husband praises them in his own memoir. His wife, he writes,

> ...was invaluable to me in the days which followed, and it is not too much to say that throughout the week of active fighting she and I, with one of my principal clerks...constituted the General Post Office...there was no Post Office, save the room which I had commandeered at the Hibernian Hotel, and the Telephone circuit which I had appropriated. At that Telephone my wife, or I, sat all day long. Her cool pluck, and excellent good sense, were invaluable to me, and indeed to the public interest.[21]

Secretary Norway's wording makes clear that his wife was more than a helpmate; she worked in 'the public interest'. Constituting as it did the provisional GPO, the room at the Royal Hibernian with the telephone circuit had become a public space; it was a branch of the government. With a kind of feminist sensitivity, Norway avoids any language that would make his wife's work sound secondary, though of course it was secondary: it was his government position that made the room governmental. If the GPO itself was now, temporarily as it turned out, the site of a Republican Irish government, and the women in it occupying a governmental or at least revolutionary space, then so too the room at the hotel gave a public position and status to the woman who occupied and worked at the telephone in it.

Elsie Mahaffy also, in her role as hostess to the British army, can be said to have occupied a borderland space at the Provost's House. Mahaffy and Mrs Norway did not need to find a point of entry to a new territory; the Rising came to them. Through the public roles of their male relatives their homes were transformed into sites of the state apparatus. For these women, 'home' became a way of functioning beyond the domestic arena while at the same time remaining in it.

The Easter Rising was only one of many 'borderlands' to offer Irish women a field of service between 'the female world of household and family' and 'the public, male-dominated world of politics'. In Ireland as in England, nineteenth-century women's charitable work had led them to a life beyond the home and 'an understanding and consolidation of gender identity...'.[22] Well before the Rising, in one of the most important borderlands for Irish women, the many women's religious orders also operated in a public though patriarchal site.[23] Moreover, as *Irish women's writing and traditions* (vol. v of the *Field Day anthology of Irish writing*) amply demonstrates, Irish women had had 'public voices' as early as the sixteenth century and were visibly active in politics from the middle of the nineteenth.[24] A great number of the women 'out' in the Rising were professionally qualified in teaching, medicine, nursing or art; many others worked in theatres, shops or businesses. And in the years before the Rising, the Great War as well as the Irish women's political organisations mentioned in the Introduction offered women routes into a fuller citizenship through which they could contribute to the professional, political, and economic life of the nation.[25]

The Easter Rising offered such routes also, though not means to operate from a position of significant power. It was a site where women's efforts were at the same time auxiliary and essential. Commenting on the absence of women from the Boland's Mills garrison, Margaret Ward notes that 'The role in which many of the women visualised themselves did little to threaten the ingrained conservatism' of some of the men.[26] And yet as Senia Pašeta observes, '...the women who chose to take part unambiguously understood themselves to have been active participants in a military campaign'.[27]

The women's letters, diaries, and other accounts report the complexities of their position in 1916. They were indeed proud of their contributions; that note is clear in Catherine Byrne's letter to the Department of Defence when her application for a pension was rejected: 'Apart from the matter of finance I feel a reflection is being cast on my National past'.[28] And yet their stories show the limits of their participation. The promise of the Volunteer 'Manifesto'—'There will also be work for women to do'—was true for all the women, with an emphasis on 'also'. Their narratives show male territories incompletely occupied by women, but their presence in public space, wherever it was, gave them the authority to write and record.

# ENDNOTES

## Introduction

[1] Bureau of Military History (BMH), witness statement (WS) 648, Rooney (née Byrne), Catherine, 2. According to her military service pension statement, it was five minutes after twelve noon when she arrived at the Post Office, Military Archives, Ireland (IE/MA), Military service pension (MSP) 34REF3935, Rooney (née Byrne), Catherine, Sworn statement before the Advisory Committee, 22 February 1937, 1.

[2] BMH, WS 648, 2.

[3] In the narrative given in her 1952 witness statement, Gahan is recorded as saying 'What the bloody hell are you doing there?' In the episode as told to the interviewer for the military service pension application in 1937, however, the person taking dictation appears to have gotten the pronouns confused. The statement says, 'Joe Gahan lifted me in through the window and I said to him "where the devil did you come from" and as I said that there was an explosion and we thought we were gone, and he said "come quick, there is a case for you"...' (IE/MA, MSP 34REF3935, Rooney (née Byrne), Catherine, Sworn statement before the Advisory Committee, 22 February 1937, 3). That version does not make sense, because Gahan is the one who would be confused at her unusual arrival through the window; she would not be confused at his presence in the Post Office. Moreover, as a young woman, she is unlikely to have cursed; or if she did, she would not have quoted herself swearing.

[4] Erving Goffman, *Interaction ritual* (New York, 1982), 1. In this paragraph, I have borrowed some words from the introduction to a previous book of my own. See Lucy McDiarmid, 'Introduction: the Irish controversy', in *The Irish art of controversy* (Ithaca, NY, 2005), 1–9.

[5] BMH, WS 648, 3. See also Lucy Smyth attesting to Byrne's membership of Cumann na mBan, IE/MA, MSP 34REF3935, Rooney, Letter from Lucy Byrne (née Smyth) to the Advisory Committee, 13 January 1937; and Byrne's reference to her mobilisation order, IE/MA, MSP 34REF3935, Rooney, Sworn statement before the Advisory Committee, 22 February 1937, 3.

[6] For more background on these developments, see Seth Koven and Sonya Michel (eds), *Mothers of a new world: maternalist politics and the origins of welfare states* (New York and London, 1993). See therein especially Seth Koven, 'Borderlands: women, voluntary action, and child welfare in Britain, 1840–1914', 94–135.

[7] Kathryn Kish Sklar, 'The historical foundations of women's power in the creation of the American welfare state, 1830–1930', in Koven and Michel (eds), *Mothers of a new world*, 43–93: 61, 63.

[8] Senia Pašeta, *Irish nationalist women, 1900–1918* (Cambridge, 2013), 45.

[9] See Rosemary Cullen Owens, *Smashing times: a history of the Irish women's suffrage movement 1889–1922* (Dublin, 1984), and Pašeta, *Irish nationalist women 1900–1918*.

[10] *Manifesto of the Irish Volunteers* (Dublin, 1913, re-issued 1914), http://source.southdublinlibraries.ie/bitstream/10599/9706/3/wm_DSC_0480.jpg (9 May 2015).

[11] 'Cumann na mBan manifesto', ed. Maria Luddy, 'Women and politics in Ireland, 1860–1918', in Angela Bourke *et al.* (eds), *Field Day anthology of Irish writing (vol. v): Irish women's writing and traditions* (Cork, 2001), 69–74:104.

[12] BMH, WS 399, Mulcahy (née Ryan), Mary Josephine ('Min'), 5.

[13] Pašeta, *Irish nationalist women*, 136; see also 33–169 for a discussion of the various feminisms and debates among the major Irish women's organisations in the years before the Rising; and Margaret Ward, *Hanna Sheehy Skeffington: a life* (Dublin, 1997).

[14] BMH, WS 391, Molony, Helena, 39.

[15] Maryann Gialanella Valiulis, 'Introduction: gender, power and patriarchy', in Maryann Gialanella Valiulis (ed.), *Gender and power in Irish history* (Dublin and Portland, OR, 2009), 1–8: 3.

[16] IE/MA, MSP 34REF15389, McLoughlin, Mary, Sworn statement to the Advisory Committee, 22 February 1937, 2–6.

[17] According to McLoughlin's Bureau of Military History witness statement, Clan na Gael was 'attached to the Hibernian Rifles', BMH, WS 934, 1. See also Padraig Óg Ó Ruairc, 'The Irish story, a short history of the Hibernian Rifles', *The Irish story* (2013), http://www.theirishstory.com/2013/03/31/a-short-history-of-the-hibernian-rifles-1912-1916/#.VUVhlvlViko (9 May 2015): 'The Clann [*sic*] Na Gael Girl Scouts founded in 1911 by sisters May and Elizabeth Kelly also used the hall for training and May Kelly the O/C of this group was attached to the Hibernian Rifles unit during Easter Week'. Clan na Gael was a Dublin division of the Irish branch of the Irish–American organisation the Hibernian Rifles.

[18] Mary Hamilton Norway, 'The Sinn Fein rebellion as I saw it', in Keith Jeffery (ed.), *The Sinn Féin rebellion as they saw it: Mary Louisa and Arthur Hamilton Norway* (Dublin, 1999), 35, 69.

[19] National Library of Ireland (NLI), MS 24553, Letter from Mrs Arthur J.C. Mitchell to her sister Flora, 24–7 April 1916.

[20] Trinity College Dublin, Digital Humanities (TCDDH), *The diary of Mary Martin*, 28 April 1916, see http://dh.tcd.ie/martindiary/ (9 May 2015). Francis ('Frank') Sheehy Skeffington was killed on 26 April 1916; Connolly was executed on 12 May; and Markievicz was sentenced to death on 4 May. Her sentence was commuted to life imprisonment.

[21] After the surrender on Saturday, 29 April, the rebels from the GPO and Four Courts garrisons were made to sleep on the grounds of the Rotunda Hospital. The executed rebels (in addition to Connolly) were Patrick Pearse, Thomas Clarke, Thomas MacDonagh (3 May 1916); Joseph Plunkett, Ned Daly, Michael O'Hanrahan, Willie Pearse (4 May 1916); John MacBride (5 May 1916); Éamonn Ceannt, Michael Mallin, Seán Heuston, Con Colbert (8 May 1916); Thomas Kent (9 May 1916); Seán MacDermott (12 May 1916); and Roger Casement (3 August 1916).

[22] These and other important books in Irish women's history are listed in the bibliography of secondary sources at the end of the book.

[23] See the bibliography for the list of manuscript sources used in this book.

[24] IE/MA, MSP 34REF3935, Rooney. (Date application sent: 11 October 1934; received by the Military Service Pension Board: 23 February 1935.) According to the

Military Archives web site, 'Legislation was introduced, commencing in 1924 and continuing in 1934 and 1949, to recognize the service of veterans from Easter Week, 1916 through to the 30 September 1923, who were proven to have had active service during the week commencing 23 April 1916, and in the War of Independence and the Civil War, through the payment of service pensions' (http://www.militaryarchives.ie/collections/online-collections/military-service-pensions-collection/about-the-collection/origin-and-scope).

[25] BMH, WS 648, 3: 'When the Cumann na mBan representative—afterwards Tom Byrne's wife [Lucy Smyth], I forget her maiden name—came to mobilise me, my mother told her that Alice and I had been gone for some time but she did not know where. Afterwards, when applying for my pension, I got very little assistance from the Cumann ma mBan authorities, as some of them who were in the G.P.O. did not remember my presence at the place of mobilisation or at the Post Office'. Lucy Smyth (see Chapter Three) did supply a letter for Byrne. In March 1940, Byrne was awarded a pension, although she appealed the amount granted and sought the help of solicitors, IE/MA, MSP 34REF3935, Letter to the MSP Board from C. Rooney, 3 April 1940. See also IE/MA, MSP 34REF3935, Memorandum, 25 November 1940. For the granting of the pension, see IE/MA, MSP W34E4971, Letter from the Department of Finance, 10 February 1941. Note that she writes 'I always carried a gun' (IE/MA, MSP 34REF3935, Sworn statement to the Advisory Board, 22 February 1937, 9).

[26] The word is written the same way on several other pages with the same question, IE/MA, MSP 34REF3935.

[27] IE/MA, MSP 34REF3935; W34E4971, Letter from C. Rooney to F. Aiken, 2.

[28] IE/MA, MSP 34REF3935; W34E4971, MSP Certificate, 7 February 1941.

[29] Diarmaid Ferriter, *The transformation of Ireland, 1900–2000* (London, 2005), 6.

[30] Eve Morrison, 'The Bureau of Military History and female Republican activism, 1913–23', in Maryann Gialanella Valiulis (ed.), *Gender and power in Irish history* (Dublin and Portland, OR, 2009), 59–83: 59.

[31] BMH, WS 648, Rooney (née Byrne), Catherine, 14.

[32] R.F. Foster, *Vivid faces: the revolutionary generation in Ireland 1890–1923* (London, 2014), xxii.

[33] Helen Litton, 'Introduction', in Kathleen Clarke, *Revolutionary woman*, ed. Helen Litton (Dublin, 1991), 7–8: 7.

[34] BMH, WS 359, de Burca, Aoife, 25. Some of the women's witness statements have tables of contents, evidence that they were carefully written autobiographies. See, for instance, those of Elizabeth Bloxham (BMH, WS 632) and Catherine Rooney (BMH, WS 648).

[35] See Chapter 7 for a discussion of this episode.

[36] BMH, WS 216, Duffy, Louise Gavan, *passim*.

[37] BMH, WS 257, Plunkett (née Gifford), Grace, 12.

[38] Clarke, *Revolutionary woman*, 78.

[39] Arlie Russell Hochschild, *The managed heart: commercialization of human feeling* (Berkeley and Los Angeles: CA), vii, ix, *passim*.

## Chapter One

[1] The man who inspired Gavan Duffy's response was General Lowe's son, John, later to become a Hollywood actor and the third of Hedy Lamarr's six husbands. Lamarr was the third of his five wives. See John Loder, *Hollywood hussar* (London, 1977).

[2] TCDDH, *The 1916 diary of Dorothy Stopford Price*, 27 April 1916, http://dh.tcd.ie/pricediary/ (10 May 2015).

[3] University College Dublin Archives (UCDA), Papers of Sighle Humphreys, P106/384(13), Nell Humphreys to Nora Humphreys, May 1916.

[4] UCDA, Humphreys, P106/384(13), 8.

[5] Joyce Kilmer, 'Irish girl rebel tells of Dublin fighting', *New York Times,* 20 August 1916. Kilmer wrote a sympathetic introduction to the interview with Regan. The 'absolute equality' Regan praises did not, of course, last after the creation of the Irish Free State. Máire Comerford writes in her unpublished memoir, 'Cumann na mBan allowed itself to be pushed aside when the time came to implement the ideals for which we had been fighting—but that is another story!' (UCDA, Papers of Máire Comerford, LA18/60).

[6] Kilmer had met Joseph Plunkett when he was in the U.S. in 1915 and wrote an article on the literary talents of the men executed after the Rising ('Poets marched in the van of Irish revolt', *New York Times*, 7 May 1916, 63).

[7] Kitty O'Doherty's husband Seamus O'Doherty was a member of the Irish Republican Brotherhood military council.

[8] BMH, WS 355, O'Doherty, Kitty, 24.

[9] See http://www.irishtimes.com/opinion/an-irishman-s-diary-1.499929 (1 July 2015).

[10] All the rebel garrisons in 1916 had women working in them except for Boland's Mills. Nell Humphreys writes, 'The only place where [women] were not present, Bolands [*sic*] Mills (as de Valera, the Commandant, would have none of them) they [the 3rd Battalion] became so highly strung that a young Volunteer lost his head and shot one of their best men' (UCDA, Humphreys, P106/384(13), Nell Humphreys to Nora Humphreys, May 1916). In the Dáil Debate of 13 May 1937, de Valera said, '...In 1916 it is true that some Cumann na mBán [*sic*] section offered to serve with us. I do not remember whether it was directly or through some officer. I said we have anxieties of a certain kind here and I do not want to add to them at the moment by getting untrained women, women who were clearly un-trained for soldiering. I did not want them as soldiers in any case. I am not saying for a moment that they may not fight as well as men. That was not the question I had to decide, but I said I did not want them. I did appreciate their services but I did not want them to accept any such work at the time. I said we may have some people wounded, and I would be very glad indeed if we can get some women to take over the dispensary in Grand Canal Street. I think [463] I also indicated that we would have to take some of the men out of the firing line for the purpose of cooking food and that sort of thing. Perhaps that is the origin of the suggestion that I wanted to put women in the kitchen. I think any sensible woman will admit, in these circumstances, that it was not disregard for women's rights that impelled me to act like that. That is the only thing I can remember that could give rise to

the suggestion about women in the kitchen' (*Dáil Debates*, vol. 67, cols 462–3 (13 May 1937)).

[11] Máire Nic Shiubhlaigh, *The splendid years*, as told to Edward Kenny (Dublin, 1955), 154, 155.

[12] 'Julia Grenan', in Donncha Ó Dúlaing (ed.), *Voices of Ireland* (Dublin, 1984), 68–77: 72.

[13] IE/MA, MSP, 34REF15389, McLoughlin, Mary, Letter from the secretary of the Department of Finance to the secretary of the Department of Defence (P. 20/761/39), 19 December 1939.

[14] BMH, WS 934, McLoughlin, Mary, 3–4.

[15] The Seán who told his sister Mary McLoughlin that their mother would kill her is the subject of a biography by Charlie McGuire, *Sean McLoughlin: Ireland's forgotten revolutionary*. It was he, after the evacuation of the GPO, to whom the leaders delegated 'the military command'. Seán MacDermott said that McLoughlin was 'the only one likely to get us out of here'. His final plans were not carried out, however, because Pearse decided to surrender (McGuire, 32, 34).

[16] The 1911 Census returns may be found online at www.census.nationalarchives.ie (10 May 2015).

[17] This and all subsequent quotations from Comerford are taken from an untitled typescript memoir, revised in holograph, a copy of which was given to me by Hilary Dully (Comerford) whose husband, Joe Comerford, is Máire Comerford's nephew.

[18] The description of Máire Comerford on the UCDA website says she was a 'witness' to the Rising; see http://www.ucd.ie/archives/html/collections/comerford-maire.htm (10 May 2015). However, the Comerford family blog says she 'carried dispatches for the G.P.O.'; see http://comerfordfamily.blogspot.com/2009/09/comerford-profiles-21-maire-comerford.html (10 May 2015).

[19] The National Archives (TNA), War Office (WO) 141/19, Letter from J.G. Maxwell, Commander in Chief, Ireland, to the secretary, War Office, 10 May 1916, in Maria Luddy (ed.), *Women in Ireland, 1800–1918: a documentary history* (Cork, 1995), 317.

[20] BMH WS 610, Daly, Una, 4. Sometimes women entered a sacred male space by accident. On Sunday night, 23 April 1916, Rosie Hackett was delivering messages for Connolly and was summoned to a room in Liberty Hall: the message, she writes, 'must have been in connection with the Proclamation, because the type was being fitted at the time. It was right at the back of the hall, and when I went in, one of the men was astounded that I should be allowed in. I just went in with messages to the men', BMH, WS 546, Hackett, Rose, 4–5. Even in Liberty Hall, with the Irish Citizen Army's reputation for gender equality, boundaries, however permeable, obtained. The man was 'astounded' that Hackett should be allowed near the inner sanctum of the Proclamation, but whether the surprise was because of her gender or because she was not a signatory is not clear.

[21] BMH, WS 919, Heron (née Connolly), Ina, 109.

[22] BMH, WS 919, 90.

[23] BMH, WS 805, O'Brien (née Cooney), Annie, and Curran (née Cooney), Lily, 3.

[24] BMH, WS 648, 1.

[25] BMH, WS 391, 33–4.

[26] BMH, WS 805, 9.

27 BMH, WS 482, McNamara, Rose, 8.

28 BMH, WS 399, Mulcahy (née Ryan), Mary Josephine ('Min'), 18.

29 BMH, WS 648, 10.

30 BMH, WS 270, O'Reilly (née O'Hanrahan), Eily, 11–12.

31 BMH, WS 258, MacDowell (née Cavanagh), Maeve, 6. The 'women poets' Cavanagh referred to wrote during the (failed) Young Ireland rising of 1848. She may have been remembering the famous poems of 'Speranza', aka Jane Elgee, later the mother of Oscar Wilde.

32 Mrs Thomas [Helena] Concannon, *Women of 'Ninety-Eight* (Dublin, 1920), vii.

33 BMH, WS 259, Thornton (née Lyons), Brigid, 11. On this subject, the art of women's deceit, but from the male point of view, see Louise Ryan, '"In the line of fire": representations of women and war (1919–1923) through the writings of Republican men', in Louise Ryan and Margaret Ward (eds), *Irish women and nationalism: soldiers, new women and wicked hags* (Dublin and Portland, OR, 2004), 45–61.

34 BMH, WS 210, Morkan, Phyllis, 3.

35 In the 1911 Census, Ní Cheallaigh registered her name in Irish, so this book will follow the spelling that she apparently preferred; see http://www.census.nationalarchives.ie/pages/1911/Dublin/Rotunda/Belvidere_Avenue/29790/ (16 May 2015).

36 BMH, WS 925, Ni Cheallaigh, Mairéad, 8.

37 BMH, WS 648, 9.

38 BMH, WS 398, Martin (née Foley), Brigid, 11.

39 BMH, WS 937, McCarthy (née Ryan), Cathleen, 3.

40 BMH, WS 919, 100–01.

41 On this subject, see Eve Morrison's interesting discussion of how women's 'invisibility' aided their participation in the War of Independence (Morrison, 'The Bureau of Military History and female Republican activism', 62–3).

42 BMH, WS 648, 7–8.

43 In her witness statement, Catherine Byrne names so many of her siblings (Paddy, Jack and Alice) that it is possible to find her among the many Catherine Byrnes in the 1911 Census. Her family lived on Richmond Street North, and as her statement makes clear, they were all, including her parents, militant nationalists, hiding guns in their house and otherwise active in the movement for independence.

44 Plunkett's accoutrements drew much attention, not all of it pleasant. When the Volunteers were seated on the wet grass outside the Rotunda after the surrender, Seán McLoughlin records, 'an officer came up, kicked me on the feet. He also kicked Plunkett on the feet and said: "I suppose you looted those boots"' (BMH, WS 290, McLoughlin, Sean, 32). According to another account, when the rebels were prisoners in Richmond Barracks, British soldiers were 'endeavouring to get hold of a ring which Comdt. Joseph Plunkett was wearing, but which he refused to give up' (BMH, WS 533, Dowling, Thomas, 3–4). Grace Plunkett mentions that ring in her witness statement: 'I am now wearing a ring, which Joe wore during the Rising. It is an Irish-made one. Miss MacDermott of Belfast made it' (BMH, WS 257, Plunkett (née Gifford), Grace, 14).

45 Special Collections Library at the University of Limerick, Daly Papers (UL SCL, P/2 Daly), Madge Daly, 'The memoirs of Madge Daly', typescript draft, Folder 76, 231–2.

[45] BMH, WS 391, 39–40.

[47] BMH, WS 357, Lynn, Kathleen, 6.

[48] BMH, WS 398, Martin (née Foley), Brigid, 15.

[49] BMH, WS 259, 6.

[50] For a more detailed discussion of sexual harassment during the Rising, see Chapter Four.

[51] BMH, WS 648, 4.

[52] BMH, WS 293, Heron, Áine, 4.

[53] 'Miss Hayes' later became Mrs O'Gorman, and she appears in the Military Service Pensions Collection as Mary Christina O'Gorman.

[54] It is interesting that in Eamon Morkan's witness statement he never mentions this wound, possibly because of the somewhat embarrassing way he got it (BMH, WS 411, Morkan, Eamon).

[55] Vera Brittain, *Testament of youth* (London, 1994 edition; originally published 1933), 165–6.

[56] BMH, Report by the Director of the Bureau of Military History to the Minister of Defence, Kevin Boland, for the year ending 31 December, 1957.

[57] For an excellent articulation of this idea, see Karen Steele, 'When female activists say "I": veiled rebels and the counterhistory of Irish independence', in Gillian McIntosh and Diane Urquart (eds), *Irish women at war: the twentieth century* (Dublin and Portland, OR, 2010), 51–68.

## Chapter Two

[1] BMH, WS 648, 15.

[2] BMH, WS 925, Ní Cheallaigh, Mairéad, 2.

[3] BMH, WS 210, Morkan, Phyllis, 3.

[4] BMH, WS 482, 5.

[5] Mary Spring Rice, 'Diary of the *Asgard*, July 1914', in F.X. Martin (ed.), *The Howth gun-running and the Kilcoole gun-running; recollections & documents* (Sallins, 2014), 65–98: 81.

[6] Trinity College Dublin (TCD), Manuscripts and Archives Research Library (MARL), MS 2074, Elsie Mahaffy, 'The Irish rebellion' (diary). I have estimated Mahaffy's age from information in the 1911 Census, where she is listed as 42 years old.

[7] UCDA, Papers of The O'Rahilly, (The O'Rahilly P102), UCHGR/355.

[8] TCD, MARL, MS 2074, Mahaffy, 'The Irish rebellion', 97/113.

[9] The country is England; the hymn was the favourite of the late Diana, Princess of Wales.

[10] W.B. Stanford and R.B. McDowell, *John Pentland Mahaffy: biography of an Anglo–Irishman* (London, 1971), 90.

[11] Montgomery Hyde, *Oscar Wilde: a biography* (London, 1977), 18.

[12] Gerald Griffin, *The Wild Geese* (Norwich, Norf., 1938), 24.

[13] NLI, MS 43332/2, Mary Spring Rice, 'Log of the gun-running cruise in the "Asgard" July 1914', corrected typescript.

[14] TCD, MARL, MS 2074, Mahaffy, 'The Irish rebellion', 1r.

[15] TCD, MARL, MS 2074, Mahaffy, 'The Irish rebellion', 123r.

[16] TCD, MARL, MS 2074, Mahaffy, 'The Irish rebellion', 122v. It begins, 'Says Lady Aberdeen / "I'm a step below your Queen. / She lives beyond the sea, and loves you dearly / I love you just as well / And I've come with you to dwell / For the paltry sum of twenty-thousand yearly."'

[17] F.X. Martin, *The Howth gun-running and the Kilcoole gun-running: recollections and documents* (Sallins, 2014), 54.

[18] Martin, *The Howth gun-running*, 54.

[19] Spring Rice, 'Diary of the *Asgard*', 85. The six people were Erskine and Molly Childers, Mary Spring Rice, Gordon Shephard, and two men from Gola Island, Co. Donegal, Charles Duggan and Patrick McGinley.

[20] Spring Rice, 'Diary of the *Asgard*', 66.

[21] Spring Rice, 'Diary of the *Asgard*', 98.

[22] No attribution for the corrections is given, but the handwriting looks similar to that in letters from Spring Rice to The O'Rahilly.

[23] All deletion marks are taken from NLI, MS 43,332/1, Mary Spring Rice, 'Log of the gun-running cruise in the "Asgard" July 1914'.

[24] See also her letters to The O'Rahilly, UCDA, The O'Rahilly P102/335, which also focus exclusively on practical details and not politics.

[25] Spring Rice, 'Diary of the *Asgard*', 92.

[26] Spring Rice, 'Diary of the *Asgard*', 69.

[27] Spring Rice, 'Diary of the *Asgard*', 69.

[28] Spring Rice, 'Diary of the *Asgard*', 76.

[29] Spring Rice, 'Diary of the *Asgard*', 77.

[30] Spring Rice, 'Diary of the *Asgard*', 78.

[31] Spring Rice, 'Diary of the *Asgard*', 78.

[32] Spring Rice, 'Diary of the *Asgard*', 79.

[33] Spring Rice, 'Diary of the *Asgard*', 79.

[34] Spring Rice, 'Diary of the *Asgard*', 82.

[35] Molly Childers, 'Letters to Alice Stopford Green', in Martin, *The Howth gun-running*, 98–109: 104.

[36] Spring Rice, 'Diary of the *Asgard*', 83.

[37] Spring Rice, 'Diary of the *Asgard*', 71.

[38] Spring Rice, 'Diary of the *Asgard*', 69.

[39] Spring Rice, 'Diary of the *Asgard*', 82.

[40] Elsie Henry, *The world upturning: Elsie Henry's Irish wartime diaries 1913–1919*, ed. Clara Cullen (Dublin, 2012), 46.

[41] TCD, MARL, MS 2074, Mahaffy, 'The Irish rebellion', 36r.

[42] Declan Kiberd, *1916 rebellion handbook* (Belfast, 1998), 16.

[43] TCD, MARL, MS 2074, Mahaffy, 'The Irish rebellion', 18r.

[44] TCD, MARL, MS 2074, Mahaffy, 'The Irish rebellion', 17r–18r.

[45] TCD, MARL, MS 2074, Mahaffy, 'The Irish rebellion', 111r.

[46] The National Volunteers split with the Irish Volunteers in September 1914 and supported John Redmond's appeal for Irish men to enlist in the British army.

[47] Stanford and McDowell, *John Pentland Mahaffy*, 222.

[48] TCD, MARL, MS 2074, Mahaffy, 'The Irish rebellion', 24r.

[49] TCD, MARL, MS 2074, Mahaffy, 'The Irish rebellion', 24r.

[50] The dead Volunteer was Gerald Keogh. For his story, see Raymond M. Keogh, 'Well dressed and from a respectable street', *History Ireland* 17:2 (2009), 32–3.

[51] TCD, MARL, MS 2074, Mahaffy, 'The Irish rebellion', 30r.

[52] TCD, MARL, MS 2074, Mahaffy, 'The Irish rebellion', 100r.

[53] Earlscliffe House, Baily, Co. Dublin, was owned by John Pentland Mahaffy between 1901 and 1922. For further information see http://www.earlscliffe.com/residents_1901_1922.htm (11 May 2015).

[54] BMH, WS 270, O'Reilly (née O'Hanrahan), Eily, 15.

[55] TCD, MARL, MS 2074, Mahaffy, 'The Irish rebellion', 31r.

[56] TCD, MARL, MS 2074, Mahaffy, 'The Irish rebellion', 32r.

[57] TCD, MARL, MS 2074, Mahaffy, 'The Irish rebellion', 37r–38r.

[58] TCD, MARL, MS 2074, Mahaffy, 'The Irish rebellion', 49r. See Chapter Seven for the accounts of the women in these houses.

[59] TCD, MARL, MS 2074, Mahaffy, 'The Irish rebellion', 75r–76r.

[60] TCD, MARL, MS 2074, Mahaffy, 'The Irish rebellion', 73r.

[61] TCD, MARL, MS 2074, Mahaffy, 'The Irish rebellion', 60r.

[62] TCD, MARL, MS 2074, Mahaffy, 'The Irish rebellion', 113r.

[63] TCD, MARL, MS 2074, Mahaffy, 'The Irish rebellion', 82r.

[64] *Hansard Commons* vol. 82, cols 935–70 (11 May 1916).

[65] TCD, MARL, MS 2074, Mahaffy, 'The Irish rebellion', 83r.

[66] TCD, MARL, MS 2074, Mahaffy, 'The Irish rebellion', 93r–93v.

[67] In the following pages, she describes her own visit to North King Street the previous day. Although she is sympathetic to the sufferings inflicted on the British soldiers, her main response is revulsion at the Irish 'girls' who are soliciting the favours of the soldiers: 'In the old days we all believed that Irish women were dignified and pure,—these hussies were more than forward' (97r).

[68] TCD, MARL, MS 2074, Mahaffy, 'The Irish rebellion', 84r–85r.

[69] TCD, MARL, MS 2074, Mahaffy, 'The Irish rebellion', 86r.

[70] TCD, MARL, MS 2074, Mahaffy, 'The Irish rebellion', 86r–87r.

[71] Very little information of any sort exists about Elsie Mahaffy. There is, however, one small piece of evidence connecting her with Margot Asquith: 'Very modern and up to date is Miss Mahaffy's Knitting Industry: and it is particularly interesting as from its cottages come some of the most popular fashions of the day! This industry has been working for many years, having been started by Lady Margaret Domville in Howth Village in the "Eighties"; but since 1899 it has much increased, as in that year Lady Ribblesdale invented the universal "Golf Jersey", which now abounds in all shapes and styles in every mercer's shop over Europe. Mrs. Asquith furnished another design in 1900...' ('The work of the women's world', in Chalmers Roberts (ed.), *The world's work* (London, 1907), vol. ix, 638).

[72] TCD, MARL, MS 2074, Mahaffy, 'The Irish rebellion', 14v–14v/1.

[73] 'Miss Mahaffy', *Irish Times,* 6 November 1926, 7. The short obituary calls her 'a lady of high intelligence and wide reading' and mentions her knitting business.

[74] Mahaffy's diary was digitised in 2013, and posted online by Trinity College, Dublin, 2014.

## Chapter Three

[1] Gerard MacAtasney, *Tom Clarke: life, liberty, revolution* (Sallins, 2013), 232.

[2] See http://www.census.nationalarchives.ie/reels/nai000075502/

[3] BMH, WS 411, Morkan, Eamon, 18.

[4] It is interesting, though hardly surprising, that babies born to wives of men 'out' in 1916 were named after 1916 leaders: Agnes Mallin's daughter was Maura Constance Connolly, after Constance Markievicz, the second-in-command at the College of Surgeons, where Mallin's husband Michael was Commandant, and James Connolly. Sinéad and Éamon de Valera's son Rúaidhrí was named after Roger Casement; Maeve Brennan's full name was Maeve Bridget Clarke Brennan, after Tom Clarke. Phyllis Morkan's baby was named Edward Daly Morkan; and the son of Volunteer John Furlong and his wife Kathleen was named Rory, after Roger Casement. For information on Furlong, see http://mspcsearch.militaryarchives.ie/docs/files//PDF_Pensions/R3/DP1012JOHNFURLONG/WDP1012JOHNFURL-ONG.pdf (1 July 2015). Furlong also appears in Robert Brennan's memoir *Allegiance*.

[5] BMH, WS 293, 3; BMH, WS 210, 4ff and BMH, WS 411, 18; BMH, WS 779, Brennan, Robert, 111; and see Yvonne Jerrold's website: http://www.yvonnejer-rold.com/RBrennan/Robert%20Brennan%201881-1964.html (12 May 2015).

[6] Tessa Finn (ed.), *Letters—May and James: a private love in a revolutionary year* (Dublin, 2012), 125.

[7] BMH, WS 314, O'Carroll, Liam, 5.

[8] Clarke, *Revolutionary woman*, 68.

[9] Finn, *Letters—May and James*, 137.

[10] Finn, *Letters—May and James*, 138.

[11] Finn, *Letters—May and James*, 10.

[12] Finn, *Letters—May and James*, 137.

[13] Finn, *Letters—May and James*, 152.

[14] Finn, *Letters—May and James*, 155. In the event, they honeymooned in West Cork, possibly to avoid the imminent 'second rebellion'.

[15] Finn, *Letters—May and James*, 148.

[16] Finn, *Letters—May and James*, 161.

[17] Charles Townshend, *Easter 1916: the Irish rebellion* (London, 2005), 305.

[18] Cesca Trench, *Cesca's diary 1913–1916*, ed. Hilary Pyle (Dublin, 2005), 149.

[19] Trench, *Cesca's diary*, 208.

[20] Trench, *Cesca's diary*, 279–80; see also http://www.ainm.ie/Bio.aspx?ID=415 (1 July 2015).

[21] Finn, *Letters—May and James*, 171–2.

[22] BMH, WS 246, Flanagan (née Perolz), Marie, 4.

[23] BMH, WS 118, O'Mahony, Patrick C., 5.

[24] BMH, WS 259, 2.

[25] As quoted in Ferriter, *The transformation of Ireland*, 92.

[26] TCD, MARL, MS 2074, Mahaffy, *Irish rebellion*, 60r.

[27] Stanford and McDowell, *John Pentland Mahaffy*, 27.

[28] Lilly Stokes, 'Easter Week diary', in Roger McHugh (ed.), *Dublin 1916* (Dublin and London, 1966), 63–79: 66.

[29] Stokes, 'Easter Week diary', 75–6.

[30] BMH, WS 805, 7.

[31] BMH, WS 856, Colbert, Elizabeth ('Lila'), 3.

[32] The story of Lucy Smyth and Tom Byrne is the subject of a short documentary, *A terrible beauty*, directed by Keith Farrell and produced by David Farrell. See www.storiesfrom1916.com/tomandlucy/ (11 May 2015).

[33] BMH, WS 805, 2.

[34] BMH, WS 805, 4 and 5.

[35] BMH, WS 805, 6. Eileen Cooney also performed nationalist work with her future husband. Her sister Lily Cooney's statement notes, 'We were to accompany two Volunteers, Sean Harbourne—who is now Eileen's husband—and Andy Healy who was adjutant of F/Coy. to the vicinity of the prison...We were to play the part of courting couples' (BMH, WS 805, 30).

[36] Annie Cooney was 15 years old at the time of the 1911 Census; if she was born in 1896, she would have been about 57 years of age when she wrote her witness statement.

[37] BMH, WS 805, 10.

[38] BMH, WS 805, 13.

[39] BMH, WS 805, 16.

[40] BMH, WS 805, supplementary statement, 3 May 1963.

[41] Clarke, *Revolutionary woman*, 68.

[42] BMH, WS 328, Holohan, Garry, 50.

[43] BMH, WS 564, Byrne, Thomas P., 25.

[44] Mary J. Ryan, 'Sean McDermott' [*sic*], in Maurice Joy (ed.), *The Irish rebellion of 1916 and its martyrs: Erin's tragic Easter* (New York, 1916), 372–9: 377.

[45] Clarke, *Revolutionary woman*, 68. To which Clarke replied, that he'd better dance now, because he might be 'dancing at the end of a rope' sometime soon.

[46] BMH, WS 399, 12–13.

[47] BMH, WS 1765, O'Kelly, Seán T., 243.

[48] BMH, WS 399, 14.

[49] BMH, WS 399, 17.

[50] Risteárd Mulcahy, *Richard Mulcahy (1886–1971): a family memoir* (Dublin, 1999), 279.

[51] For a discussion of the last meeting of Ryan and MacDermott, see Chapter Six.

[52] BMH, WS 257, 9.

[53] Geraldine Plunkett Dillon, *All in the blood*, ed. Honor O Brolchain (Dublin, 2012), 221.

[54] Dillon, *All in the blood*, 221.

[55] Marie O'Neill, *Grace Gifford Plunkett and Irish freedom: tragic bride of 1916* (Dublin, 2000), 44.

[56] Dillon, *All in the blood*, 221.

[57] Dillon, *All in the blood*, 222.

[58] BMH, WS 257, 12.

[59] Anne Mac Lellan, *Dorothy Stopford Price: rebel doctor* (Sallins, 2014), 26.

[60] Bodleian Library of Commonwealth and African Studies at Rhodes House, Oxford (Bodl. RH), Nathan Papers, Ms. N. 476, Estelle Nathan, Letter 'Thursday Morning'.

[61] Bodl. RH, Nathan Papers, Ms. N. 476.

[62] TCDDH, 'The 1916 diary of Dorothy Stopford Price', 28 April 1916.

[63] J. Harvey et al. (eds), *Biographical dictionary of women in science*, (Abingdon, Oxon, 2000), 1054.

[64] Mac Lellan, *Dorothy Stopford Price*, 39, 40.

[65] See http://dh.tcd.ie/pricediary/about-dorothy-price-her-family/about-dorothy-price/ (21 July 2015).

## Chapter Four

[1] Angela Bourke, 'More in anger than in sorrow', in Joan Radnor (ed.), *Feminist messages: coding in women's folk culture* (Urbana, IL, 1993), 160–82: 167. Translated by Angela Bourke.

[2] Bourke, 'More in anger than in sorrow', 161.

[3] See http://www.gaelchultur.com/en/newsletters/newsletterarticle.aspx?id=156 (12 May 2015).

[4] Bourke, 'More in anger than in sorrow', 172.

[5] Ward, *Hanna Sheehy Skeffington*, 86–96.

[6] Ward, *Hanna Sheehy Skeffington*, 71.

[7] Ward, *Hanna Sheehy Skeffington*, 283.

[8] Hanna Sheehy Skeffington, 'A pacifist dies', in McHugh (ed.), *Dublin 1916*, 276–88: 283.

[9] BMH, WS 1754, Barry (née Price), Leslie, 11.

[10] Price calls the priest 'Father O'Flanagan', but he was actually Father Flanagan, not to be confused with the Sinn Féin priest Father O'Flanagan.

[11] BMH, WS 1754, 12–13. See also Aoife de Burca's very different account of this same episode (BMH, WS 359, 14–15).

[12] BMH, WS 1754, 12–20.

[13] UL SCL, P/2 Daly, 'Memoirs of Madge Daly', 117A–17B.

[14] Clarke, *Revolutionary woman*, 92–3.

[15] For a similar (though fictional) episode in which an angry woman attacks a priest, see Aunt Kate's attack on the Pope in 'The Dead' (in James Joyce's *Dubliners*).

[16] BMH, WS 398, 14.

[17] BMH, WS 246, 11.

[18] Mary Douglas, *Purity and danger: an analysis of the concepts of pollution and taboo* (Abingdon, Oxon, 1984), 115.

[19] McGarry, *Rebels*, 313.

[20] Joe Sweeney, *Curious journey: an oral history of Ireland's unfinished revolution* (Cork, 1998), 7.

[21] These and all subsequent quotations from Elizabeth O'Farrell are taken from the Allen Library, Dublin, IE/AL/1916/95/2, 'The personal account of the surrender at the G.P.O. and other posts', annotated typescript. 'C. of the B.F. in I' is the Commander of the British Forces in Ireland and 'the Irish R. Army' is the IRA; also note the misspelling of Portal.

[22] Ward, *Hanna Sheehy Skeffington*, 159.

[23] Hanna Sheehy Skeffington's account of her attempts to get information about the murder of her husband has been identified in Roger McHugh's book *Dublin 1916* as 'From her lecture, delivered in 1917'.

[24] Ward, *Hanna Sheehy Skeffington*, 165, gives the figure eighteen months.

[25] Ward, *Hanna Sheehy Skeffington*, 184.

[26] Ward, *Hanna Sheehy Skeffington*, 205.

[27] Sheehy Skeffington 'A pacifist dies', 282.

[28] Sheehy Skeffington 'A pacifist dies', 283.

[29] Sheehy Skeffington 'A pacifist dies', 283–4. Hanna Sheehy Skeffington's comment is reminiscent of what Clarke said to her husband in his cell: 'I wish the British would put a bullet in me too'.

[30] Sheehy Skeffington 'A pacifist dies', 286–7.

[31] Bourke, 'More in anger than in sorrow', 161.

[32] Gertrude Parry, 'The last days of Roger Casement', in McHugh, *Dublin 1916*, 289–305: 290.

[33] Parry, 'The last days of Roger Casement', 298.

[34] Parry, 'The last days of Roger Casement', 299.

[35] Parry, 'The last days of Roger Casement', 300.


## Chapter Five

[1] Rose McNamara writes 'Tuesday May 2nd', but the first rebels were executed early in the morning of 3 May. Either McNamara got the date wrong, or the soldiers were practising their marksmanship.

[2] The six 'girls' from the North who went from Belfast to Dublin on Saturday, 22 April (and back to Belfast on Monday morning, 24 April) were sisters Elizabeth and Nell Corr, sisters Nora and Ina Connolly, Kathleen O'Kelly (later Murphy), and Eilis Allen (information taken BMH, WS 179, Corr, Elizabeth and Nell, 2). They are called 'girls' by Nora Connolly O'Brien frequently in her memoir *The unbroken tradition* and also by James Connolly, as quoted by the Corr sisters: 'Well, girls, we start operations at noon today. This is the Proclamation of the Republic' (BMH, WS 179, 5).

[3] BMH, WS 805, 5.

[4] BMH, WS 805, 10.

[5] BMH, WS 259, 7.

[6] BMH, WS 805, 11–12.

[7] BMH, WS 432, Keating (née Morkan), Pauline, 5.

[8] Spring Rice, 'Diary of the *Asgard*', 75, 85.

[9] Spring Rice, 'Diary of the *Asgard*', 104.

[10] Spring Rice, 'Diary of the *Asgard*', 93.

[11] Spring Rice, 'Diary of the *Asgard*', 94.

[12] Spring Rice, 'Diary of the *Asgard*', 94.

[13] Spring Rice, 'Diary of the *Asgard*', 88.

[14] Spring Rice, 'Diary of the *Asgard*', 98.

[15] Clarke, *Revolutionary woman*, 84.

[16] Clarke, *Revolutionary woman*, 84. According to Helen Litton, Clarke's grand-niece, the funds were £2,000 in gold.

[17] Clarke, *Revolutionary woman*, 86. Helen Litton says, 'family legend holds that Kattie had difficulty retrieving the money later, but the situation was eventually resolved with the aid of a local priest' (private message). The bodice was not the only place that money collected by Tom Clarke was hidden. Máire Smartt had also secreted funds in domestic space, as she explains in her witness statement. The raid she refers to took place at the end of Easter Week; 'Mícheál' is her fiancé, later her husband, Mícheál Ó Foghludha. She writes, 'I had a big bundle of notes which Mícheál had given me to mind. I think it was about £500. I had it in the safe at Findlater's, of which I had the key. I must have brought it home during Holy Week when I knew the Rising was coming off. I ripped a feather bolster and put the bundle of notes among the feathers. I was trembling in fear lest the soldiers would find it during the raid, but they did not. Mícheál, with whom I discussed this matter recently, told me that this money had been given him by Tom Clarke some time before the Rising and having collected the money from me, when he saw me after the Rising, he handed it over to Mrs. Clarke subsequent to her release from Kilmainham' BMH, WS 539, Smartt, 4–5.

[18] TCD, MARL, MS 2074, Mahaffy, 'The Irish rebellion', 161r.

[19] Dillon, *All in the blood*, 234.

[20] Dillon, *All in the blood*, 247.

[21] For a double biography of Constance Markievicz and her husband Casimir, see Lauren Arrington, *Revolutionary lives: Constance and Casimir Markievicz* (Princeton, NJ, 2015).

[22] Nurse Margaretta Keogh was also killed in the Rising, but not in combat; she was stationed at the South Dublin Union and had gone to look after people who might have been hurt by a volley of gunfire when soldiers hiding in a corridor shot and killed her (Ruth Taillon, *When history was made: the women of 1916* (Belfast, 1996), 60–1). See also Aoife de Burca: 'I met a nurse of my acquaintance who told me her best friend, Nurse Keogh, had been shot dead in the S.D.U. I felt very sorry as I knew Nurse Keogh myself' (BMH, WS 359, 13). For a longer commentary, see Keith Jeffery, 'Nationalisms and gender: Ireland in the time of the Great War 1914–1918', http://www.oslo2000.uio.no/program/papers/r13/r13-jeffery.pdf (1 July 2015). Jeffery mentions that 'over 40 women bystanders were killed during the Rising', 2.

[23] Margaret Skinnider, *Doing my bit for Ireland* (New York, 1917), 6. For an analysis of Skinnider's sartorial choices, see Lisa Weihman, '*Doing my bit for Ireland*: transgressing gender in the Easter Rising', *Éire–Ireland* 39 (2004), 215–36.

[24] Skinnider, *Doing my bit for Ireland*, 7.

[25] Skinnider, *Doing my bit for Ireland*, 5.

[26] Skinnider, *Doing my bit for Ireland*, 4.

[27] Skinnider, *Doing my bit for Ireland*, 3.

[28] Skinnider, *Doing my bit for Ireland*, 4.

[29] Skinnider, *Doing my bit for Ireland*, 12.

[30] Skinnider, *Doing my bit for Ireland*, 15.

[31] Skinnider, *Doing my bit for Ireland*, 31. According to Lauren Arrington, author of *Revolutionary lives: Constance and Casimir Markievicz*, 'Markievicz was in the

Citizen Army, not the Volunteers.' Arrington believes Skinnider may simply be wrong about Markievicz or she may be assuming that that once the Rising had started, there was only one army, that of the Irish Republic.

[32] Skinnider, *Doing my bit for Ireland*, 38.

[33] Skinnider, *Doing my bit for Ireland*, 39.

[34] Skinnider, *Doing my bit for Ireland*, 40.

[35] Skinnider, *Doing my bit for Ireland*, 39, 40.

[36] See the end of Chapter One for a discussion of Vera Brittain's *Testament of youth*.

[37] Elaine Showalter, 'Dark places', *New York Times*, Sunday Book Review, 6 June 2013, BR 35.

[38] BMH, WS 398, 13.

[39] Quotations by kind permission of the Royal College of Physicians of Ireland (RCPI) from ACC/1990/1, Kathleen Lynn diaries, KL/1.

[40] BMH, WS 398, 13.

[41] Clarke, *Revolutionary woman*, 89.

[42] Clarke, *Revolutionary woman*, 91.

[43] Clarke, *Revolutionary woman*, 90.

[44] Clarke, *Revolutionary woman*, 90–1.

## Chapter Six

[1] These words and variations of them are cited frequently (in quotation marks) with reference to the statue, but nowhere is a source given.

[2] Piaras F. Mac Lochlainn (ed.), *Last words: letters and statements of the leaders executed after the Rising at Easter 1916* (Dublin, 1990), 112, 113. The editor notes that he is paraphrasing 'a statement' from Heuston's sister (116).

[3] Mac Lochlainn, *Last words*, 79.

[4] BMH, WS 257, 12.

[5] Mac Lochlainn, *Last words*, 96–7.

[6] Nora Connolly O'Brien, *The unbroken tradition* (New York, 1918, repr. Memphis, TN, 2010), 184–5.

[7] BMH, WS 286, 51 and Mac Lochlainn, *Last words*, 191.

[8] Mac Lochlainn, *Last words*, 146.

[9] Mac Lochlainn, *Last words*, 149.

[10] Mac Lochlainn, *Last words*, 150–1. The soldier in Seán Heuston's cell was also crying (Mac Lochlainn, *Last words*, 112).

[11] UL SCL, P/2 Daly, 'Memoirs of Madge Daly', 123; Mac Lochlainn, *Last words*, 112; Ryan, 'Sean McDermott', 373–4; Nora Connolly O'Brien, *Unbroken tradition*, 183.

[12] UL SCL, P/2 Daly, 'Memoirs of Madge Daly', 123.

[13] UL SCL, P/2 Daly, 'Memoirs of Madge Daly', 124.

[14] Clarke, *Revolutionary woman*, 93.

[15] Edith Cavell was a British nurse who helped Allied soldiers hide and escape from the Germans during the First World War. She was captured and executed by a German firing squad in 1915.

[16] Clarke, *Revolutionary woman*, 95.

[17] Clarke, *Revolutionary woman*, 95–6.

[18] UL SCL, P/2 Daly, 'Memoirs of Madge Daly', 124.

[19] Clarke, *Revolutionary woman*, 118.

[20] UL SCL, P/2 Daly, 'Memoirs of Madge Daly', 125.

[21] UL SCL, P/2 Daly, 'Memoirs of Madge Daly', 125.

[22] UL SCL, P/2 Daly, 'Memoirs of Madge Daly', 126.

[23] UL SCL, P/2 Daly, 'Memoirs of Madge Daly', 128.

[24] UL SCL, P/2 Daly, 'Memoirs of Madge Daly', 22.

[25] Clarke, *Revolutionary woman*, 119.

[26] BMH, WS 270, 10–11.

[27] Constance Markievicz, 'The women of '98', *Irish Citizen* (1915), 4 December 1915; see https://www.marxists.org/archive/markievicz/1915/11/women98.html, (13 May 2015).

[28] BMH, WS 270, 11; Anna M'Cleery, 'Life of Mary Ann McCracken', in Robert M. Young (ed.), *Historical notices of old Belfast and its vicinity; a selection from the mss. collected by William Pinkerton, F.S.A., for his intended history of Belfast, additional documents, letters, and ballads, O'Mellan's narrative of the wars of 1641, biography of Mary Ann McCracken, now first printed. With maps and illustrations/edited, with notes, by Robert M. Young* (Belfast 1896), 175–97: 186; see https://archive.org/stream/historicalnotice00youn/historicalnotice00youn_djvu.txt (13 May 2015).

[29] M'Cleery, 'Life of Mary Ann McCracken'.

[30] Mac Lochlainn, *Last words*, 172.

[31] BMH, WS 257, 12–13.

[32] Mac Lochlainn, *Last words*, 172.

[33] Ryan, 'Sean McDermott', 374.

[34] Mac Lochlainn, *Last words*, 170.

[35] Ryan, 'Sean McDermott', 375.

[36] Ryan, 'Sean McDermott', 375.

[37] Parry, 'The last days of Roger Casement', 304–5.

[38] As quoted in Jeffrey Dudgeon, *Roger Casement: the Black Diaries—with a study of his background, sexuality and Irish political life* (Belfast, 2002), 9.

[39] The comments from the Pentonville priests are as quoted in Dudgeon, *Roger Casement*, 9.

## Chapter Seven

[1] UCDA, Humphreys, P106/976.

[2] BMH, WS 563, Cremen, Michael, 6 and BMH, WS 724, Ryan, Desmond, 9. Cremen's account records Connolly's words as 'Thank God, Pearse, we (or I) have lived to see this day!'

[3] BMH, WS 779, Brennan, Robert, 94–5.

[4] BMH, WS, 359, 27.

[5] 'After some time Paddy was not saying anything. Jim spoke to him and got no reply. He pulled him by the coat and he fell over into his arms. He was shot

through the head. We told Dick Murphy about him and we three said a prayer for his soul.' (BMH, WS 198, Walsh, Thomas and Walsh, James, 19).

[6] BMH, WS 416, Cregan, Máirín, 6.

[7] Elizabeth Bloxham, a Protestant nationalist working in County Down, also inspired arguments during the Rising, though they were mostly one-on-one; see BMH, WS 632, 22.

[8] Dillon, *All in the blood,* 233.

[9] Clarke, *Revolutionary woman,* 127.

[10] Mary Louisa Hamilton Norway, 'The Sinn Féin Rebellion as I saw it', in Jeffery, *Sinn Féin rebellion,* 33–86: 69.

[11] BMH, WS 779, 154–5. It is interesting to note that Brennan did not include this exchange in the published version of his memoir, the book *Allegiance.*

[12] I considered looking at the idea of 'emotion' in terms of 'writing trauma', but decided against it because most of the women were concerned with getting on the record the events they witnessed or took part in; they were not writing to 'heal' a trauma. Of course, their documents could still be understood in that context, but the idea of emotions as major events seemed to me a more useful conceptual framework.

[13] BMH, WS 779, 102.

[14] BMH, WS 258, MacDowell (née Cavanagh), Maeve, 12.

[15] From 'They went forth to battle but they always fell', by Shaemas O'Sheel [*sic*].

[16] As several people have pointed out to me, Cavanagh's witness statement was written (or spoken) in 1949, a date long after the Civil War. The tone of her comments about O'Connell may reflect her Republican perspective on his Free State politics, just as his word 'hysterical' reflects the opinion of a Free-Stater about a republican. Her comments on his tears remain significant.

[17] Margaret O'Callaghan, 'Women and politics in independent Ireland, 1921–68', in Angela Bourke *et al.* (eds), *The Field Day anthology of Irish writing vol. v: Irish women's writing and traditions,* 120–34: xlii + 1711, (Cork, 2002), 123.

[18] BMH, WS 298, Monahan, Alf, 48.

[19] See witness statements by Christopher (Christy) Byrne (BMH, WS 167), Liam Tobin (BMH, WS 1753), Arthur Greene (BMH, WS 238) and Thomas Cleary (BMH, WS 972), among many others.

[20] BMH, WS 333, O'Rahilly, Áine, 5. See also Aodagán O'Rahilly's emphasis on his father's singing in his biography *Winding the clock: O'Rahilly and the 1916 Rising* (Dublin, 1991).

[21] BMH, WS 195, Reynolds, Molly, 3.

[22] W.B. Yeats, 'The O'Rahilly', *The variorum edition of the poems of W.B. Yeats,* eds Peter Allt and Russell K. Alspach (New York, 1977), 585.

[23] BMH, WS 805, O'Brien (née Cooney), Annie and Curran (née Cooney), Lily, 5.

[24] BMH, WS 286, O'Brien (née Connolly), Nora, 33. For the lyrics, see Padraic O'Farrell (ed.), *The '98 Reader* (Minneapolis, MN, 1998), 164.

[25] BMH, WS 934, McLoughlin, Mary, 4.

[26] She also remembered it in 1938 when she was interviewed for a military service pension application: IE/MA, MSP 34REF15389, McLoughlin, Mary, Sworn statement before the Advisory Committee, 4 February 1938, 5.

[27] Both quotations are from MacDonagh's translation.

[28] Honor O Brolchain, *Joseph Plunkett* (Dublin, 2012), 398.

[29] Angela Bourke, 'Performing, not writing: the reception of an Irish woman's lament', in Yopie Prins and Maeera Schreiber (eds), *Dwelling in possibility: women poets and critics on poetry* (Ithaca, NY, 1997), 132–46: 134.

[30] John Millington Synge, *The Aran Islands*, ed. Tim Robinson (London, 1992), 31.

[31] McHugh, *Dublin 1916*, 220 ff.

[32] McHugh, *Dublin 1916*, 223.

[33] McHugh, *Dublin 1916*, 224.

[34] McHugh, *Dublin 1916*, 224.

[35] McHugh, *Dublin 1916*, 225.

[36] Seán Ó Tuama and Thomas Kinsella, *An Dunaire. 1600–1900: poems of the dispossessed* (Portlaoise, 1981), 204, 206, 212.

[37] Clarke, *Revolutionary woman*, 127.

[38] See http://www.crystalinks.com/nde.html (15 May 2015).

[39] George Eliot, *Middlemarch* (Boston, MA, 1956; 1968 impression), 578.

[40] Clarke, *Revolutionary woman*, 118.

[41] BMH, WS 850, Colgan, Patrick, 24.

[42] Nevil Shute, *Slide rule: an autobiography* (London, 1954), 14.

[43] Shute, *Slide rule*, 15.

[44] Máirtín Mac Con Iomaire, 'Kenneth George Besson', in James McGuire and James Quinn (eds), *Dictionary of Irish biography* (9 vols, Cambridge, 2009), vol. 1, 505–06, available online at dib.cambridge.org.

[45] Mary Louisa Hamilton Norway, 'The Sinn Fein rebellion as I saw it', in Jeffery, *Sinn Féin rebellion*, 33–86: 41, 59.

[46] Arthur Hamilton Norway, 'Irish experiences in war', in Jeffery, *Sinn Féin rebellion*, 87–122: 117.

[47] Mary Louisa Hamilton Norway, 'The Sinn Fein rebellion as I saw it', 58.

[48] Mary Louisa Hamilton Norway, 'The Sinn Fein rebellion as I saw it', 67.

[49] Mary Louisa Hamilton Norway, 'The Sinn Fein rebellion as I saw it', 55.

[50] Mary Louisa Hamilton Norway, 'The Sinn Fein rebellion as I saw it', 62.

[51] Mary Louisa Hamilton Norway, 'The Sinn Fein rebellion as I saw it', 77.

[52] Mary Louisa Hamilton Norway, 'The Sinn Fein rebellion as I saw it', 79–80.

[53] Mary Louisa Hamilton Norway, 'The Sinn Fein rebellion as I saw it', 48.

[54] BMH, WS 359, 20–1.

[55] See, for instance, the accounts of Louise Gavan Duffy (BMH, WS 216), Patrick Colgan (BMH, WS 850), and Molly Reynolds (BMH, WS 195), who also describe the evacuation through the Coliseum but who do not mention the contagious laughter.

[56] Mary Borden, *The forbidden zone* (New York: Doubleday, 1930) 143.

[57] Hochschild, *The managed heart*.

[58] Interview with Éanna de Búrca in Maurice O'Keefe (ed.), *1916 Rising oral history collection*. Irish Life and Lore, CD 15 Tralee, 2013.

## Conclusion

[1] BMH, WS 432, 3.

[2] Margaret MacCurtain, 'The historical image', in Eiléan Ní Chuilleanáin (ed.), *Irish women: image and achievement* (Dublin, 1985), 37–50: 49.

[3] Maryann Gialanella Valiulis, 'Virtuous mothers and dutiful wives: the politics of sexuality in the Irish Free State', in Valiulis (ed.), *Gender and power in Irish history*, 100–14: 101.

[4] Morrison, 'The Bureau of Military History and female Republican activism', 73.

[5] Morrison, 'The Bureau of Military History and female Republican activism', 73.

[6] For a history of Irish women's activism and achievements in the twentieth century, see Linda Connolly, *The Irish women's movement: from revolution to devolution* (Houndmills, Basingstoke, 2002).

[7] Rosita Boland, 'Micheline Sheehy Skeffington: "I'm from a family of feminists. I took this case to honour them"', *Irish Times*, 6 December 2014.

[8] A discussion of this passage appears in Chapter Three.

[9] 'Sean T. O'Kelly's sister dies', *Irish Independent*, 30 December 1971.

[10] BMH, WS 925, Ní Cheallaigh, Mairéad, 2.

[11] That 'last morning' is almost a trope in the women's accounts, remembered also in reverential detail by Annie Cooney (about Con Colbert) and Kathleen Clarke (about Tom Clarke).

[12] BMH, WS 925, 5.

[13] In those pre-Rising days, the leaders were great meat-eaters. Foster mentions Min Ryan's disapproval when she saw Seán MacDermott 'ordering a large steak' on Good Friday (Foster, *Vivid faces*, 229).

[14] BMH, WS 925, 4.

[15] BMH, WS 925, 4.

[16] BMH, WS 925, 6–7.

[17] BMH, WS 925, 7.

[18] BMH, WS 925, 7–8.

[19] Seth Koven, 'Borderlands' in Koven and Michel (eds), *Mothers of a new world*, 94–135: 95–6.

[20] Constance Markievicz and Margaret Skinnider did not function on such a 'borderland': they were shooting with the men on the front lines, though it took some argument for Skinnider to get there. Their sartorial experiments, however, suggest that they perceived and constructed themselves on a border of gender, either alternating between women's and men's clothing, as Skinnider did, or wearing both together, as Markievicz did in the famous photograph of her in a soldier's uniform and a feathered woman's hat. See Chapter Five for a fuller discussion and see also Weihman, '*Doing my bit for Ireland*: transgressing gender', 215–36.

[21] Arthur Hamilton Norway, 'Irish experiences in war', in Jeffery, *Sinn Féin rebellion*, 87–122: 113, 117.

[22] Maria Luddy, *Women and philanthropy in nineteenth century Ireland* (Cambridge, 1995), 4.

[23] See Jacinta Prunty, 'Margaret Louisa Aylward', in Mary Cullen and Maria Luddy (eds), *Women, power and consciousness in 19th century Ireland* (Dublin, 1995), 55–

88; and Mary Peckham Magray, *The transforming power of the nuns: women, religion, and cultural change in Ireland, 1750–1900* (New York and Oxford, 1998).

[24] Bourke *et al.*, *Irish women's writing and traditions.*

[25] In an essay on gender in 'Ireland during the Great War', Keith Jeffery notes that the war had changed the arena in which women 'noncombatants' could operate by making more and different labours available to them, labours previously open only to men. Women 'who had never before stepped out of the domestic environment' were 'socially, if not also economically, empowered by their experience' (Keith Jeffery, 'Nationalisms and gender: Ireland in the time of the Great War 1914–1918'; see http://www.oslo2000.uio.no/program/papers/r13/r13jeffery.pdf).

[26] Ward, *Unmanageable revolutionaries*, 111. Ward's book, published in 1983, was one of the earliest to focus on the participation of women in Irish national politics.

[27] Pašeta, *Irish nationalist women*, 183.

[28] IE/MA, MSP 34REF3935, Rooney, W34E4971, Letter from C. Rooney to F. Aiken, 2.

# LIST OF ILLUSTRATIONS

## Introduction

## Chapter One

## Chapter Two

## Chapter Three

## Chapter Four

p. 118    Elizabeth O'Farrell, reproduced from the *Catholic Bulletin* 1917, p. 267, by permission of the Royal Irish Academy.

p. 118    Leslie Barry, reproduced by persmission of Meda Ryan and Mercier Press.

p. 119    Hanna Sheehy Skeffington and her son, Owen; courtesy of the Library of Congress Prints and Photographs Division, George Grantham Bain Collection [LC-DIG-ggbain-23442].

## Chapter Five

p. 138    Marie Perolz, reproduced by permission of the Irish Labour History Society.

p. 138    Margaret Skinnider, reproduced from Margaret Skinnider, *Doing my bit for Ireland*, New York, 1917.

p. 139    Kathleen Clarke, *c.* 1902; photo by Otto Boye, John J. Burns Library, Boston College, reproduced by permission of Boston College.

## Chapter Six

p. 162    Nora Connolly; reproduced by permission of Seamus Connolly.

p. 163    Eily, Anna and Mary Margaret O'Hanrahan with their mother, date unknown; reproduced by permission of Emer Greif.

p. 163    17BC-1B52-05, Daly family in mourning; reproduced by permission of Máiréad de hÓir and Kilmainham Gaol.

## Chapter Seven

p. 191    Michael 'The' O'Rahilly and his sister Nell, 1914; courtesy of Mark Humphrys at humphrysfamilytree.com.

p. 192    Hanna Sheehy Skeffington, Kathleen Lynn and Mary McLoughlin, *c.* 1941; reproduced by permission of Christina McLoughlin.

p. 192    Máirín Cregan with her husband Dr James Ryan; reproduced by permission of Mercier Press.

# BIBLIOGRAPHY

## PRIMARY SOURCES

## Archives

### Allen Library

Madeleine ffrench Mullen, Transcript of memoir/diary written in Kilmainham and Mountjoy jails, 5–20 May 1916, 201/File B.

IE/AL/1916/95/2, Elizabeth O'Farrell, 'The personal account of the surrender at the G.P.O. and other posts', annotated typescript.

### Bodleian and Rhodes House libraries, Oxford University

Papers of Sir Matthew Nathan, MS N 476, Estelle Nathan, Letters to George Nathan. Undated (25 April–28 April 1916).

### Kilmainham Goal Archives

Helena Molony Papers KMGLM 2011.0282.01-02
                                              KMGLM 2011.0284.01-37 Box 25
Elizabeth O'Farrell Papers 17MS-1B51-08
Mary/May Gahan O'Carroll Papers 20MS-1B53-10

### Manuscripts and Archives Research Library, Trinity College Library

MS 2074, Elsie Mahaffy, 'The Irish rebellion', diary.

### National Library of Ireland

MS 24,553, Letter from Mrs Arthur (Mary Agnes) Mitchell to her sister Flora, 24–7 April 1916.

MS 43,332/1–2, Mary Spring Rice, 'Log of the gun-running cruise in the "Asgard" July 1914', corrected typescript.

MS 31,112 (28), Lily Yeats, Holograph letter to John Butler Yeats, 26 April 1916.

### Royal College of Physicians of Ireland

ACC/1990/1, KL/1, Kathleen Lynn, holograph diary 1966–1955.

**University College Dublin Archives**

> Papers of Máire Comerford, UCDA LA18 (http://www.ucd.ie/
> archives/html/collections/comerford-maire.htm, Accessed 10 May
> 2015).
> Papers of Sighle Humphreys, UCDA P106
> Papers of The O'Rahilly, UCDA P102
> Papers of Ernie O'Malley, UCDA P17

**University of Limerick Library, Special Collections**

> Daly Papers, P/2, Folder 76: Madge Daly, 'The memoirs of Madge
> Daly', typescript draft.

## Private collection

Joe and Hilary Comerford

> Máire Comerford, Untitled memoir, typescript draft.

## Official publications

*Dáil Debates*, vol. 67, cols 462–3 (13 May 1937).

## Newspapers

*Irish Independent*
*Irish Times*
*New York Times*
*Woman's Dreadnought*

## Women's Accounts of 1916

**Bureau of Military History: witness statements**

| | |
|---|---|
| Barry (née Price), Leslie | BMH, WS 1754 |
| Bloxham, Elizabeth | BMH, WS 632 |
| Colbert, Lila | BMH, WS 856 |
| Corr, Elizabeth and Nell | BMH, WS 179 |
| Curran (née Cooney), Lily | BMH, WS 805 |
| de Burca, Aoife | BMH, WS 359 |
| Duffy, Louise Gavan | BMH, WS 216 |
| Flanagan (née Perolz), Marie | BMH, WS 246 |
| Foley (neé Smartt), Máire | BMH, WS 539 |

Hackett, Rose/Rosanna                   BMH, WS 546
Heron, Áine                                 BMH, WS 293

| Hackett, Rose/Rosanna | BMH, WS 546 |
|---|---|
| Heron, Áine | BMH, WS 293 |
| Heron (née Connolly), Ina | BMH, WS 919 |
| Keating (née Morkan), Pauline | BMH, WS 432 |
| Kennedy, Margaret | BMH, WS 185 |
| Lynn, Kathleen | BMH, WS 357 |
| Martin (née Foley), Brigid | BMH, WS 398 |
| McCarthy (née Ryan), Cathleen | BMH, WS 937 |
| McGarry, Maeve | BMH, WS 826 |
| MacDowell (née Cavanagh), Maeve | BMH, WS 258 |
| McLoughlin, Mary | BMH, WS 934 |
| McNamara, Rose | BMH, WS 482 |
| McWhinney (née Kearns), Linda | BMH, WS 404 |
| Molony, Helena | BMH, WS 391 |
| Morkan (née Lucas), Phyllis | BMH, WS 210 |
| Mulcahy (née Ryan), Mary Josephine ('Min') | BMH, WS 399 |
| Ní Cheallaigh, Mairéad | BMH, WS 925 |
| O'Brien (née Cooney), Annie | BMH, WS 805 |
| O'Brien (née Connolly), Nora | BMH, WS 286 |
| O'Doherty (née Gibbons), Kitty | BMH, WS 355 |
| O'Donnell (née Coyle), Eithne | BMH, WS 750 |
| O'Rahilly, Áine | BMH, WS 333 |
| O'Reilly (née O'Hanrahan), Eily | BMH, WS 270 |
| Plunkett (née Gifford), Grace | BMH, WS 257 |
| Reynolds, Molly | BMH, WS 195 |
| Rooney (née Byrne), Catherine | BMH, WS 648 |
| Ryan (née Cregan), Máirín | BMH, WS 416 |
| Thornton (née Lyons), Brigid | BMH, WS 259 |

## Military Service Pensions Collection

| Byrne (née Smyth), Lucy | MSP 34REF2055 |
|---|---|
| de Burca, Aoife | MSP 34REF53445 |
| Ledwith (née Elliott), Emily | MSP 34 REF9307 |
| McLoughlin, Mary | MSP 34REF15389 |
| O'Brien (née Cooney), Annie | MSP 34REF8809 |
| O'Brien (née Elliott) Eilis | MSP 34REF21833 |
| O'Gorman (née Hayes), Mary Christina | MSP 34REF2044 |
| Rooney (née Byrne), Catherine | MSP 34REF3935 |

## Digitised diaries

Trinity College Dublin, Digital Humanities (TCDDH), A family at war: the diary of Mary Martin, 1 January–25 May 1916; http://dh.tcd.ie/martindiary/ (Accessed 9 May 2015).

TCDDH, The 1916 diary of Dorothy Stopford Price, 21 April–6 May 1916; http://dh.tcd.ie/pricediary/ (Accessed 10 May 2015).

### Books, articles and chapters

Childers, M. 2014 Letters to Alice Stopford Green. In F. X. Martin (ed.), *The Howth gun-running and the Kilcoole gun-running: recollections and documents*, 98–109. Dublin. Merrion.

Clarke, K. 1991 *Revolutionary woman*, ed. H. Litton. Dublin. O'Brien Press.

Czira, S. 2000 *The years flew by: the recollections of Madame Sydney Czira*, ed. A. Hayes. Galway. Arlen House.

Dillon, Geraldine Plunkett 2006 *All in the blood: a memoir*, ed. Honor O Brolchain. Dublin. A&A Farmar.

Fay, M. and Finn, J. 2012 *May and James: a private love in a revolutionary year, 1916*, ed. T. Finn. Dublin. Createspace.

Fennell, A., Ennis, K., Hickey, Mrs T., Kelly, K., Connolly, Mrs P., Hughes, S., Walsh, E., Beirnes, E. and Lawless, Mrs 1966 Dubliners: Statements concerning civilian deaths in the North King Street area. In R. McHugh (ed.), *Dublin 1916*, 220–39 Dublin and London. Arlington Books.

Gore-Booth, E. 1966 The countess in prison. In R. McHugh (ed.), *Dublin 1916*, 306–15. Dublin and London. Arlington Books.

Grenan, J. 1984 Women of the revolution. In D. Ó Dúlaing (ed.), *Voices of Ireland*, 68–77. Dublin. O'Brien Press in association with Radio Teilifís Éireann.

Henry, E. 2012 *The world upturning: Elsie Henry's Irish wartime diaries 1913–1919*, ed. C. Cullen. Dublin. Merrion.

Kilmer, J. 1916 Irish girl rebel tells of Dublin fighting. *New York Times*, 20 August.

Lynch, P. 1916 'Scenes from the Irish rebellion', *Woman's Dreadnought* III:7, 473, 475.

Lynch, P. 1966 Aftermath. In R. McHugh (ed.), *Dublin 1916*, 316–22. Dublin and London. Arlington Books.

Mac Lochlainn, P.F. (ed.) 1990 *Last words: letters and statements of the leaders executed after the Rising at Easter 1916*. Dublin. The Stationery Office. (Including letters, interviews and other materials by 'John Brennan' (Sidney Czira); Madge, Nora, and Carrie Daly; Teresa Heuston; Ina Connolly Heron; Mary Josephine (Ryan) Mulcahy; Mrs Seamus (Kate) Murphy, Nora Connolly O'Brien; Eily O'Hanrahan O'Reilly; Margaret Pearse and Countess Plunkett.)

[de] Markievicz, C. 1966 Women in the fight. In R. McHugh (ed.), *Dublin 1916*, 122–5. Dublin and London. Arlington Books.

Nic Shiubhlaigh, M. 1955 *The splendid years*, ed. E. Kenny. Dublin. James Duffy.

Norway, M.L. Hamilton 1999 The Sinn Féin rebellion as I saw it. In K. Jeffery (ed.), *The Sinn Féin rebellion as they saw it*, 33–86. Dublin. Irish Academic Press.

Nurse L (Voluntary Aid Detachment Nurse), 1966 A nurse in Dublin Castle. In R. McHugh (ed.), *Dublin 1916*, 89–121. Dublin and London. Arlington Books.

O'Brien, N. Connolly. 2010 *The unbroken tradition* (reprint). Memphis, TN. General Books LLC.

O'Farrell, E. 1966 The surrender. In R. McHugh (ed.), *Dublin 1916*, 206–19. Dublin and London. Arlington Books.

Parry, G. 1966 The last days of Roger Casement. In R. McHugh (ed.), *Dublin 1916*, 289–305. Dublin and London. Arlington Books.

Roberts, M. 2008 Monica Roberts's diary of Easter Week 1916, ed B. MacMahon. *Obelisk: Journal of Kilmacud-Stillorgan Local History Society* 3, 8–14.

Ryan, M. Sean McDermott. In Joy, M. 1916 *The Irish rebellion of 1916 and its martyrs: Erin's tragic Easter*. 372–9. New York. The Devin-Adair Company.

Sheehy Skeffington, H. 1966 A pacifist dies. In R. McHugh (ed.), *Dublin 1916*, 276–88. Dublin and London. Arlington Books.

Skinnider, M. 1917 *Doing my bit for Ireland*. New York. The Century Company.

Spring Rice, M. 2014 Diary of the *Asgard*. In F.X. Martin (ed.), *The Howth gun-running and the Kilcoole gun-running: recollections and documents*, 65–98. Dublin. Merrion.

Stokes, L. 1966 Easter Week diary. In R. McHugh (ed.), *Dublin 1916*, 63–79. Dublin and London. Arlington Books.

Swanton, D. Lawrenson. 1994. *Emerging from the shadow: the lives of Sarah Anne Lawrenson and Lucy Olive Kingston. Based on personal diaries, 1883–1969*. Dublin. Attic Press.

Trench, C. 2005 *Cesca's diary 1913–1916: where art and nationalism meet*, ed. H. Pyle. Dublin. Woodfield Press.

## Men's Accounts of 1916

### Bureau of Military History: witness statements

| | |
|---|---|
| Brennan, Robert | BMH, WS 779 |
| Byrne, Christopher ('Christy') | BMH, WS 118 |
| Byrne, Thomas ('Tom') | BMH, WS 564 |
| Cleary, Thomas | BMH, WS 972 |
| Colgan, Patrick | BMH, WS 850 |
| Cremen, Michael | BMH, WS 563 |
| Dowling, Thomas | BMH, WS 533 |
| Greene, Arthur | BMH, WS 238 |
| Holohan, Garry | BMH, WS 328 |
| McLoughlin, Sean | BMH, WS 290 |
| Monahan, Alf | BMH, WS 298 |
| Morkan, Eamon ('Eddie') | BMH, WS 411 |
| O'Kelly, Seán T. | BMH, WSs 611 and 1765 |
| O'Mahony, Patrick | BMH, WSs 118 and 745 |
| Ryan, Desmond | BMH, WS 724 |
| Tobin, Liam | BMH, WS 1753 |
| Walsh, James and Thomas | BMH, WS 198 |

### Military Service Pensions Collection

Furlong, John     DP1012

### Books, articles and chapters

Brennan, R. 1950 *Allegiance*. Dublin. Browne and Nolan.

Brennan Whitmore, W.J. 1996 *Dublin burning: the Easter Rising from behind the barricades* (reprint), ed. P. Travers. Dublin. Gill and Macmillan.

Fannin, A. 1995 *Letters from Dublin, Easter 1916: Albert Fannin's diary*, eds A. and S. Warwick Haller. Dublin. Irish Academic Press.

Henderson, F. 1998 *Frank Henderson's Easter Rising: recollections of a Dublin Volunteer*, ed. M. Hopkinson. Cork. Cork University Press.

Norway, A. Hamilton 1999 Irish experiences in war. In K. Jeffery (ed.), *The Sinn Féin rebellion as they saw it*, 87–122. Dublin. Irish Academic Press.

O'Malley, E. 2013 *On another man's wound: a personal history of Ireland's War of Independence*. Cork. Mercier Press

Robbins, F. 1977 *Under the Starry Plough: recollections of the Irish Citizen Army.* Dublin. The Academy Press.

Stephens, J. 1992 *The insurrection in Dublin* (reprint). Gerrards Cross, Bucks. Colin Smythe.

Sweeney, J. 1998 Interview. In K. Griffith and T. E. O'Grady (eds), *Curious journey: an oral history of Ireland's unfinished revolution,* 78–80. London. Hutchinson.


# SECONDARY SOURCES


### Newspaper articles

Boland, R. 2014 'Micheline Sheehy Skeffington: "I'm from a family of feminists. I took this case to honour them"', *Irish Times,* 6 December.

Gibbons, J. 2012 'An Irishman's diary', *Irish Times,* 12 April.

Kilmer, J. 1916 'Poets marched in the Van of Irish revolt', *New York Times,* 7 May.

### Reference works

McGuire, J. and Quinn, J. (eds) 2009 *Dictionary of Irish Biography.* Cambridge and Dublin. Cambridge University Press and the Royal Irish Academy.


### Websites

Census of Ireland 1901 and 1911, www.census.nationalarchives.ie (Accessed 4 August 2015).

Breathnach, Diarmuid and Ní Mhurchú, Maire, 'Diarmuid Coffey 1888–1964', http://www.ainm.ie/Bio.aspx?ID=415 (Accessed 7 August 2015).

Comerford, Patrick, 'A blog devoted to the history of the Comerford, Comberford and Quemford families', http://comerfordfamily.blogspot.com (Accessed 4 August 2015).

Farell, Colin, 'Stories from 1916: Tom and Lucy Byrne', www.storiesfrom1916.com/tomandlucybyrne (Accessed 11 May 2015).

Foley, Karen, 'The Robinson garden at Earlscliffe, Baily, Co. Dublin, Ireland', www.earlscliffe.com (Accessed 5 August 2015).

Gaelchultur newsletter, 'September 2011', http://www.gaelchultur.com/en/newsletters/newsletterarticle.aspx?id=156 (Accessed 12 May 2015).

Hansard Parliamentary Papers 1803–2005, http://hansard.millbanksystems.com/ (Accessed 4 August 2015).

History Ireland, www.historyireland.com (Accessed 5 August 2015).

Jeffery, Keith, 'Nationalisms and gender: Ireland in the time of the Great War 1914–1918', http://www.oslo2000.uio.no/program/papers/r13/r13-jeffery. pdf (Accessed 7 August 2015).

Jerrold, Yvonne, 'Robert Brennan 1881–1964', http://www.yvonnejerrold.com/ RBrennan/Robert%20Brennan%201881-1964.html (Accessed 7 August 2015).

Manifesto of the Irish Volunteers (Dublin, 1913, re-issued 1914), http://source. southdublinlibraries.ie/bitstream/10599/9706/3/wm_DSC_0480.jpg (Accessed 9 May 2015).

Markievicz, Constance. 'The women of '98', Marxists Internet Archive, https://www.marxists.org/archive/markievicz/1915/11/women98.html (Accessed 13 May 2015).

Ó Ruairc, Padraig Óg, 'A short history of the Hibernian Rifles', The Irish story, http://www.theirishstory.com/2013/03/31/a-short-history-of-the-hibern- ian-rifles-1912-1916 (Accessed 9 May 2015).

Pinkerton, William, Historical notices of old Belfast and its vicinity, 1896, https://archive.org/stream/historicalnotice00youn/historicalnotice00youn_ djvu.txt (Accessed 13 May 2015).

## CD
de Búrca, Éanna. 2013 Interview. In M. O'Keefe (ed.), 1916 Rising Oral History Collection, Irish Life and Lore, CD 15. Tralee. Irish Life and Lore.

## Books and articles
Beatty, J.D. (ed.) 2001 Protestant women's narratives of the Irish rebellion of 1798. Dublin. Four Courts Press.

Bourke, A. 1993 More in anger than in sorrow: Irish women's lament poetry. In Joan Newlon Radner (ed.), Feminist messages: coding in women's folk culture, 160–82. Urbana, IL. Illinois University Press.

Bourke, A. 1997 Performing not writing: the reception of an Irish woman's lament. In Y. Prins and M. Schreiber (ed.), Dwelling in possibility: women poets and critics on poetry, 132–46. Ithaca, NY. Cornell University Press.

Bourke, A. 1999 The burning of Bridget Cleary. London. Pimlico.

Brittain, V. 1993 Testament of youth: an autobiographical study of the years 1900–1925. London. Penguin Books.

Childers, E. 2013 *The riddle of the sands.* London. Vintage Classics.

Clare, A. 2011 *Unlikely rebels: the Gifford girls and the fight for Irish freedom.* Cork. Mercier Press.

Collins, L. 2012 *16 lives. James Connolly.* Dublin. O'Brien Press.

Colum, M. 1947 *Life and the dream.* New York. Doubleday and Company.

Concannon, Mrs T. 1920 *Women of 'ninety-eight.* Dublin. M.H. Gill and Son Ltd.

Conlon, L. 1969 *Cumann na mBan and the women of Ireland.* Kilkenny. Kilkenny People.

Connolly, L. 2002 *The Irish women's movement: from revolution to devolution.* Houndmills, Basingstoke, Hants. Palgrave.

Coulter, C. 1993 *The hidden tradition: feminism, women and nationalism in Ireland.* Cork. Cork University Press.

Cowell, J. 2005 *A noontide blazing: Brigid Lyons Thornton: rebel, soldier, doctor.* Dublin. Currach Press.

Cullen, M. and Luddy, M. (eds) 1995 *Women, power and consciousness in 19th century Ireland.* Dublin. Attic Press.

Cullen, M. and Luddy M. (eds) 2001 *Female activists: Irish women and change 1900–1960.* Dublin. Woodfield Press.

Cullen Owens, R. 1984 *Smashing times: a history of the women's suffrage movement, 1889–1922.* Dublin. Attic Press.

Daly, M.E. and O'Callaghan, M. (eds) 2007 *1916 in 1966: commemorating the Easter Rising.* Dublin. Royal Irish Academy.

Donnelly, M. (ed.) 1932 *The last post.* Dublin. National Graves Association.

Douglas, M. 1984 *Purity and danger: an analysis of the concepts of pollution and taboo.* Abingdon, Oxon. Routledge.

Dudley Edwards, R. 1978 *Patrick Pearse: the triumph of failure.* New York. Taplinger.

Dudgeon, J. 2002 *Roger Casement: the Black Diaries—with a study of his background, sexuality and Irish political life.* Belfast. Belfast Press.

Dunsany, Lord E. 1938 *Patches of sunlight.* London. W. Heinemann.

Eliot, George 1956 *Middlemarch.* Boston. Houghton Mifflin,

Feeney, B. 2014 *16 lives. Seán MacDiarmada.* Dublin. O'Brien Press.

Ferriter, D. 2005 *The transformation of Ireland 1900—2000.* London. Profile Books.

Ferriter, D. 2015 *A nation and not a rabble: the Irish revolution 1913–1923.* London. Profile Books.

Foster, R.F. 2014 *Vivid faces: the revolutionary generation in Ireland 1890–1923.* London. Allen Lane.

Foy, M. and Barton, B. 2011 *The Easter Rising.* Stroud, Glos. History Press.

Gallagher, A.-M., Lubelska, C. and Ryan, L. (eds) 2001 *Re-presenting the past: women and history.* New York. Routledge.

Gillis, L. 2014 *Women of the Irish revolution 1913–1923: a photographic history.* Cork. Mercier Press.

Goffman, E. 1967 *Interaction ritual: essays on face-to-face behavior.* New York. Doubleday.

Griffin, G. 1900 *The Wild Geese: pen portraits of famous Irish exiles.* Norwich, Norf. Jarrolds.

Griffith, K. and O'Grady, T. 1998 *Curious journey: an oral history of Ireland's unfinished revolution.* Cork. Mercier Press.

Harvey, J., Ogilvie, M. and Rossiter, M. (eds) 2000 *The biographical dictionary of women in science.* Abingdon, Oxon. Routledge.

Haverty, A. 1988 *Constance Markievicz: an independent life.* London. Pandora.

Hegarty, S. and O'Toole, F. 2006 *The Irish Times book of the 1916 Rising.* Dublin. Gill and Macmillan.

Higgins, R. and Uí Chollatáin, R. 2009 *The life and after-life of P.H. Pearse.* Dublin. Irish Academic Press.

Hochschild, A.R. 1983 *The managed heart: commercialization of human feeling.* Berkeley and Los Angeles, CA. University of California Press.

Jeffery, K. 2006 *The GPO and the Easter Rising.* Dublin. Irish Academic Press.

Kenna, S. 2014 *16 lives. Thomas MacDonagh.* Dublin. O'Brien Press.

Keogh, D. and Furlong, N. (eds) 1998 *The women of 1798.* Dublin. Four Courts Press.

Keogh, R.M. 2009 Well dressed and from a respectable street. *History Ireland* 17:2, 32–3.

Kiberd, D. 1998 *1916 rebellion handbook.* Belfast. Mourne River Press.

Kilfeather, S. 2005 *Dublin: a cultural and social history.* Dublin. Liffey Press.

Kinsella, T. and Ó Tuama, S. 1981 *An Dunaire. 1600–1900: Poems of the dispossessed.* Mountrath. Dolmen.

Koven, S. 1993 Borderlands: women, voluntary action, and child welfare in Britain, 1840 to 1914. In S. Koven and S. Michel (eds), *Mothers of a new world: maternalist politics and the origins of welfare states,* 94–135. New York. Routledge.

Koven, S. and Michel, S. (eds) 1993 *Mothers of a new world: maternalist politics and the origins of welfare states.* New York. Routledge.

Lane, L. 2010 *Rosamond Jacob: third person singular.* Dublin. University College Dublin Press.

Levenson, L. 1983 *With wooden sword: a portrait of Francis Sheehy-Skeffington, militant pacifist.* Boston. Northeastern University Press.

Levenson, L. and Natterstad, J.H. 1986 *Hanna Sheehy-Skeffington: Irish feminist.* Syracuse, NY. Syracuse University Press.

Lewis, G. 1988 *Eva Gore-Booth and Esther Roper: a biography.* London. Pandora.

Litton, H. 2013 *16 lives. Edward Daly.* Dublin. O'Brien Press.

Litton, H. 2014 *16 lives. Thomas Clarke.* Dublin. O'Brien Press.

Loder, J. 1977 *Hollywood hussar: the life and times of John Loder.* London. Howard Baker.

Luddy, M. 1995a *Women and philanthropy in 19th-century Ireland.* Cambridge. Cambridge University Press.

Luddy, M. 1995b *Women in Ireland: a documentary history 1800–1918.* Cork. Cork University Press.

Luddy, M. 2002 Women and politics in Ireland, 1860–1918. In A. Bourke *et al.* (eds), *The Field Day anthology of Irish women's writing and traditions* (2 vols; vol. v), 69–74. Cork. Cork University Press.

MacAtasney, G. (ed.) 2013 *Tom Clarke: life, liberty, revolution.* Sallins, Co Kildare. Merrion.

McCarthy, C. 2007 *Cumann na mBan and the Irish revolution 1914–1923.* Cork. Collins.

MacCurtain, M. 1995 The historical image. In E. Ní Chuilleanáin (ed.), *Irish women: image and achievement*, 37–50. Dublin. Arlen House.

MacCurtain, M. 2008 *Ariadne's thread: writing women into Irish history.* Galway. Arlen House.

M'Cleery, A. 1896 Life of Mary Ann McCracken. In Robert M. Young (ed.), *Historical notices of old Belfast and its vicinity; a selection from the mss. collected by William Pinkerton, F.S.A., for his intended history of Belfast, additional documents, letters, and ballads, O'Mellan's narrative of the wars of 1641, biography of Mary Ann M'Cracken, now first printed. With maps and illustrations/edited, with notes, by Robert M. Young*, 175–97. Belfast. Marcus Ward & Co.

McCoole, S. 1997 *Guns and chiffon: women revolutionaries and Kilmainham Gaol 1916–1923.* Dublin. Stationery Office.

McCoole, S. 2004 *No ordinary women: Irish female activists in the revolutionary years 1900–1923.* Dublin. O'Brien Press.

McCoole, S. 2014 *Easter widows.* Dublin. Doubleday Ireland.

McDiarmid, L. 2005 *The Irish art of controversy.* Dublin. Lilliput Press.

McDowell, R.B. 1967 *Alice Stopford Green: a passionate historian.* Dublin. A. Figgis.

McGarry, F. 2010 *The Rising: Ireland. Easter 1916.* Oxford. Oxford University Press.

McGarry, F. 2011 *Rebels: voices from the Easter Rising.* Dublin. Penguin Ireland.

McGuire, C. 2011 *Sean McLoughlin: Ireland's forgotten revolutionary.* Pontypool, Gwent. Merlin.

McHugh, R. 1966 *Dublin 1916.* London. Arlington Books.

McIntosh, G. and Urquhart, D. (eds) 2010 *Irish women at war: the twentieth century.* Dublin. Irish Academic Press.

McKenna, K. 2014 *A Dáil girl's revolutionary recollections.* Dublin. Original Writing.

McKillen, B. 1982a Irish feminism and nationalist separatism, 1914–1923. *Éire-Ireland* 17:3, 52–67.

McKillen, B. 1982b Irish feminism and nationalist separatism, 1914–1923. *Éire-Ireland* 17:4, 74–90.

Mac Lellan, A. 2014 *Dorothy Stopford Price: rebel doctor.* Sallins. Irish Academic Press.

MacMahon, D. (ed.) 2004 *The Moynihan brothers in peace and war 1908–1918: their new Ireland.* Dublin. Irish Academic Press.

Magray, M.P. 1998 *The transforming power of the nuns: women, religion, and cultural change in Ireland, 1750–1900.* Oxford. Oxford University Press.

Matthews, A. 2010a *Renegades: Irish Republican women 1900–1922.* Cork. Mercier Press.

Matthews, A. 2010b *The Kimmage garrison, 1916: making billy-can bombs at Larkfield.* Dublin. Four Courts Press.

Montgomery Hyde, H. 1977 *Oscar Wilde: a biography.* London. Eyre Methuen.

Morrison, E. 2009 The Bureau of Military History and female Republican activism, 1913–1923. In M. G. Valiulis (ed.), *Gender and power in Irish history,* 59–83. Dublin. Irish Academic Press.

Mulcahy, R. 1999 *Richard Mulcahy (1886–1971): a family memoir.* Dublin. Aurelian Press.

Ní Dhonnchadha M. and Dorgan, T. (eds) 1991 *Revising the Rising.* Derry. Field Day.

Ó Broin, L. 1971 *Dublin Castle and the 1916 Rising.* New York. New York University Press.

Ó Broin, L. 1985 *Protestant nationalists in revolutionary Ireland: the Stopford connection.* Dublin. Gill and MacMillan.

O Brolchain, H. 2012 *16 Lives. Joseph Plunkett.* Dublin. O'Brien Press.

O'Callaghan, J. 2015 *16 lives. Con Colbert.* Dublin. O'Brien Press.

O'Callaghan, M. 2002 Women and politics in independent Ireland, 1921–68. In A. Bourke, S. Kilfeather, M. Luddy, M. MacCurtain, G. Meaney, M. Ní Dhonnchadha, M. O'Dowd and C. Wills (eds), *The Field Day anthology of Irish writing* (vol v), 120–34. *Cork.* Cork University Press.

O'Casey, S. 1994 *Autobiographies.* New York. Carroll and Graf.

Ó Dúlaing, D. and Boylan, H. 1984 *Voices of Ireland.* Dublin. O'Brien Press.

O'Farrell, P. (ed.) 1998 *The '98 reader.* Minneapolis. Irish Books and Media.

Ó hÓgartaigh, M. 2006 *Kathleen Lynn: Irishwoman, patriot, doctor.* Dublin. Irish Academic Press.

Ó hÓgartaigh, M. 2011 *Quiet revolutionaries: Irish women in education, medicine and sport, 1861–1964.* Dublin, History Press.

O'Neill, M. 2000 *Grace Gifford Plunkett and Irish freedom: tragic bride of 1916.* Dublin. Irish Academic Press.

O'Rahilly, A. 1991 *Winding the clock: O'Rahilly and the 1916 Rising.* Dublin. Lilliput Press.

O'Riordan, M. 2006 What if a patriot priest has been traduced? In defence of Father O'Flanagan. *Irish Political Review* 21:7, 11–13.

Ó Ruairc, P. Óg 2011. *Revolution: a photographic history of revolutionary Ireland 1913–1923*. Cork. Mercier Press.

Pašeta, S. 2013 *Irish nationalist women, 1900–1918*. Cambridge. Cambridge University Press.

Pearse, M.B. 1979 *The home life of Pádraig Pearse: as told by himself, his family and friends*. Dublin. Mercier Press.

Pearse, P.H. 1917 *Collected works of Padraic H. Pearse: plays, stories, poems*. Dublin. Maunsel and Co. Ltd.

Pearse, P.H. 2012 *The coming revolution: the political writings and speeches of Patrick Pearse*. Cork. Mercier Press.

Prunty, J. 1995 Margaret Louisa Aylward. In M. Cullen and M. Luddy (eds), *Women, power and consciousness in 19th-century Ireland*, 55–88. Dublin. Attic Press.

Pyle, H. 1998 *Red-headed rebel: Susan L. Mitchell: poet and mystic of the Irish cultural renaissance*. Dublin. Woodfield Press.

Ryan, A. 2005 *Witnesses inside the Easter Rising*. Dublin. Liberties Press.

Ryan, L. 2003 'In the line of fire': representations of women and war (1919–1923) through the writings of republican men. In L. Ryan and M. Ward (eds), *Irish women and nationalism: soldiers, new women and wicked hags*, 45–61. Dublin and Portland, OR. Irish Academic Press.

Showalter, E. 2013 Dark places. *New York Times, Sunday Book Review* 6 June, BR 35.

Shute, N. 1954 *Slide rule: autobiography of an engineer*. London. William Heinemann Ltd.

Sklar, K. Kish 1993 The historical foundations of women's power in the creation of the American welfare state, 1830–1930. In S. Koven and S. Michel (eds), *Mothers of a new world: maternalist politics and the origins of welfare states*, 43–93. New York. Routledge.

Smedley, C. (ed.) 1907 What women have done for Ireland. In *The work of the women's world*, 638; *The World's Work*, vol. ix (Henry Chalmers Roberts, ed.). London. Heineman.

Smith, S. and Watson, J. 1998 *Women, autobiography, theory: a reader* Madison, WI. University of Wisconsin Press.

Stanford, W.B. and McDowell, R.B. 1971 *John Pentland Mahaffy: a biography of an Anglo-Irishman*. London. Routledge and Kegan Paul.

Steele, K. 2007 *Women, press and politics during the Irish revival*. Syracuse. Syracuse University Press.

Steele, K. 2010 When female activists say 'I': veiled rebels and the counter-history of Irish independence. In G. McIntosh and D. Urquhart (eds), *Irish women at war: the twentieth century*, 51–68. Dublin and Portland, OR. Irish Academic Press.

Stephens, J. 1916 *The insurrection in Dublin.* New York. The Macmillan Company.

Synge, J.M. 1992 *The Aran Islands*, ed. T. Robinson. London. Penguin Group.

Taillon, R. 1996 *When history was made: the women of 1916.* Belfast. Beyond the Pale.

Tiernan, S. 2012 *Eva Gore-Booth: an image of such politics.* Manchester. Manchester University Press.

Townshend, C. 2005 *Easter 1916: the Irish rebellion.* London. Allen Lane.

Valiulis, M.G. 2009a Introduction. In Valiulis, M.G. (ed.), *Gender and power in Irish history*, 1–8. Dublin. Irish Academic Press.

Valiulis, M.G. 2009b Virtuous mothers and dutiful wives: the politics of sexuality in the Irish Free State. In Valiulis, M.G. (ed.), *Gender and power in Irish history*, 100–14. Dublin. Irish Academic Press.

Valiulis, M.G. and O'Dowd, M. (eds) 1997 *Women and Irish history: essays in honour of Margaret MacCurtain.* Dublin. Wolfhound Press.

Ward, M. 1983 *Unmanageable revolutionaries: women and Irish nationalism.* Dingle. Brandon.

Ward, M. 1990 *Maud Gonne: Ireland's Joan of Arc.* London. Pandora.

Ward, M. 1995 *In their own voice: women and Irish nationalism.* Dublin. Attic Press.

Ward, M. 1997 *Hanna Sheehy Skeffington: a life.* Dublin. Attic Press.

Webb, T. Tears: an introduction. In *Towards a lachrymology: Tears in literature and cultural history*, Webb, T. (ed.), *Litteraria Pragensia: Studies in Literature and Culture*, 22, no. 43, 2012, 1–25.

Weihman, L. 2004 'Doing my bit for Ireland': transgressing gender in the Easter Rising. *Éire–Ireland* 39, 215–36.

Wills, C. 2009 *Dublin 1916: the siege of the GPO.* London. Profile Books.

Yeats, W.B. 1977. *The Variorum edition of the Poems of W.B. Yeats*, ed. Peter Allt and Russell K. Alspach. New York: Macmillan, 1977.

# BIOGRAPHICAL APPENDIX

*(with Fionnuala Walsh)*

ASQUITH, H.H. (1852–1928)

Born in Morley, West Yorkshire; prime minister of the United Kingdom, April 1908–December 1916; leader of the Liberal Party.

BANNISTER, GERTRUDE *SEE* PARRY, GERTRUDE

BARRY, LESLIE (NÉE PRICE) (1893–1984)

Member of Cumann na mBan; based at the GPO and the Hibernian Bank during the Easter Rising; later became director of organisation for Cumann na mBan; married IRA guerrilla leader Tom Barry in 1921; served as president of the Irish Red Cross Society, 1939–62.

BIBBY, FR ALBERT (1877–1925)

Roman Catholic priest of the Capuchin order; ministered to the rebels in Kilmainham Gaol; wrote an account of the final hours of Seán Heuston.

BLACKWELL, SIR ERNLEY (1868–1941)

Scottish lawyer and civil servant; acted as chief legal advisor to the British Cabinet, 1913–33; involved in the prosecution of Roger Casement and the distribution of his diaries.

BLAKE, SIR HENRY (1840–1918)

Grew up in Limerick; Royal Irish Constabulary (RIC) officer and Resident Magistrate; British colonial administrator and governor-general of Hong Kong, 1898–1903; governor of Ceylon (Sri Lanka), 1903–07; leading southern Irish unionist; living in Cork at the time of the Easter Rising.

BLOXHAM, ELIZABETH (B. 1878)

Protestant nationalist from Co. Mayo; member of the executive and organiser of Cumann na mBan; dismissed from her post as teacher in Newtownards, Co. Down, for her Republican sympathies following the Easter Rising; also involved in the suffrage movement.

## BOLAND, HENRY JAMES ('HARRY') (1887–1922)

Grew up in Dublin; member of the Irish Volunteers and the Irish Republican Brotherhood (IRB); stationed at the GPO during the Easter Rising; after the surrender interned until June 1917; subsequently served as joint-secretary of Sinn Féin and as envoy to the United States in 1919; close friend of Michael Collins; opposed the Anglo–Irish Treaty of 1921; killed during the Civil War.

## BOWEN-COLTHURST, JOHN COLTHURST (1880–1965)

Born into a prominent Anglo–Irish family in Co. Cork; British army officer with the Royal Irish Rifles during the First World War; based at Portobello Barracks during the Easter Rising and was responsible for the execution without trial of Frank Sheehy Skeffington and two others; court-martialled following the Rising and found guilty but insane; committed to Broadmoor Asylum for the Criminally Insane and released in 1919; subsequently emigrated to Canada.

## BRENNAN, ROBERT (1881–1964)

Born in Co. Wexford; member of the IRB; commanded the rebels in Wexford during the Easter Rising; sentenced to death but sentence commuted to imprisonment; acted as Sinn Féin director of elections in December 1918; one of the co-founders of the *Irish Press*, of which he was general manager, 1930–4; Irish minister in Washington, 1938–47; autobiography, *Allegiance*, covers 1916 and later; father of the writer Maeve Brennan.

## BRENNAN, UNA (NÉE ANASTASIA BOLGER) (1888–1958)

Adopted an Irish name when she became active in radical nationalist politics; married Robert Brennan; joined Cumann na mBan in 1915; actively involved in the Easter Rising in Wexford; mother of the writer Maeve Brennan.

## BRITTAIN, VERA (1893–1970)

English writer and prominent pacifist; served as a Red Cross nurse during the First World War, an experience which inspired her best-selling memoir *Testament of youth* (1933).

## BROCKWAY, BARON ARCHIBALD FENNER (1888–1988)

Born in India but grew up in Great Britain; conscientious objector during the First World War and imprisoned in Pentonville Prison at the same time as Roger Casement; Labour Party MP, 1929–31 and 1950–64.

BROWNE, FR PADDY (1889–1960)

Roman Catholic priest; taught mathematics at St Patrick's College, Maynooth; visited Seán MacDermott in Kilmainham Gaol before his execution; wrote an article condemning the executions that was discussed in the House of Commons; president of University College Galway, 1945–59.

BYRNE, ALICE *SEE* COOGAN, ALICE

BYRNE, CATHERINE *SEE* ROONEY, CATHERINE

BYRNE, CHRISTOPHER ('CHRISTY') (1885–1960)

General labourer and lieutenant, 'F' Company, 4th Battalion, Irish Volunteers; stationed at Watkins Distillery on Ardee Street and at Marrowbone Lane Distillery during the Rising; close friend of Con Colbert; boarded with the Cooney family in the years before the Rising.

BYRNE, LUCY AGNES (NÉE SMYTH) (1882–1972)

Grew up in Dublin, the daughter of a clerk; member of Cumann na mBan; called by Con Colbert (according to his sister Lila Colbert) 'the nicest girl in Dublin'; attached to the first-aid post at the GPO during the Rising; married Tom Byrne.

BYRNE, THOMAS ('TOM') (1877–1962)

Member of 'B' Company, 1st Battalion, Irish Volunteers; later staff officer of the Dublin Brigade; at Pearse's order, took charge of the Volunteers in Co. Kildare and travelled from Maynooth to take part in the Rising; stationed at the GPO for Easter Week; escaped imprisonment following the surrender; commandant, 1st Battalion, Dublin Brigade of the IRA, 1919–22; appointed by Michael Collins as first captain of the guard at Leinster House.

CAREY, FR THOMAS (N.D.)

Elderly Roman Catholic priest who visited Irish rebels in prison in England after the Rising and showed his support for their cause.

CARLETON, GENERAL LANCELOT RICHARD (N.D.)

Brigadier-general, commander, 177th infantry brigade, 2nd Staffordshire Regiment, British army; accepted the surrender of Thomas MacDonagh and others in Dublin during Easter Week.

CARNEY, WINIFRED *SEE* MCBRIDE, WINIFRED

## CARROLL, TERESA (B. 1869)

Born in Dublin; married Edward Carroll, a labourer for Dublin Corporation; had one child, a daughter Marcella; living on North King Street in Dublin in 1916; witness to neighbours' murder by the British Army during Easter Week.

## CASEMENT, ROGER (1864–1916)

Born in Dublin; surveyor and explorer in the Congo Free State; joined the British consular service; produced reports on atrocities in the Congo and in the Putomayo region of the Upper Amazon; knighted in 1911; member of the Irish Volunteers; met with Alice Stopford Green and others to plan the Howth gun-running in 1914; attempted to win German support for an Irish rebellion but on realising that the rebels had insufficient arms travelled to Ireland to try to prevent the Rising; captured on Banna Strand, Co. Kerry, arrested, taken to London, tried for high treason, found guilty and executed in August 1916; author of the so-called 'Black Diaries', which contain descriptions of homosexual encounters.

## CAVANAGH, MAEVE *SEE* MACDOWELL, MAEVE

## CEANNT, ÉAMONN (EDWARD KENT) (1881–1916)

Born in Co. Galway, the son of an RIC officer; member of the IRB supreme council and commandant of the 4th Battalion, Dublin Brigade of the Irish Volunteers; a signatory of the Proclamation of the Irish Republic in 1916 and commander at the South Dublin Union; executed following the surrender.

## CHILDERS, MARY ALDEN ('MOLLY') (NÉE OSGOOD) (1875–1964)

Born in Boston, Massachusetts; married Robert Erskine Childers in 1904; sailed with her husband on the *Asgard*, a wedding present from her parents, in the famous Howth gun-running in July 1914 to secure arms for the Irish Volunteers; awarded an MBE for her work in assisting Belgian refugees during the First World War; opposed the Anglo–Irish Treaty.

## CHILDERS, (ROBERT) ERSKINE (1870–1922)

Born in England but spent time in Ireland as a child; worked as a parliamentary clerk in the House of Commons; served in the British army during the Boer War and was an officer in the British navy during the First World War; member of the Irish Volunteers; navigated the *Asgard* during the Howth gun-running in July 1914; involved in Republican activities during the War of Independence; opposed the Anglo–Irish Treaty; executed during the Civil War.

### CLANCY, PEADAR (1886–1920)

Member of the Irish Volunteers; stationed at the Four Courts during the Rising; interned following the surrender until June 1917; second-in-command of the Dublin Brigade during the War of Independence; captured in 1920 and shot by the Auxiliaries in Dublin Castle.

### CLARKE, KATHLEEN (NÉE DALY) (1878–1972)

Born into a Fenian family in Limerick City; married the Fenian activist Tom Clarke in 1901; joined Cumann na mBan in 1914; her husband and her brother (Ned Daly) executed for their roles in the Easter Rising; established the Irish Volunteer Dependants Fund to assist dependants of those killed or imprisoned as a result of the Rising; from 1917, was a member of the Sinn Féin executive; served as a district judge of the Republican courts in Dublin during the War of Independence; first woman lord mayor of Dublin, 1939–41.

### CLARKE, LIAM (1893–1941)

Member of the Dublin Brigade of the Irish Volunteers; stationed at the GPO during the Rising; injured by a dropped grenade on the first day of the Rising and treated first by Catherine Byrne; sent to Richmond Hospital and therefore not imprisoned after the surrender.

### CLARKE, THOMAS ('TOM') (1858–1916)

Born in Hampshire; imprisoned for Fenian activity between 1883 and 1898; married Kathleen Daly in 1901; served as treasurer of the supreme council of the IRB from 1907; first signatory of the Proclamation; fought in the GPO during the Rising and was executed following the surrender.

### COFFEY, (HUGH) DIARMID (1888–1964)

Member of the Volunteers; after the split in 1914 member of the National Volunteers; secretary to Colonel Maurice Moore; sailed on the *Kelpie* for the Kilcoole gun-running in August 1914; married the nationalist activist and artist Cesca Trench on 17 April 1918.

### COLBERT, CORNELIUS ('CON') (1888–1916)

Born in Moanlena, Castlemahon, Co. Limerick to a nationalist family; moved to Dublin, where he worked as a clerk in Kennedy's Bakery;

drill instructor at Patrick Pearse's school St Enda's; active member of the Irish Volunteers and the IRB; involved in fighting at Watkins Brewery and Jameson's Distillery in Marrowbone Lane; executed following the surrender.

### COLBERT, ELIZABETH ('LILA') (1887–1976)

Sister of Con Colbert; worked at Lafayette's (photographers and publishers); met with Lucy Smyth (later Byrne) after Colbert's execution; later involved with the Volunteer Dependants Fund.

### COLGAN, PATRICK (1890–1960)

Joined the Irish Volunteers in 1913; served with the Maynooth Company of the Kildare Battalion; marched from Maynooth to participate in the Rising; based at the GPO and the Exchange Hotel on Parliament Street; interned following the surrender until December 1916; active in the IRA during the War of Independence.

### COMERFORD, MÁIRE (1892–1982)

Born in Ardavon, Co. Wicklow; grew up in Wexford; in Dublin taking care of an invalid relative during the week of the Rising; left an incomplete memoir describing her frustration at being unable to participate in the Rising, but it is said by some sources that she carried dispatches for the GPO garrison; after the Rising, joined the local Sinn Féin branch in Wexford and supported the IRA during the War of Independence; worked as secretary to Alice Stopford Green during the War of Independence; active in Republican politics as a journalist and protester until her death.

### CONCANNON, HELENA (NÉE WALSH) (1878–1952)

Grew up in Co. Derry; professor of history at University College Galway; wrote books on Irish women, including the women of 1798 and nuns in penal Ireland; elected as TD for Fianna Fáil in 1933; member of the Seanad for the National University of Ireland constituency, 1938–52.

### CONNOLLY, INA *SEE* HERON, INA

### CONNOLLY, JAMES (1868–1916)

Born in Scotland; co-founder of the Irish Labour Party and commander of the Irish Citizen Army; led the Irish Citizen Army during the Rising; commandant-general of the Dublin division at the GPO; sustained injuries in the arm and the ankle on the Thursday of Easter Week; executed following the surrender.

### CONNOLLY, LILLIE (NÉE REYNOLDS) (1869–1938)

Born into a Protestant family in Co. Wicklow; in 1890 married James Connolly, with whom she had six children; received into the Catholic Church in August 1916 following her husband's execution.

### CONNOLLY, NORA *SEE* O'BRIEN, NORA CONNOLLY

### COOGAN, ALICE (NÉE BYRNE) (1898–1972)

Member of Cumann na mBan; sister of Catherine Rooney (née Byrne); based at Liberty Hall and the GPO during Easter Week; also carried food and supplies to the Hibernian Bank and Reiss's Building; after the Rising, worked in Glasgow and involved in nationalist activities there; married in 1922 and remained in Scotland.

### COONEY, ANNIE *SEE* O'BRIEN, ANNE

### COONEY, EILEEN *SEE* HARBOURNE, EILEEN

### COONEY, LILY *SEE* CURRAN, LILY

### COYLE, EITHNE *SEE* O'DONNELL, EITHNE

### CREGAN, MÁIRÍN *SEE* RYAN, MÁIRÍN

### CULHANE, MARGARET (NÉE SHEEHY) (1879–1956)

Born in Co. Cork; one of four daughters of David Sheehy, MP and member of the Irish Parliamentary Party; sister of Hanna Sheehy Skeffington; married first to John Culhane, later to Michael Casey; went with another sister, Mary Kettle, to Portobello Barracks during the Rising in attempt to get information about Frank Sheehy Skeffington.

### CURRAN, LILY (NÉE COONEY) (B. 1897/8)

Joined Cumann na mBan in 1915; based in Marrowbone Lane during the Easter Rising, along with her sisters Annie and Eileen; imprisoned in Richmond Barracks and Kilmainham Gaol after the surrender; involved with the National Aid Association and the anti-conscription movement; active with Cumann na mBan and the IRA throughout the War of Independence and the Civil War.

### DALY, AGNES (ALSO KNOWN AS ÚNA) (1881–1969)

Born in Limerick City into a Republican family; niece of Fenian John Daly, sister of Madge Daly and Kathleen Clarke; brother Edward ('Ned') Daly executed for his role in the Easter Rising; member of Cumann na mBan; delivered dispatches to the Volunteers in Limerick on behalf of Seán MacDermott at the start of Easter Week; attacked by the Black and Tans in a raid on the Daly family house during the War of Independence; worked in the Daly bakery shop in Limerick.

### DALY, CATHARINE (NÉE O'MARA) (D. 1937)

Daughter of a coachman and the governess of a 'big house'; according to her great-granddaughter Helen Litton, she sang her children to sleep with the 'Marseillaise'; mother of nine daughters (one died at birth) and one son, Edward ('Ned') Daly; during the Civil War was part of a group of women charged by soldiers and attacked while they prayed outside a barracks in Limerick; her house was raided during the War of Independence and the contents taken out and burned in the middle of the Ennis Road in Limerick City; honoured with a large funeral in 1937.

### DALY, EDWARD ('NED') (1891–1916)

Born into a prominent republican family in Limerick City; as commandant, led the 1st Battalion of the Dublin Brigade of the Irish Volunteers during the Rising; commanded the Four Courts garrison and buildings along Church Street; executed following the surrender.

### DALY, JOHN (1845–1916)

Well-known Fenian and member of the IRB from the 1860s on; uncle of Commandant Edward ('Ned') Daly; his Limerick home was raided during the Rising; died following an illness in June 1916.

### DALY, LAURA *SEE* O'SULLIVAN, LAURA

### DALY, MARGARET ('MADGE') (1877–1969)

Born in Limerick City to the famous republican Daly family; sister of Commandant Ned Daly; with her sister Laura founded the Limerick branch of Cumann na mBan; led that branch until 1924; helped Ernest Blythe set up a second Limerick Volunteer battalion after 1916; became manager of Daly's bakery, inherited from her uncle John Daly; left a long, unpublished memoir in manuscript.

### DE BURCA, AOIFE (EVA BURKE) (1885–1974)

Public health nurse with Dublin Corporation; member of Cumann na mBan; attended to the wounded at the GPO and participated in the evacuation to Jervis Street Hospital, about which she left a detailed account; her brother Frank Burke was also stationed in the GPO during Easter Week.

## DE VALERA, ÉAMON (1882–1975)

Born in Brooklyn, New York; raised in Bruree, Co. Limerick; school-teacher and college lecturer; member of the IRB and commandant of the 3rd Battalion of the Dublin Brigade of the Irish Volunteers; commanded the Boland's Mills garrison during the Rising; death sentence commuted; released from prison in June 1917; elected president of Sinn Féin in 1917; president of Dáil Éireann in 1919; after 1922, nominal head of the anti-treaty forces; founded Fianna Fáil in 1926; taoiseach, 1937–48, 1951–4 and 1957–9; president of Ireland, 1959–73.

## DE VALERA, SINÉAD (NÉE FLANAGAN) (1875–1975)

Born in Dublin; national schoolteacher and member of the Gaelic League and Inghinidhe na hÉireann; married Éamon de Valera in 1910; mother of five sons and two daughters and author of children's books.

## DICKSON, THOMAS (D. 1916)

Journalist and editor of the loyalist newspaper *Searchlight*; summarily executed along with Frank Sheehy Skeffington and Patrick MacIntyre on the order of Captain J.C. Bowen-Colthurst on the Wednesday of Easter Week.

## DILLON, ELIZABETH (NÉE KIRBY SULLIVAN) (N.D.)

Daughter of William Kirby Sullivan, a chemist, Young Irelander and president of Queen's College Cork; wife of John Dillon, an engineer; mother of five, including Thomas Dillon, a chemistry professor who was active in the Republican movement during the War of Independence; mother-in-law of Geraldine Dillon.

## DILLON, GERALDINE (NÉE PLUNKETT) (1891–1986)

Born in Dublin, one of seven children of Count George Noble Plunkett and Josephine Cranny; aide-de-camp for her brother Joseph, executed for his role in the Easter Rising; married Thomas Dillon, a chemistry professor, on Easter Sunday 1916; honeymooned at the Imperial Hotel, directly opposite the GPO, but was not actively involved in the Rising; endured many raids along with her children during the War of Independence; imprisoned in Galway Gaol in 1920 for Republican activities; mother of five; left a long memoir edited and published by her granddaughter Honor O Brolchain.

## DILLON, JOHN (1851–1927)

MP for the Irish Parliamentary Party, 1885–1918; leader of the Irish Party in 1918; constitutional nationalist opposed to the Easter Rising who nevertheless gave emotional speeches to the House of Commons attacking the murder of civilians living on North King Street in Dublin and the executions of the Rising's leaders.

### DILLON, THOMAS ('TOMMY') (1884–1971)

Chemistry professor in University College Galway; married Geraldine Plunkett, sister of Joseph Plunkett, on Easter Sunday, 1916; a member of the IRB from 1919.

### DORE, EAMONN (B. 1896)

Member of the Irish Volunteers and the IRB; married Nora Daly, sister of Edward ('Ned') Daly and Kathleen Clarke; travelled from Limerick to Dublin to participate in the Rising; stationed at the GPO; interned following the surrender.

### DUFFY, GEORGE GAVAN (1882–1951)

Born in England to an Irish nationalist family; trained as a solicitor; represented Roger Casement during his trial for high treason in 1916; Sinn Féin TD; involved in the Anglo–Irish Treaty negotiations in 1921; became president of the High Court in 1946.

### DUFFY, LOUISE GAVAN (1884–1969)

Born in France, daughter of journalist and politician Charles Gavan Duffy; moved to Ireland in 1907; after graduation from University College Dublin taught in St Ita's, the girls school founded by P.H. Pearse; joined Cumann na mBan in 1914; joint secretary with Mary Colum; opposed the Rising but worked in the GPO kitchen; founded Scoil Bhríde, a bilingual school in Dublin, in 1917; at the start of the Civil War joined Cumann na Saoirse, the women's organisation that supported the Free State government.

### DUGGAN, CHARLES (B. 1877)

One of two fishermen from Gola Island, Co. Donegal, who sailed on the *Asgard* during the Howth gun-running.

### ENNIS, GEORGE (1866–1916)

Coachmaker; one of fifteen unarmed civilians living on North King Street killed by the South Staffordshire Regiment of the British army during the Rising.

### ENNIS, KATE (B. 1874)

Born in Co. Wexford; wife of George Ennis; married seven years with no children; gave evidence to the Military Court of Inquiry about her husband's murder.

FAHY, FRANCIS ('FRANK') (1879–1953)
Born in Galway; member of the Irish Volunteers; commander, 'C' Company of the 1st Battalion of the Dublin Brigade during the Rising; based at the Four Courts; imprisoned after the Rising until June 1917; Ceann Comhairle of Dáil Éireann, 1932–51.

FAY, MAY *SEE* FINN, MARY

FENNELL, ANNE (B. 1842)
Housekeeper; lived as a tenant at 174 North King Street in 1916; gave evidence to the Military Court of Inquiry about the murder of two of her neighbours by the British army during Easter Week.

FINN, JAMES (1877–1922)
Senior civil servant; worked for the National Health Insurance Commission in Dublin; wrote a series of letters to his fiancée, May Fay, between January and June 1916; married Fay in June 1916; died from endocarditis, a side effect of influenza; correspondence published by their granddaughter Tessa Finn in 2012.

FINN, MARY ('MAY') (NÉE FAY) (B. 1896)
Born in Co. Westmeath; engaged to James Finn during the winter and spring of 1916; widowed, aged 25, in 1922, while pregnant with her fourth child; their courtship correspondence was published by their granddaughter Tessa Finn in 2012.

FLANAGAN, FR JOHN (B. 1884)
Roman Catholic priest who heard confessions at the GPO during the Rising; attended the wounded in Jervis Street Hospital; features in witness statement of Leslie Barry; often confused with the Sinn Féin priest Father Michael O'Flanagan.

FLANAGAN, MÁIRE, MARIE/MARY (NÉE PEROLZ) (1874–1950)
Born in Limerick; member of Inghinidhe na hÉireann, Cumann na mBan and the Irish Citizen Army; delivered dispatches to Waterford during Holy Week and sent to Cork and Kerry during Easter Week; held in Ship Street Barracks, then Kilmainham Gaol, Mountjoy Prison and Lewes Prison; freed in July 1916; active during the War of Independence; also involved with the Irish Women Workers Union; in 1919 married James Flanagan.

**FFRENCH-MULLEN, MADELEINE (1880–1944)**
Born in Malta, daughter of a Royal Navy surgeon; family returned to Ireland when she was a child; one of the original contributors to *Bean na hÉireann*, the journal of Inghinidhe na hÉireann; worked in the soup kitchens during the 1913 Lockout; active with the Irish Citizen Army during the Rising; imprisoned briefly after the surrender; in 1919, with her partner Kathleen Lynn, established Teach Ultáin, the first infants hospital in Ireland.

**FOLEY, BRIGID *SEE* MARTIN, BRIGID**

**FURLONG, JOHN (1889–1918)**
Member of a nationalist family in Wexford; Irish Volunteer, 1913–18; mentioned in Robert Brennan's memoir *Allegiance* and in his statement for the Bureau of Military History; married to Kathleen (née Kearney); their son, born in 1917, was named after Roger Casement; after his death from influenza in 1918, his wife remarried and later became the mother of Brendan Behan.

**GAHAN, JOSEPH ('JOE') (1895–1969)**
Painter; member of the Dublin Brigade of the Irish Volunteers, Kimmage garrison; stationed at the GPO for most of the Rising; also involved in the occupation of Ship Inn on Abbey Street and Pillar House on O'Connell Street; interned until July 1916; mentioned by Catherine Rooney (née Byrne) as the Volunteer she landed on when she jumped through a window of the GPO.

**GIBBONS, MOTHER COLUMBA (MARIA) (1875–1961)**
Grew up in Co. Westmeath; became a nun in 1906, taking the name Columba and joining the Loreto convent in Navan; wrote the ballad 'Who fears to speak of Easter Week' after the 1916 executions; sister of Kitty O'Doherty.

**GIFFORD, GRACE *SEE* PLUNKETT, GRACE**

**GORE-BOOTH, CONSTANCE, *SEE* MARKIEVICZ, COUNTESS CONSTANCE**

**GREEN, ALICE SOPHIA AMELIA STOPFORD (1847–1929)**
Born in Co. Meath; moved to England in 1874 where she married the historian J.R. Green; supported Home Rule and wrote numerous books on Irish history (which argued for Irish self-government); best known for *The making of Ireland and its undoing*, 1908; gave generous financial

aid to and helped organise the Howth and Kilcoole gun-runnings; did not support the Easter Rising; returned to Ireland in 1918, living in Dublin; was pro-treaty and served in the first Free State Senate until her death.

### GRENAN, JULIA (1884–1972)

Born in Dublin; member of Inghinidhe na hÉireann, Cumann na mBan and the Irish Citizen Army; active in the Rising, carried messages to Dundalk, Co. Louth, the week before and dispatches during Easter Week; imprisoned after the surrender; later worked for the Irish Hospital Sweepstakes; lived with her friend Elizabeth O'Farrell in Dublin until the latter's death.

### GWYNN, EDWARD (1868–1941)

Lecturer in Old Irish at Trinity College Dublin; provost of Trinity College, 1927–37; brother of Stephen Gwynn, the Irish Party MP; son of John Gwynn.

### GWYNN, JOHN (1827–1917)

Regius professor of divinity at Trinity College Dublin, 1888–1917; father of Stephen Gwynn, the Irish Party MP and of Edward Gwynn.

### HACKETT, ROSANNA, ROSE ('ROSIE') (1893–1976)

Born in Dublin to a working-class family; worker in Jacob's Biscuit Factory while active in the nationalist and labour movements; founder member of the Irish Women Workers Union; supported the strikers during the 1913 Dublin Lockout; helped print the Proclamation of the Republic; during Easter Week, served with the Irish Citizen Army in St Stephen's Green and at the College of Surgeons; in 2014, a bridge over the River Liffey was named after her.

### HAMILTON-GORDON, DAME ISHBEL MARIA, MARCHIONESS OF ABERDEEN AND TEMAIR (NÉE MARJORIBANKS) (1857–1939)

Known as Lady Aberdeen; philanthropist and the wife of the Lord-Lieutenant of Ireland (1886 and 1905–15); founded the Women's National Health Association in 1907; active in the anti-tuberculosis campaign.

### HARBOURNE, EILEEN (NÉE COONEY) (1899–1982)

Born in Dublin; joined Cumann na mBan in 1915; based at the Jameson Distillery in Marrowbone Lane with her sisters Annie and Lily during the Rising; imprisoned in Richmond Barracks and Kilmainham Gaol until 8 May; later involved with the National Aid Association and the anti-conscription movement; active with Cumann na mBan until 1923; married Sean Harbourne, who had also been active in the Rising and the War of Independence.

### HAYDEN, FR AUGUSTINE (1870–1954)

Roman Catholic priest of the Capuchin order; Irish language enthusiast; active during the Rising, helping to secure the surrenders of Thomas MacDonagh and Éamonn Ceannt; visited many of the Rising's leaders in Kilmainham Gaol before their executions.

### HAYES, MARY *SEE* O'GORMAN, MARY CHRISTINA

### HENRY, ALICE HELEN ('ELSIE') (NÉE BRUNTON) (1881–1956)

Born in London; niece of Alice Stopford Green and cousin of Dorothy Stopford Price; in 1908, married Augustine Henry, a botanist; moved to Dublin in 1913; quartermaster of the sphagnum department of the Irish War Hospital Supply Depot, 1915–19; awarded an OBE in 1918 for her contribution to the war effort; kept a detailed diary that records her experiences during the Easter Rising, which included delivering sphagnum bandages to the temporary hospital at Merrion Square.

### HENRY, AUGUSTINE (1857–1930)

Professor of forestry at the Royal College of Science for Ireland; married Elsie Brunton; was in London when the Easter Rising began.

### HERON, ÁINE (1884–1952)

Married to Thomas Heron, a general labourer; claimed to have been storing ammunition in her husband's Dublin shop from January 1916 in preparation for rebellion; one of several pregnant women 'out' in the Rising; performed first-aid work at the Hibernian Bank, the Four Courts and Church Street; actively involved with the National Aid Association and with the Irish Republican Prisoners Defence Fund after the Rising; member of the executive committee of Cumann na mBan in 1922.

### HERON, INA (NÉE CONNOLLY) (1896–1980)

Fourth child of James Connolly and Lillie Reynolds, and first to be born in Ireland; member of the Fianna (from 1911) and of Cumann na mBan; delivered dispatches from Patrick Pearse to the Irish Volunteers in Co. Tyrone at the beginning of Easter Week; active in first aid during the Civil War; married Archie Heron, an Irish Labour Party politician.

### HEUSTON, SEÁN (1891–1916)

Born in Dublin; worked as a railway clerk; officer in the Fianna; captain of 'D' Company, 1st Battalion, of the Dublin Brigade of the Irish Volunteers; during the Rising led the force at the Mendicity Institute; executed following the surrender.

### HEUSTON, TERESA (B. 1893)

Sister of Seán Heuston; visited him in Kilmainham Gaol before he was executed and left an account of the visit quoted in Piaras Mac Lochlainn's *Last words*; successfully applied for a dependant's allowance under the military service pension scheme in 1953.

### HICKEY, CHRISTOPHER (1900–16)

Raised in a working-class household in Dublin; son of Thomas Hickey; both men among the fifteen unarmed civilians living on North King Street killed by the South Staffordshire Regiment of the British army during the Rising.

### HICKEY, TERESA (B. 1877)

Wife of Thomas Hickey, a butcher; her husband and teenage son, Christopher, killed by the South Staffordshire Regiment of the British army during Easter Week at North King Street; gave evidence to the Military Court of Inquiry about their murders.

### HICKEY, THOMAS (1878–1916)

Butcher living in Dublin with his family in 1916; killed by the South Staffordshire Regiment of the British army on Friday, 28 April 1916, along with his son Christopher and thirteen other unarmed civilians from North King Street.

### HOLOHAN, GERARD ('GARRY') (1894–1967)

Brigade officer of the Fianna Éireann during the Rising; involved in the attack on the Magazine Fort in the Phoenix Park; stationed at Broadstone railway station, North King Street and Church Street for the remainder of the week; interned following the surrender until December 1916; later joined the Irish Volunteers and the IRA.

### HUMPHREYS, MARY ELLEN ('NELL') (NÉE O'RAHILLY) (1871–1939)

Born in Ballylongford, Co. Kerry; in 1895 married Dr David Humphreys, with whom she had three children, including Sighle; sister of The O'Rahilly, who was killed in action during the Easter Rising; briefly imprisoned following the Rising; in 1920, elected a Republican member of

Pembroke Urban District Council; imprisoned also during the Civil War for anti-treaty agitation.

### HUMPHREYS, HONORA ('NORA') (B. 1864)

Born in Co. Limerick; sister of David Humphreys (husband of Nell O'Rahilly); became a nun, taking the name Sister Nora Francis, and moved to New South Wales, Australia, where she was living at the time of the Rising.

### HUMPHREYS, SIGHLE *SEE* O'DONOGHUE, SIGHLE

### JOLY, PROFESSOR JOHN (1857–1933)

Chair of geology and mineralogy at Trinity College Dublin, 1897–1933; known for the development of radiotherapy in the treatment of cancer; assisted the Officers Training Corps in the defence of the college during the Rising.

### KEATING, PAULINE (NÉE MORKAN) (1892–1973)

Born in Dublin; joined Cumann na mBan in 1915; stationed at the Four Courts during the Rising; imprisoned briefly after the surrender and lost her job at Brown Thomas department store; married in 1920.

### KELLY, KATE (B. 1884)

Worked as a domestic servant for a family living on North King Street in 1916; gave evidence to the Military Court of Inquiry about the murders of two of her neighbours who were killed by the British army during Easter Week.

### KETTLE, MARY (NÉE SHEEHY) (1884–1967)

Born in Co. Cork; daughter of nationalist MP David Sheehy; studied at University College Dublin; active in the suffragist movement; married the Irish party politician Tom Kettle in 1909; went to Portobello Barracks with her sister Margaret Culhane to find out what had happened to their brother-in-law Frank Sheehy Skeffington; Mary's husband was killed with the British army at Ginchy, France, on the Western Front, in 1916.

### KILMER, (ALFRED) JOYCE (1886–1918)

American journalist and poet born in New Brunswick, New Jersey; wrote an extensive article on the Easter Rising for the *New York Times* in 1916; most famous as author of the poem 'Trees'; served with the New York National Guard in France in the First World War; killed in action in 1918.

## LEA WILSON, CAPTAIN PERCEVAL (1887–1920)

Born in England; district inspector, RIC, in Galway in 1911; served in France with the Royal Irish Rifles during the First World War; in charge of the captured rebels when they were held and guarded at the Rotunda, where he publically humiliated Tom Clarke, Edward ('Ned') Daly and others; killed in revenge by the IRA during the War of Independence.

## LEDWIDGE, FRANCIS (1887–1917)

Born in Co. Meath; farm labourer and poet; member of the Irish Volunteers; fought with the Royal Inniskilling Fusiliers at Gallipoli and in Serbia; felt sympathy for the rebels in the Easter Rising but nevertheless returned to the war and died near Ypres, Belgium, in July 1917; had been a close friend of Thomas MacDonagh and wrote the famous elegy 'Lament for Thomas MacDonagh', beginning with the line, 'He shall not hear the bittern cry...'

## LOWE, GENERAL WILLIAM HENRY MUIR (1861–1944)

Brigadier-general in the British army in 1916; stationed at the Curragh, Co. Kildare, at the outbreak of the Rising; assumed command of British forces in Dublin and ordered the shelling of Liberty Hall; negotiated the surrender with Patrick Pearse.

## LYNN, KATHLEEN (1874–1955)

Born in Mullafarry, Killala, Co. Mayo; trained as a medical doctor; assisted the strikers during the 1913 Dublin Lockout; joined the Irish Citizen Army; served as medical officer in the City Hall garrison during the Rising; imprisoned afterwards in Mountjoy and briefly deported to England; later served as vice-president of the Sinn Féin executive; also active in the suffrage and Labour movements; in 1919, with her partner Madeleine ffrench-Mullen, established Teach Ultáin, the first infants hospital in Ireland.

## LYONS, BRIGID SEE THORNTON, BRIGID LYONS

## MCBRIDE, (MARIA) WINIFRED ('WINNIE') (NÉE CARNEY) (1887–1943)

Suffragist, trade unionist and Irish Republican; in 1912, led the women's section of the Irish Textile Workers' Union in Belfast; made personal secretary to James Connolly; joined Cumann na mBan, 1914, and served in the GPO during Easter Week; interned following the surrender until December 1916; in 1928, married George McBride, former member of the Ulster Volunteers.

### McCarroll, Fr James

Scottish Roman Catholic priest; chaplain at Holloway Prison in London; attended Roger Casement in prison and received him into the Roman Catholic Church (Casement had already been baptised as a Catholic in childhood).

### McCarthy, Cathleen (née Ryan) (b. 1901)

Raised in Dublin in a nationalist family; brother Pádraic Ó Riain one of the founders of the Fianna; on Easter Monday, 1916, delivered a suitcase of ammunition to the Volunteers in Omagh, Co. Tyrone; married Paddy McCarthy, a worker in the GPO.

### McCracken, Henry Joy (1767–98)

Born in Belfast; Ulster industrialist and member of the Society of the United Irishmen; brother of Mary Ann McCracken; executed for his role in the Antrim rebellion in 1798.

### McCracken, Mary Ann (1770–1866)

Born in Belfast; sister of Henry Joy McCracken; led the Women's Abolitionary Committee in Belfast during the anti-slavery movement; social worker and active in promoting education for the poor of Belfast; left an account of her brother's execution in letters later published in Anna M'Cleery's 'Life of Mary Ann M'Cracken' (1896).

### MacDermott, Seán (Seán Mac Diarmada) (1883–1916)

Born in Corranmore, near Kiltyclogher, Co. Leitrim; worked as a tram driver in Belfast but soon became national organiser for Sinn Féin and later national organiser for the IRB; manager of the newspaper *Irish Freedom*; close friend of John Daly, Tom Clarke and Kathleen Clarke; romantically attached to Min Ryan; signatory of the Proclamation of the Republic; stationed at the GPO during the Rising; executed following the surrender.

### MacDonagh, Thomas (1878–1916)

Born in Cloughjordan, Co. Tipperary; schoolteacher, university lecturer, poet and playwright; moved to Dublin in 1908; taught at St Enda's and lectured in English literature at UCD; taught Irish to Joseph Plunkett; married Muriel Gifford (sister to Grace Plunkett) in 1912; director of training for the Irish Volunteers and member of the IRB; signatory of the 'Proclamation of the Irish Republic'; led the 2nd Battalion of the Dublin Brigade in the occupation of Jacob's Biscuit Factory; executed following the surrender.

## MacDowell, Maeve (née Cavanagh) (b. 1878)

Born in Dublin; wrote patriotic poetry for the *Irish Worker*; member of the Gaelic League; member of the Irish Citizen Army; called 'the poetess of the Revolution' by James Connolly; delivered messages to the Volunteers in Waterford during Holy Week and to Waterford and Kilkenny during Easter Week; remained active in the Republican movement until 1923; married Cathal MacDowell in 1921.

## McGinley, Patrick (b. 1890)

One of two fishermen from Gola Island, Co. Donegal, who sailed on the *Asgard* during the Howth gun-running.

## Mac Giolla Ghunna, Cathal Buí (c. 1680–c. 1756)

Born in Co. Fermanagh; poet most famous for 'An bonnán buí' ('The yellow bittern'), translated into English by Thomas MacDonagh, Thomas Kinsella and Seamus Heaney, among others; translation by MacDonagh inspired Francis Ledwidge's poem 'Lament for Thomas MacDonagh'.

## McGuinness, Francis ('Frank') (1868–1934)

Republican; travelled from Longford with his niece Brigid Lyons (later Thornton) to participate in the Rising; stationed at the Four Courts during Easter Week; served as chairman of Longford County Council and later as TD and senator; brother of the politician Joseph McGuinness.

## McGuinness, Joseph ('Joe') (1875–1922)

Member of the Irish Volunteers; helped establish a Gaelic League branch in Longford town; fought at the Four Courts during Easter Week with his brother Frank; interned after the Rising; elected a Sinn Féin MP in the 1917 South Longford by-election while in Lewes Prison.

## McIntyre, Patrick (d. 1916)

Journalist and editor of the loyalist paper *The Eye-opener*; previously editor of the *Toiler*, a paper that attacked Jim Larkin during the Dublin Lockout in 1913; summarily executed during the Rising on the orders of Captain Bowen-Colthurst along with Frank Sheehy Skeffington and Thomas Dickson.

## McLoughlin, Mary (1901–54)

Born in Dublin; member of Clan na Gael Scouts in 1915; one of the youngest women 'out' in the Rising; carried supplies and messages between the GPO and other garrisons, including the final message from Thomas MacDonagh to Joseph Plunkett on the Friday of Easter Week, a message that could not be delivered; active with Clan na Gael after the Rising; joined Cumann na mBan in 1918; sister of Seán McLoughlin.

## McLOUGHLIN, SEÁN (1895–1960)

Born in Dublin; officer in Fianna Éireann and lieutenant in the Irish Volunteers; stationed at the GPO during the Rising; given command (by James Connolly) of the forces retreating from the GPO to Moore Street; interned until December 1916; active in Republican and Communist politics; moved permanently to England in 1924; brother of Mary McLoughlin.

## MacMAHON, SORCHA *SEE* ROGERS, SORCHA (SARAH)

## McNAMARA, ROSE (1885–1957)

Born in Dublin; member of Inghinidhe na hÉireann; vice-commandant of the Inghinidhe branch of Cumann na mBan; stationed at the Jameson Distillery on Marrowbone Lane during the Rising; arrested following the surrender and imprisoned until 9 May 1916; involved with Cumann na mBan throughout the War of Independence and on the anti-treaty side in the Civil War.

## MacNEILL, EOIN (JOHN) (1867–1945)

Born in Glenarm, Co. Antrim; Gaelic scholar, university lecturer and commander-in-chief of the Irish Volunteers; countermanded the order for the Volunteers to mobilise on Easter Sunday because of Roger Casement's capture and the scuttling of the *Aud*, the ship carrying guns from Germany; arrested after the Rising; imprisoned in England; released in 1917; served as minister for education, 1922–5, in the Free State and as the Free State's representative on the Boundary Commission.

## MAHAFFY, ELIZABETH ('ELSIE') (1869–1926)

Born in Dublin; older daughter of Trinity College Dublin Classics professor and provost John Pentland Mahaffy; managed a knitting business marketing the work of local women from Howth; living in the Provost's House at the time of the Rising and kept a detailed diary of the events of Easter Week.

## MAHAFFY, JOHN PENTLAND (1839–1919)

Born in Switzerland; moved to Ireland as a child; Classical scholar and provost of Trinity College Dublin, 1914–19; Oscar Wilde's tutor; helped to organise the defence of the college during the Easter Rising.

## MAHAFFY, RACHEL (1876–1944)

Born in Dublin; younger daughter of John Pentland Mahaffy; amateur botanist who published accounts of rare plants; living in Trinity College Dublin at the time of the Easter Rising; involved with the British Red Cross during the First World War and helped to establish the Dublin University Voluntary Aid Detachment Hospital in Mountjoy Square for wounded soldiers.

## MALLIN, AGNES (NÉE HICKEY) (1878–1932)

Born in Dublin to a nationalist family; worked as a nurse before her marriage in 1903 to Michael Mallin; pregnant with their fifth child when he was executed for his role in the Rising; returned to nursing to support her family after his death; died of tuberculosis.

## MALLIN, MICHAEL (1874–1916)

Born in Dublin; drummer in the Royal Scots Fusiliers; served with the British army in India and Afghanistan; active in the trade union movement; was chief-of-staff of the Irish Citizen Army and a commandant in the Irish Volunteers; led the Irish Citizen Army division at St Stephen's Green and later at the Royal College of Surgeons during the Rising; executed following the surrender.

## MANSFIELD, MAUDE (1850–1921)

Born in Co. Kildare; relative of Máire Comerford; never married and lived on 'independent means' (according to the 1911 Census) primarily at Earlsfort Terrace in Dublin.

## MARKIEVICZ, COUNTESS CONSTANCE (NÉE GORE-BOOTH) (1868–1927)

Born in London into an Anglo–Irish landholding family from Co. Sligo; youthful friendship with Yeats; married Count Casimir Markievicz in 1900; studied painting in London and Paris; joined Inghinidhe na hÉireann and established Fianna Éireann in 1909; became an executive member of Sinn Féin in 1911; honorary secretary of the Irish Citizen Army; second-in-command at the College of Surgeons during the Easter Rising; the death sentence for her role in the Rising was commuted to life imprisonment; president of Cumann na mBan in 1917; in 1918, elected Sinn Féin MP for Dublin; first woman to be elected to the House of Commons; minister for labour in the first Dáil, 1919–21.

MARTIN, BRIGID (NÉE FOLEY) (B. C.1887)

Born in Dublin to a nationalist family with Irish-speaking parents; joined the Gaelic League at age 15; member of Cumann na mBan; carried dispatches to Cork for Seán MacDermott three times during the week before the Rising; according to her Bureau of Military History witness statement, MacDermott advised her when she began helping the Volunteers, 'Always have a nightie and a toothbrush ready as you never know when you may be sent with a dispatch'; carried messages between MacDermott and Captain Thomas Weafer during the first part of Easter Week; set up a First Aid station at Skelton's shop on O'Connell Street; held in Ship Street barracks, Kilmainham and Mountjoy after the Rising; deported to England and imprisoned in Lewes for about a month; later worked for the anti-conscription movement and did typing for the government of the First Dáil; present at Croke Park on Bloody Sunday.

MARTIN, MARY (NÉE MOORE) (1866–1955)

Born in Dublin; in 1890 married Thomas P. Martin, a prosperous business man with whom she had twelve children; widowed in 1907; son Charlie killed on active service in the First World War; kept a diary that covers spring 1916.

MATHEWS, SIR CHARLES (1850–1920)

Born in New York; lawyer; director of public prosecutions in Britain, 1908–20.

MAXWELL, GENERAL SIR JOHN GRENFELL (1859–1929)

Born in Liverpool; British army officer; held the rank of major-general in 1916; sent to Dublin on 28 April to quell the Rising; acted as commander-in-chief in Ireland; attacked in the House of Commons by John Dillon of the Irish Parliamentary Party for his handling of the executions of the Rising's leaders and for the murder by British troops of unarmed civilians living on North King Street; corresponded with Provost J.P. Mahaffy of Trinity College Dublin about Irish public opinion of the British army.

MITCHELL, MARY AGNES (B. 1884)

Born in Co. Tyrone; married to Arthur Mitchell, a manufacturer of carriage trimmings; wrote a letter to her sister describing what she saw and heard of the Rising from her home in Rathmines.

### Molony, Helena (1883–1967)

Born in Dublin; active member of Inghinidhe na hÉireann and editor of *Bean na hÉireann* from 1908–11; actress in the Abbey Theatre and other companies; active in the trade union movement and in Fianna Éireann; general secretary of the Irish Women Workers Union in 1915; secretary of the women's section of the Irish Citizen Army; based at City Hall for the first day of the Rising, then arrested after the garrison surrendered; remained involved with republican, labour and feminist movements for many years; elected president of the Irish Trade Union Congress in 1936.

### Monahan, Alf (1889–1967)

Born in Belfast; member of the Irish Volunteers and the IRB from 1914; involved in the Easter Rising in Galway; on the run with Liam Mellows and Frank Hynes after the Rising; worked with the Volunteers in Cork during the War of Independence; later wrote fiction in Irish under the name Ailbhe Ó Monacháin; in 1949 wrote a long, detailed, entertaining witness statement for the Bureau of Military History describing his adventures while on the run.

### Moran, Patrick (1888–1921)

Member of the Irish Volunteers and the IRB; stationed at Jacob's Biscuit Factory during the Rising; interned in Frongoch, Wales, until July 1916; served as captain of 'D' company, 2nd Battalion of the Dublin Brigade of the IRA; executed for alleged involvement in the murder of an intelligence officer.

### Morkan, Eamon ('Eddie') (b. 1888)

Born in Dublin; member of 'A' Company, 1st Battalion, Dublin Brigade, 1913–16; member of the IRB; based at Father Matthew Hall and the Four Courts during the Rising; interned until December 1916; involved with the Volunteers during the War of Independence; husband of Phyllis Morkan.

### Morkan, Pauline *see* Keating, Pauline

### Morkan, Phyllis (née Lucas) (1889–1975)

Trained nurse; married Eamon Morkan; member of Cumann na mBan; based at Father Matthew Hall during the Rising; taught nursing to members of Cumann na mBan in Co. Offaly in 1917.

## MULCAHY, MARY JOSEPHINE ('MIN') (NÉE RYAN) (1884–1977)

Born in Co. Wexford; studied in London and established a branch of Cumann na mBan at London University; based at the GPO during the Rising and served as a courier; girlfriend of Seán MacDermott and (along with her sister Phyllis) visited him in Kilmainham Gaol in the hours before his execution; travelled to the United States to report to Fenian John Devoy in New York about the Rising; married Richard Mulcahy in 1919.

## MULCAHY, RICHARD (1886–1971)

Born in Waterford; member of the IRB; 1st lieutenant of the 3rd Battalion, Dublin Brigade of the Irish Volunteers; active in raids on RIC barracks in Donabate, Swords and Ashbourne during the Rising; interned until December 1916; IRA chief-of-staff (1918–1921); commander-in-chief of the National Army during the Civil War; Cumann na nGaedheal TD, cabinet minister, leader of Fine Gael from 1944 to 1959; married to Mary Josephine Mulcahy (née Ryan).

## MURPHY, FR COLUMBUS (1881–1952)

Roman Catholic Capuchin priest; ministered to the prisoners at Kilmainham Gaol after the Rising.

## MURPHY, KATHLEEN ('KATE') (1897–1946)

Lived in Dublin; married to Seamus Murphy; stationed at the Marrowbone Lane Distillery garrison, engaged in cooking and 'relief night duty' (her words in pension application); imprisoned in Kilmainham Gaol after the surrender; visited Con Colbert before his execution and left an account of their conversation; involved in Republican activities throughout the War of Independence.

## MURPHY, SEAMUS

Captain of 'A' Company, and adjutant of 4th Battalion, Dublin Brigade of the Irish Volunteers; commanded the forces at Marrowbone Lane Distillery; interned after the Rising in Frongoch; married to Kate Murphy.

## MURTAGH, FRANCIS ('FRANK') (1899–1969)

Member of the Dublin Brigade of the Irish Volunteers; stationed at the GPO during the Rising; one of the two Volunteers who helped Catherine Byrne jump through the side window of the GPO; interned after the Rising until August 1916.

## NATHAN, ESTELLE (NÉE D'AVIGDOR) (1870–1949)

Artist married to George Nathan, brother of Sir Mathew Nathan; lived in London; guest at the undersecretary's lodge in the Phoenix Park, Dublin with her young daughters Maude and Pamela when the Rising broke out.

## NATHAN, SIR GEORGE (1869–1937)

Book publisher in London; younger brother of Sir Matthew Nathan; married to Estelle Nathan, who wrote detailed letters to him from the undersecretary's lodge during Easter Week.

## NATHAN, SIR MATTHEW (1862–1939)

British army officer and colonial administrator; undersecretary to Ireland, 1914–16; based at and unable to leave Dublin Castle during the Rising; resigned as undersecretary 3 May 1916.

## NÍ CHEALLAIGH, MAIRÉAD (MARGARET O'KELLY) (1893–1971)

Younger sister of Seán T. O'Kelly; member of Cumann na mBan; served last home-cooked breakfast to the Pearse brothers on Easter Monday; during the Rising, helped Volunteers with cooking and nursing in the North King Street area; worked with the National Aid Association and Volunteer Dependants Fund after the Rising and involved on the Republican side in the Civil War; according to a short article on her death 'led a quiet life and was rarely seen publicly'.

## NIC SHIUBHLAIGH, MÁIRE (MARY WALKER) (1883–1958)

Born in Dublin; member of the Gaelic League, Inghinidhe na hÉireann and Cumann na mBan; stationed at Jacob's Biscuit Factory during the Rising; actress in the Irish National Theatre Society, later known as the Abbey Theatre, and the Theatre of Ireland; married Major General Eamonn Price, former IRA director of organisations, in 1928.

## NOBLETT, HENRY JOHN (B. 1874)

Assistant head manager of the GPO; worked with Arthur Hamilton Norway.

## NOONAN, MICHAEL (1882–1916)

Messenger for Dublin Corporation; one of fifteen unarmed civilians killed by the South Staffordshire Regiment of the British army at North King Street during the Rising.

### NORWAY, ARTHUR HAMILTON (1859–1938)

Born in England; moved to Dublin in 1912 as manager of the General Post Office and secretary to the General Post Office in Ireland; married to Mary Louisa Hamilton Norway; during the Rising lived at the Royal Hibernian Hotel on Dawson Street where he and his wife maintained the telephone link with London.

### NORWAY, FREDERICK HAMILTON (1896–1915)

Son of Mary Louisa and Arthur Hamilton Norway; served as second lieutenant in the 2nd Battalion, Duke of Cornwall's Light Infantry; killed at Epinette, near Armentières, France, in 1915.

### NORWAY, MARY LOUISA HAMILTON (NÉE GADSDEN) (1861–1932)

Grew up in England in 'a family of British imperial soldiers and civil servants' (Jeffery, 1999); married to Arthur Hamilton Norway; mother of Frederick and Nevil; during the Easter Rising manned the only functioning telephone link between Dublin and London; wrote a series of letters to her sister during Easter Week describing the Rising as experienced from the Royal Hibernian Hotel on Dawson Street.

### NORWAY, NEVIL SHUTE (1899–1960)

Son of Mary Louisa and Arthur Hamilton Norway; on holiday from school for Easter, worked with the Red Cross as a stretcher bearer during the Rising; served in the Suffolk Regiment during the First World War; later known as the writer Nevil Shute, author of *On the beach*, among other novels.

### O'BRIEN, ANNE ('ANNIE') (NÉE COONEY) (1896–1959)

Born in Dublin; member of the Inghinidhe branch of Cumann na mBan from 1915; worked as a seamstress and made her uniform, creating the pattern from Con Colbert's Volunteer uniform; participated in the Easter Rising, along with her two sisters and her brother; stationed at the Marrowbone Lane garrison for the week; briefly imprisoned following the surrender; active in the Republican movement throughout the Civil War; married Denis O'Brien, who was also stationed at the Marrowbone Lane Distillery.

### O'BRIEN, DENIS ('DINNY') (1899–1942)

Born in Dublin; member of 'C' Company, 4th Battalion, Dublin Brigade of the Irish Volunteers; based at the South Dublin Union and then the Marrowbone Lane Distillery during the Rising; interned until

September 1916; married Annie Cooney; joined An Garda Síochána in 1933; worked as a detective based at Dublin Castle; killed by IRA members in 1942.

O'BRIEN, EDWARD CONOR MARSHALL (1880–1952)
Grandson of William Smith O'Brien; cousin of Mary Spring Rice; skippered his yacht the *Kelpie* in the Kilcoole gun-running; circumnavigated the globe in the *Saoirse*, 1923–5.

O'BRIEN, NORA CONNOLLY (1893–1981)
Born in Edinburgh; second daughter of James Connolly and Lillie Reynolds; grew up in Dublin; factory worker in Belfast; founded Belfast branch of Cumann na mBan; travelled to the north of Ireland on Easter Sunday 1916 to recruit 'the men of the North' to the Rising; returned to Dublin at the end of the week and visited her father when he was imprisoned in Dublin Castle; travelled to the United States following the Rising to rally support and raise money for the national cause; wrote a memoir of her experiences at the time of the Rising, *The unbroken tradition*; remained active in Republican politics through the Civil War; married Seamus O'Brien, whom she met in the United States.

O'BRIEN, WILLIAM SMITH (1803–64)
MP and Young Irelander; transported to Van Diemen's Land for his role in the 1848 Rebellion but returned to Ireland, having been pardoned, in 1856.

O'CARROLL, LIAM (B. 1894)
Born in Dublin; member of the IRB; lieutenant, 'A' Company, 1st Battalion, Dublin Brigade, Irish Volunteers, 1916; erected barricades at North King Street and stationed at the Four Courts during the Rising; interned afterwards until October 1916; captain in the same reorganised battalion after 1917; his father was murdered at home by Crown Forces in 1920.

O'CONNELL, JEREMIAH JOSEPH ('J.J.', 'GINGER') (1887–1944)
Born in Co. Mayo; chief of inspection of the Irish Volunteers from late 1915; refused to mobilise the Volunteers of Wexford and Kilkenny, according to Robert Brennan's memoir *Allegiance;* interned until December 1916; assistant director and director of training in the IRA during the War of Independence; pro-treaty in the Civil War.

## O'Connor, Roderick ('Rory') (1883–1922)

Born in Dublin; close friend of Joseph Mary Plunkett; attended the Easter morning wedding of Geraldine Plunkett and Thomas Dillon; stationed at the GPO during the Rising; director of engineering during the War of Independence; opposed the Anglo–Irish Treaty and led the takeover of the Four Courts in April 1922; executed by the Free State government in December that year.

## O'Doherty, Kitty (née Gibbons) (b. 1888)

Born in Co. Westmeath; married to Seamus O'Doherty (member of the supreme council of the IRB); lived in Dublin in 1916; quartermaster of Cumann na mBan in 1916; delivered messages to the Volunteers in Kilkenny before the Rising; sister of Mother Columba; active in the National Aid Association and Volunteer Dependants Fund following the Rising; travelled to the United States with Éamon de Valera in 1919 to get support for the Irish Republic.

## O'Donnell, Eithne (née Coyle) (1897–1985)

Born in Co. Donegal; joined Cumann na mBan in 1918 and established a branch in Donegal; active in fundraising and anti-conscription campaigns; imprisoned during the War of Independence and as a Republican during the Civil War; president of Cumann na mBan, 1926–41.

## O'Donoghue, Sighle (Sighle Bean Uí Dhonnchadha) (née Humphreys) (1899–1994)

Born in Limerick to a nationalist family; moved to Dublin 1909; wrote an account of saying goodbye to her uncle, The O'Rahilly, as he left to join the Rising; member of Cumann na mBan from 1919; involved in the War of Independence; imprisoned during the Civil War for her active opposition to the Free State; married the IRA activist Donal O'Donoghue in 1935.

## O'Donovan, Kathleen (née Boland) (n.d.)

Grew up in Dublin; delivered ammunition to an outpost of the 2nd Battalion of the Volunteers during the Rising; brothers Gerald, Harry and Edmund all in the Volunteers; joined Cumann na mBan after the Rising; travelled to the United States with Hanna Sheehy Skeffington to raise funds for the Volunteers' dependants; married Seán O'Donovan.

## O'Duffy, Eimar (1893–1935)

Born in Dublin; member of the IRB and the Irish Volunteers; contributor to the *Irish Volunteer*; opposed the Rising and informed Eoin

MacNeill that it was imminent; in 1919, published *The wasted island*, a roman-à-clef about the Rising.

O'DWYER, BISHOP EDWARD THOMAS (1842–1917)

Born in Co. Tipperary; Catholic bishop of Limerick, 1886–1917; supporter of Home Rule; in a private letter to General Maxwell, which was leaked and made public, attacked Maxwell's policies in suppressing the Rising and said that the execution of the leaders had 'outraged the conscience of the country'; his letter is mentioned in the correspondence of May Fay and James Finn.

O'FARRELL, ELIZABETH (1884–1957)

Born in Dublin; member of Inghinidhe na hÉireann, Cumann na mBan and the Irish Citizen Army; based in the GPO during the Rising; carried a white flag, as ordered by Seán MacDermott, and the message of surrender from Patrick Pearse to the British army on the Saturday of Easter Week; stood next to Pearse in the famous photograph of the surrender; brought information about the surrender to all the remaining garrisons; wrote a detailed account of her role in the surrender and subsequent brief imprisonment published in the *Catholic Bulletin*; active in the Republican movement; worked as a midwife and nurse.

O'GORMAN, MARY CHRISTINA (NÉE HAYES) (B. 1876)

Born in Dublin; dressmaker; joined the central branch of Cumann na mBan in 1914; in charge of the first-aid station at Father Matthew Hall during the Rising; remained active with Cumann na mBan following the Rising and throughout the War of Independence.

O'HANRAHAN, EILY *SEE* O'REILLY, EILEEN ('EILY')

O'HANRAHAN, MICHAEL (Ó HANNRACHÁIN, MICHEÁL) (1883–1916)

Born in Wexford; member of the Gaelic League, the IRB, and the Irish Volunteers; during the Rising, was third in command at Jacob's Biscuit Factory, where Thomas MacDonagh was first- and John MacBride was second-in-command; executed following the surrender.

O'KELLY, PHILOMENA ('PHYLLIS') (NÉE RYAN) (1895–1983)

Born in Co. Wexford; carried dispatches from the GPO on several days of the Rising; with her sister Min, visited Seán MacDermott in his cell in Kilmainham Gaol hours before his execution; joined Cumann na mBan; involved in the War of Independence; married Seán T. O'Kelly after the death of his first wife, her sister Mary Kate.

## O'KELLY, SEÁN T. (1882–1966)

Born in Dublin; member of the Gaelic League; manager of *An Claidheamh Soluis*; captain of staff for Patrick Pearse during the Rising; Speaker, Dáil Éireann, 1920; Irish Representative, Paris and Rome, 1920–21; Minister for Local Government and Finance, 1932–45; President of Ireland, 1945–59; married Mary Kate Ryan (1918–34) and, after her death, her sister Phyllis Ryan (1936–66).

## O'MULLANE, BRIGHID (1893–1967)

Born in Sligo; organiser for Cumann na mBan after the Rising; imprisoned in the War of Independence; took the anti-treaty side in the Civil War.

## O'RAHILLY, ANNA ('ÁINE', 'ANNO') (1873–1958)

Born in Co. Kerry; moved to Dublin with her sister Nell Humphreys in 1909; joined Cumann na mBan in 1914; sister of The O'Rahilly; involved with the National Aid Association and Volunteer Dependants Fund following the Rising; active in the Republican movement; imprisoned during the Civil War; active in the Women's Prisoners' Defence League.

## O'RAHILLY, MICHAEL JOSEPH ('THE O'RAHILLY') (1875–1916)

Born in Ballylongford, Co. Kerry; member of the Irish Volunteers; active in procuring arms for the Volunteers and corresponded with Mary Spring Rice about the 1914 gun-runnings; stationed at the GPO during the Rising; fatally wounded during evacuation of GPO on 28 April 1916.

## O'RAHILLY, NANCY (NÉE BROWN) (1878–1961)

Born in New York; married The O'Rahilly in 1899; joined Cumann na mBan in 1914; gave birth to the last of her six sons in July 1916.

## O'RAHILLY, NELL *SEE* HUMPHREYS, MARY ELLEN ('NELL')

## O'REILLY, EILEEN ('EILY') (NÉE O'HANRAHAN) (1891–1974)

Born in Co. Carlow; living in Dublin at the time of the Rising; member of Cumann na mBan; took dispatches to Wexford during Holy Week and Easter Week; along with her sister 'Cis' (Anna), visited their brother Micheál in his cell at Kilmainham before his execution; active in the War of Independence; married Thomas O'Reilly.

## O'SULLIVAN, GEAROID (1891–1948)

Born in Co. Cork; schoolteacher in Dublin; member of 'F' Company, 1st Battalion, Dublin Brigade of the Irish Volunteers; stationed at the GPO and aide-de-camp to Seán MacDermott; interned until December 1916; later a Cumann na nGaedheal TD and senator.

## O'SULLIVAN, LAURA (NÉE DALY) (1882–1967)

Born in Limerick; sister of Kathleen Clarke; founded Limerick branch of Cumann na mBan with her sister Madge Daly; her brother Ned Daly executed for his role in the Easter Rising; in 1918, married Jim (Seamus) O'Sullivan, a member of the Irish Volunteers and close friend of her brother Ned.

## O'SULLIVAN, JIM (SEAMUS) (1891–1973)

Born in Cork; lieutenant, later adjutant, 'B' Company, 1st Battalion, Dublin Brigade of the Irish Volunteers; based at the North Circular Road bridge and the GPO; married Laura Daly in 1918.

## OSGOOD, DR HAMILTON (1838–1907)

American medical doctor in Boston; father of Mary Alden Osgood (Molly Childers).

## PARRY, GERTRUDE (NÉE BANNISTER) (1883–1950)

Born in Liverpool; she and her sister Elizabeth first cousins of Roger Casement; fired from her job as schoolmistress when her name was mentioned in the paper with Casement's after he was charged with treason in May 1916; wrote an account of her attempts to visit him in prison and to secure decent treatment for him; married his friend Sidney Parry in October 1916.

## PEARSE, MARGARET (NÉE BRADY) (1857–1932)

Born in Dublin; in 1877 married James Pearse, with whom she had four children; mother of Patrick and William Pearse, both executed for their roles in the Easter Rising; became a political figure after their deaths, joining Sinn Féin and elected to Dáil Éireann as a Sinn Féin TD for Dublin in 1921; opposed the Anglo–Irish Treaty; later became a founder member of Fianna Fáil.

## PEARSE, MARGARET MARY (1878–1968)

Born in Dublin; teacher and politician; sister of Patrick and William; elected as Fianna Fáil TD for Dublin in 1933; served in the Seanad 1938–68.

PEARSE, PATRICK HENRY (1879–1916)

Born in Dublin; barrister, teacher, headmaster, writer; member of the IRB and the Volunteers; delivered famous oration at the funeral of Jeremiah O'Donovan Rossa in 1915; one of the signatories of the 'Proclamation of the Irish Republic'; director of military organisation in the Irish Volunteers and commander-in-chief of the Army of the Republic in 1916; president of the provisional government; stationed at the GPO during the Rising; executed following the surrender.

PEARSE, WILLIAM ('WILLIE') (1881–1916)

Born in Dublin; younger brother of Patrick Pearse; sculptor and school-teacher; stationed at the GPO during the Rising; executed following the surrender.

PEROLZ, MARIE *SEE* FLANAGAN, (MÁIRE, MARY)

PLUNKETT, GEORGE ('SEOIRSE') (1894–1944)

Born in Dublin; member of the Irish Volunteers; led the 'Liverpool lambs', volunteer Irish men formerly living in England, from his family's estate in Kimmage, south Dublin, to the Rising; stationed at the GPO; sentenced to death but his sentence commuted to penal servitude; released in 1917; fought in the War of Independence and on the Republican side in the Civil War; brother of Geraldine Dillon, Jack and Joseph Mary Plunkett.

PLUNKETT, GERALDINE *SEE* DILLON, GERALDINE PLUNKETT

PLUNKETT, GEORGE NOBLE, COUNT (1851–1948)

Born in Dublin; curator of the National Museum of Ireland, 1907–16; father of Geraldine Dillon, George, Jack and Joseph Mary Plunkett and three other daughters; imprisoned following the Rising and deported to Oxford; elected Sinn Féin TD for Roscommon in 1917.

PLUNKETT, GRACE (NÉE GIFFORD) (1888–1955)

Born in Dublin; studied at the Metropolitan School of Art in Dublin and at the Slade School of Fine Art in London; sold drawings to the *Irish Review* and other papers; sister of Muriel Gifford, who was married to Thomas MacDonagh; became engaged to Joseph Plunkett in 1915; married him in Kilmainham Gaol hours before his execution; member of the Sinn Féin executive in 1917; took the Republican side during the Civil War; continued to produce drawings inspired by contemporary cultural and political issues throughout her life.

## PLUNKETT, JOHN ('JACK') (1897–1960)

Born in Dublin; member of the Irish Volunteers; brother of Geraldine and George Plunkett and Joseph Plunkett; based at the GPO during the Rising; sentenced to death but his sentence commuted to penal servitude; released in 1917; took the Republican side in the Civil War.

## PLUNKETT, JOSEPH MARY (1887–1916)

Born in Dublin; journalist, poet, religious mystic; studied Irish with Thomas MacDonagh; ill with tuberculosis from childhood and was recovering from recent surgery throughout the week of the Rising; member of the IRB; director of military operations for the Irish Volunteers and chief military strategist for the Rising; signatory of the Proclamation; based at the GPO during Easter Week; married Grace Gifford hours before he was executed.

## POPE, PROFESSOR JOHN VAN SOMEREN (1850–1932)

Born in Devon; professor of modern East Indian languages in Trinity College Dublin from 1913; in Trinity College at the time of the Easter Rising.

## PORTAL, COLONEL BERTRAM (1866–1949)

Born in Berkshire; brigadier-general in the British army; commander of the cavalry brigade, 1916–18; commanded the cavalry column during the Easter Rising; responsible for the arrest of Patrick Pearse.

## PRICE, DOROTHY STOPFORD (1890–1954)

Born in Dublin; niece of Alice Stopford Green; medical student at Trinity College Dublin at the time of the Easter Rising, when she was staying as a guest of Sir Matthew Nathan in the undersecretary's lodge in the Phoenix Park; during the War of Independence became medical officer to a Cork brigade of the IRA; married Liam Price in 1925; authored *Tuberculosis in childhood* and made a significant contribution to controlling the tuberculosis epidemic in Ireland.

## PRICE, LESLIE *SEE* BARRY, LESLIE

## REGAN, MOIRA (N.D.)

Member of Cumann na mBan; identified only through an interview with the American journalist and poet Joyce Kilmer published in the *New York Times* in August 1916; states that she was stationed at the GPO throughout the Easter Rising and active in nursing the wounded; participated in a fundraising trip to the United States in August 1916.

REYNOLDS, MARY CATHERINE ('MOLLY') (N.D.)

Born in Dublin; joined Inghinidhe branch of Cumann na mBan in 1914; in 1915, co-founded the Cathleen Ní Houlihan branch of Cumann na mBan, also known as the Fairview branch; daughter of John R. Reynolds, auditor to the Volunteers; Casement used to bring her violets when she was in her father's office; stationed at the GPO during Easter Week providing first aid; involved with the Volunteer Dependants Fund after the Rising.

ROGERS, SORCHA (SARAH) (NÉE MACMAHON) (1888–1973)

Born in Co. Monaghan; joined Cumann na mBan in 1914; member of the executive, 1914–19; carried messages between the GPO, Four Courts and Father Matthew Hall during the Rising; actively involved in running the Volunteer Dependants Fund; worked directly for Michael Collins during the War of Independence.

ROONEY, CATHERINE (NÉE BYRNE) (1896–1971)

Born in Dublin; daughter of a coach trimmer; worked as a grocery shop assistant in 1911; joined Cumann na mBan in 1915; stationed in the GPO during the Easter Rising; involved with first aid and delivering dispatches to other garrisons; active in the War of Independence, carrying ammunition and explosives from Glasgow and Belfast to Dublin; family home used as a safe house for Michael Collins's 'squad'.

RYAN, CATHLEEN *SEE* MCCARTHY, CATHLEEN

RYAN, MÁIRÍN (NÉE CREGAN) (1891–1975)

Born in Co. Kerry; member of Cumann na mBan; sang at Volunteer concerts before the Rising; served as courier to Kerry in Holy Week, 1916; member of Cumann na mBan in Wexford during the War of Independence; worked with Robert Brennan in the Department of Foreign Affairs; wrote children's books, including *Old John* (1936); married Dr James Ryan, brother of Min Ryan.

RYAN, MIN *SEE* MULCAHY, MARY JOSEPHINE ('MIN')

RYAN, PHYLLIS *SEE* O'KELLY, PHILOMENA ('PHYLLIS')

SAMUEL, HERBERT (1870–1963)

Born in Liverpool; British Liberal politician; postmaster general, 1915–16; home secretary at the time of the Rising; leader of the Liberal Party, 1931–5.

## SEERY, MARY (B. 1871)

Born in Co. Westmeath; married a farmer, Thomas Seery, but by 1911 was a widow with two surviving children; mentioned in 1916 correspondence between her neighbour May Fay and her relative James Finn.

## SHANAHAN, JANE ('JINNY') (1891–1936)

Born in Dublin; registered as 'cook' and 'domestic servant' in the 1911 Census; joined the Irish Citizen Army in 1913; stationed at City Hall and imprisoned briefly following the surrender; took part in the posting of the Proclamation on the anniversary of the Rising in 1917; supported the Volunteers during the War of Independence.

## SHEEHY SKEFFINGTON, FRANCIS ('FRANK') (BORN FRANCIS SKEFFINGTON) (1878–1916)

Born in Bailieborough, Co. Cavan; close friend of James Joyce at University College Dublin; feminist, suffragist, pacifist, socialist, internationalist; married Hanna Sheehy in 1903; author, journalist and editor; co-founder of the *Irish Citizen*; activist in national and civic affairs; co-founded the Irish Women's Franchise League; supported the 'Save the Dublin Kiddies' campaign to feed the strikers' children in 1913; attempted to help an officer shot at the gate of Dublin Castle on the first day of the Rising; on the second day of the Rising, in order to stop looting and destruction of shops in the city, called a meeting to organise a civilian police force; arrested by Lieutenant M. C. Morris, detained and imprisoned in Portobello Barracks, shot and killed along with two other men by order of Captain Bowen-Colthurst on the morning of Wednesday, 26 April 1916.

## SHEEHY SKEFFINGTON, (JOHANNA) HANNA (NÉE SHEEHY), (1877–1946)

Born in Co. Cork; received BA and MA degrees from the Royal University of Ireland; married Frank Skeffington in 1903; founded the Irish Women's Franchise League in 1908; feminist, suffragist, socialist, internationalist; arrested several times for actions related to the women's suffrage movement and the 1913 strike and lockout; went on hunger strike every time and was released; helped edit the *Irish Citizen*; carried supplies of food to the GPO and College of Surgeons garrison during the Rising; met with Prime Minister Asquith to demand an inquiry after the murder of her husband; refused to accept financial compensation offered by Asquith; toured the United States speaking about her experiences during and after the Rising; active in Republican and feminist causes.

### Sheehy Skeffington, Owen (1909–70)

Born in Dublin; son of Frank and Hanna Sheehy Skeffington; seven years old when his father was murdered during the Easter Rising; became a lecturer at Trinity College Dublin and a senator.

### Shephard, Gordon Strachey (1885–1918)

Born in Madras, India; British; member of the Royal Cruising Club and pilot in the Royal Flying Corps; sailed on the gun-running voyage of the *Asgard* in July 1914 with Erskine and Molly Childers and Mary Spring Rice; as brigadier general, served as a commander in the Royal Flying Corps in the First World War; killed in France in 1918.

### Sinnott, Sean (n.d.)

Commanding officer of the Wexford Volunteers; involved in the uprising in Wexford during Easter Week; worked closely with Wexford Volunteer Robert Brennan; imprisoned in England after the Rising.

### Skinnider, Margaret (1893–1971)

Born in Scotland to Irish parents; teacher; member of the Volunteers, Cumann na mBan and the Irish Citizen Army; stationed at the College of Surgeons during the Rising and wounded during an attempt to cut off the retreat of British soldiers on the south side of St Stephen's Green; travelled to the United States after the Rising raising funds for the nationalist cause; active in the War of Independence and on the Republican side in the Civil War; taught in a primary school in Dublin until retiring in 1961.

### Smyth, Lucy Agnes *see* Byrne, Lucy

### Spring Rice, Sir Cecil (1859–1918)

Born in London; cousin of Mary Spring Rice; served as British ambassador to the United States, 1912–18; author of the hymn 'I vow to thee my country'.

### Spring Rice, Mary (1880–1924)

Born in London; grew up on the Spring Rice estate, Mount Trenchard, in Co. Limerick; member of the Gaelic League; active in the United Irishwomen and member of Sinn Féin; suggested to Erskine Childers and to The O'Rahilly that a private yacht be used to run guns from Germany; to that end sailed on the *Asgard* in July 1914 and kept the 'Log of the *Asgard*' during the voyage that ended at Howth in the distribution of rifles to the Volunteers; offered Mount Trenchard as a safe house for Irish men on the run during the War of Independence; died of tuberculosis.

## SPRING RICE, THOMAS, 2ND BARON MONTEAGLE OF BRANDON (1849–1926)

Anglo–Irish politician and landowner; lived on his Co. Limerick estate, Mount Trenchard; involved in the founding of the Irish Dominion League; brought his three children up to speak Irish; father of Mary Spring Rice.

## STAINES, MICHAEL JOSEPH (1885–1955)

Born in Co. Mayo; member of the IRB; quartermaster of the Dublin Brigade of the Irish Volunteers; stationed at the GPO during the Rising; interned until December 1916; after his release, active in elections and reorganisation of the Volunteers; imprisoned during the War of Independence; first commissioner of An Garda Síochána.

## STOKES, ADRIAN (1887–1927)

Born in Switzerland; member of the distinguished clerical and academic Stokes family; grew up in Ireland; brother of Henry and Lilly; officer in the British army during the First World War; on leave in Dublin during the Rising; professor of bacteriology and preventive medicine at Trinity College Dublin (1919–22); professor of pathology, Guy's Hospital, London (1922–7); died of yellow fever, which he was studying.

## STOKES, HENRY (1879–1967)

Born in India; member of the distinguished clerical and academic family; brother of Adrian and Lilly; studied medicine at Trinity College Dublin; elected a fellow of the Royal College of Surgeons in Ireland (1907); studied further at Leyden and Berne universities and at the Mayo Clinic in America; returned to Dublin and joined the staff at the Meath Hospital; at the outbreak of World War I joined the Royal Army Medical Corps and served throughout on the western front; on leave in Dublin during the Rising; tended to the wounded James Connolly in Dublin Castle; awarded an OBE (1917); returned to Dublin after the war; appointed as a consulting surgeon to the National Children's Hospital and to St Ultan's Infant Hospital; established a reputation as an expert in the area of blood transfusion and outlined methods for the prevention of clotting.

### STOKES, LILIAN ('LILLY') (1876–1955)

Born in India; member of the distinguished clerical and academic Stokes family; first cousin of Elsie Mahaffy; living in Dublin in 1916 and kept a diary during Easter Week; married her first cousin John Boxwell in 1920.

### STOPFORD, DOROTHY SEE PRICE, DOROTHY STOPFORD

### SWEENEY, JOSEPH 'JOE' (1897–1980)

Born in Donegal; member of 'E' Company, 4th Battalion, Dublin Brigade of the Irish Volunteers; stationed at the GPO during the Rising; interned after the surrender; commandant general of the Northern division of the IRA during the War of Independence; supported the Anglo–Irish Treaty and served as a major-general in the army of the Free State.

### THORNTON, BRIGID (NÉE LYONS) (1896–1987)

Born in Co. Roscommon; trained as a medical doctor in UCG; joined Cumann na mBan in 1915; travelled to Dublin with her uncle, Frank McGuinness, to participate in the Easter Rising; stationed at the Four Courts; imprisoned after the surrender; supported her uncle Joe McGuiness, in the 1917 Longford election; procured arms in the War of Independence; served as first lieutenant in the medical service of the Free State Army; married Edward Thornton in 1925; among many jobs in public health, worked as a child welfare pediatrician for Dublin Corporation.

### TRENCH, FRANCESCA ('CESCA') ('SADHBH TRINSEACH') (1891–1918)

Born in Liverpool; granddaughter of Richard Chenevix Trench, Anglican archbishop of Dublin; active in the Gaelic League and Sinn Féin; studied art in Paris and Dublin and published drawings and designs in *An Claidheamh Soluis* and created Christmas cards for Conradh na Gaeilge; involved with Cumann na mBan from 1914; after a long courtship, married National Volunteer Diarmid Coffey in April 1918 but died in October of that year from influenza.

### VANE, SIR FRANCIS (1861–1934)

Born in Dublin; British army major in the Royal Munster Fusiliers; second in command at Portobello Barracks during the Rising; protested to authorities in London against the murder of Frank Sheehy Skeffington and attempted to have Bowen-Colthurst charged with murder; for this reason, relegated to unemployment by the army.

WALKER, MARY *SEE* NIC SHIUBHLAIGH, MÁIRE

WEAFER (SOMETIMES SPELLED WAFER), THOMAS (1890–1916)

Born in Enniscorthy, Co. Wexford; captain of the 2nd Battalion of the Dublin Brigade of the Irish Volunteers; occupied the Hibernian Bank on Lower Abbey Street during the Rising; shot and killed on 26 April 1916.

WHEELER, CAPTAIN HENRY DE COURCY (B. 1872)

Born in Dublin; British army officer based at the Curragh; served as staff officer to General Lowe; involved in the suppression of the Easter Rising; married to a first cousin of Constance Markievicz; drove Elizabeth O'Farrell to the College of Surgeons and to Boland's Mills when she carried the surrender to those garrisons.

WILSON, LIEUTENANT LESLIE ORME (1876–1955)

Born in London; served in the Boer War and the First World War; based at Portobello Barracks during the Easter Rising; directly involved in the shooting of Frank Sheehy Skeffington and two other journalists; gave evidence in the subsequent investigation.

WIMBORNE, LORD IVOR CHURCHILL GUEST (1873–1939)

Born in London; Lord Lieutenant of Ireland, 1915–18; wanted militant nationalists arrested before the Rising but Sir Matthew Nathan said he did not have the power; resigned after the Rising but was reappointed Lord-Lieutenant.

WYSE POWER, JANE ('JENNIE') (NÉE O'TOOLE) (1858–1941)

Born in Co. Wicklow; active in the Ladies Land League, the Gaelic League, Inghinidhe na hÉireann (co-founder), the Irish Women's Franchise League (founder member), Cumann na mBan (co-founder), and Sinn Féin (founder and vice president); married John Wyse Power; in 1899 started a produce shop and restaurant in Dublin where active nationalists met; the Proclamation was signed in her Dublin house; supported the pro-treaty side in the Civil War; appointed as a Cumann na nGaedheal senator in 1922; became an independent senator in 1925 and a Fianna Fáil senator in 1934.

# INDEX

*Page numbers in italic refer to documents,
illustrations and photographs.*